D1413499

The Secular Priests

The Secular Priests

By MAURICE NORTH

London · George Allen & Unwin Ltd
Ruskin House · Museum Street

Printed in Great Britain
in 11 on 12 point Plantin type
by Unwin Brothers Limited
Woking and London

To
Beatrix Anderson Reinholdt
in esteem and friendship

Contents

Contents

Acknowledgments

I wish to express my indebtedness to all the authors of works cited in this book. I am especially indebted and grateful to the following authors, editors, and publishers for written permission to quote from published material:

Viktor E. Frankl and the Souvenir Press Ltd, for permission to quote from *The Doctor and the Soul*, London, 1969;
Felix P. Biestek and George Allen & Unwin Ltd, for permission to quote from *The Casework Relationship*, London, 1961;
Paul Halmos and Constable & Co. Ltd, for permission to quote from *The Personal Service Society*, London, 1970;
Alick Holden and Constable & Co. Ltd, for permission to quote from *Teachers as Counsellors*, London, 1969;
Kathleen Heasman and Constable & Co. Ltd, for permission to quote from *An Introduction to Pastoral Counselling*, London, 1969;
Carl Rogers and Constable & Co. Ltd, for permission to quote from *On Becoming a Person*, London, 1967;
Philip Rieff and Chatto and Windus Ltd, for permission to quote from *The Triumph of the Therapeutic*, London, 1966;
Robert Bessell and B. T. Batsford Ltd, for permission to quote from *Introduction to Social Work*, London, 1970;
Bernard D. Davies, Alan Gibson, and University of London Press Ltd, for permission to quote from *The Social Education of the Adolescent*, London, 1967;
Professor A. G. Joselin and The Department of Education of The University of Aston in Birmingham, for permission to quote from the Departmental brochure on their Counselling Course;
Mr M. B. Yeats, Macmillan & Co. Ltd, and A. P. Watt & Son, for permission to quote from *Collected Poems of W. B. Yeats*, London, 1950;
Richard Wollheim and the Fabian Society, for permission to quote from *Socialism and Culture*, Fabian Tract 331, London, 1961;

Charles Rycroft, Thomas Nelson & Sons Ltd, and A. D. Peters & Company, for permission to reprint an extract from *A Critical Dictionary of Psychoanalysis*, London, 1968;

Benjamin Spock and The Bodley Head Ltd, for permission to quote from *A Young Person's Guide to Life and Love*, London, 1971;

G. A. and A. G. Theodorson, Associated Book Publishers Ltd, and John Farquharson Ltd, for permission to quote from *A Modern Dictionary of Sociology*, Methuen, London, 1970;

Charles Rycroft and Constable & Co. Ltd, for permission to quote from *Psychoanalysis Observed*, London, 1966;

Tom Burns and the Editor of *New Society*, for permission to quote from 'A Meaning in Everyday Life', *New Society*, 25 May 1967;

Oxford University Press Inc., for permission to quote from the late C. Wright Mills, *The Sociological Imagination*, New York, 1959;

Marion K. Sanders, the Editor ot *Harper's Magazine*, and Minneapolis Star and Tribune Co. Inc., for permission to quote from 'Social Work: A Profession Chasing Its Tail', in the March 1957 issue of *Harper's Magazine;*

Erik H. Erikson and The Hogarth Press Ltd, for permission to quote from *Childhood and Society*, London, 1965;

Jacques Ellul and Jonathan Cape Ltd, for permission to quote from *The Technological Society*, London, 1965;

Barbara Wootton and George Allen & Unwin Ltd, for permission to quote from *Social Science and Social Pathology*, London, 1959;

Peter L. Berger and Doubleday & Company, Inc., for permission to quote from *The Precarious Vision*, New York, 1961;

Joseph Bensman and The Macmillan Company, for permission to quote from *Dollars and Sense*, New York, 1967;

David Riesman and The Macmillan Company, for permission to quote from *Individualism Reconsidered*, The Free Press, Glencoe, Illinois, 1954;

Georges Friedmann and The Macmillan Company, for permission to quote from *Industrial Society*, The Free Press, Glencoe, Illinois, 1955;

Geoffrey Rankin, and the Editor of *Social Work Today*, for permission to quote from 'Professional Social Work and the

Campaign Against Poverty' in *Social Work Today*, Vol. 1, No. 10, January 1971;

Kenneth Roberts and Longman Group Ltd, for permission to quote from *Leisure*, London, 1970;

David Silverman and Heinemann Educational Books Ltd, for permission to quote from *The Theory of Organizations*, London, 1970;

Peter L. Berger and Faber and Faber Ltd, for permission to quote from *The Social Reality of Religion*, London, 1969, published in the USA by Doubleday & Co. Inc., as *The Sacred Canopy*, New York, 1967;

Eileen Younghusband and George Allen & Unwin Ltd, for permission to quote from *Social Work and Social Values*, London, 1967;

Peter Kelvin and Holt, Rinehart and Winston Ltd, for permission to quote from *The Bases of Social Behaviour*, London, 1970;

Noel Timms and Routledge and Kegan Paul Ltd, for permission to quote from *Social Casework, Principles and Practice*, London, 1964;

Erich Fromm and Routledge and Kegan Paul Ltd, for permission to quote from *The Sane Society*, London, 1956;

J. H. Wallis and Routledge and Kegan Paul Ltd for permission to quote from *Marriage Guidance, A New Introduction*, London, 1968;

Richard Dewey and W. J. Humber and The Macmillan Company, for permission to quote from *An Introduction to Social Psychology*, New York, 1966;

Ludwig von Bertalanffy and George Braziller, Inc., for permission to quote from *Robots, Men and Minds*, New York, 1967;

Philip Rieff, Victor Gollancz Ltd, The Viking Press, Inc., and Laurence Pollinger Ltd, for permission to quote from *Freud: The Mind of the Moralist*, London, 1960;

The Editor of *Health Visitor* for allowing me to use in Chapter I some material that appeared in slightly different form in *Health Visitor*, January 1971, Vol. 44, pp. 15–17;

Helen Harris Perlman and The University of Chicago Press, for permission to quote from *Persona—Social Role and Personality*, Chicago, 1968.

Gordon Hamilton and Columbia University Press, for permission to quote from *Theory and Practice of Social Case Work*, New York, 1951.

'The day after the bomb fell, the doctor was out
binding up radiation burns. The minister prayed and
set up a soup kitchen in the ruined chapel. The
policeman herded stray children to the rubble heap
where the teacher had improvised a classroom. And
the social worker wrote a report; since two had
survived, they held a conference on Interpersonal
Relationships in a Time of Intensified Anxiety
States.'

Marion K. Sanders

'The social worker's claim to professional status
centres upon being a specialist in human relationships, an individual trained and disciplined in
human adjustments.'

Association of Social Workers

'We cannot deduce—Hume's celebrated dictum runs
—how we ought to act from what we believe is.
Neither can we deduce how anyone else ought to act
from how we believe we ought to act. In the end, if
the end comes, we just have to beat those who
disagree with us over the head.'

C. Wright Mills

Chapter 1

The Psychotherapeutic Ideology and Industrialized Society

The '*will-to-meaning* is the most human phenomenon of all' (1). It is as constant an element in social life as it is in the lives of individuals. Historians recognize and acknowledge specific 'meanings' as being characteristic of what they, from their vantage points of hindsight, discern as historical periods or epochs. The social actions of men are charged with 'meaning' both in the sense of that which informs a particular action at a given time and place, and that which bestows 'meaningfulness' on all their actions and is the set of principles that gives an order to the succession of acts that is daily life. The beliefs an individual holds about his own nature and the nature of human created society infuses a special and recognizable quality into his acts. Sometimes the 'meaning' is made explicit in a publicly agreed religious dogma, philosophy, *Weltanschauung*, value-consensus, ideology, or even a 'scientific' belief that allegedly puts an end to all ideologies. Sometimes the meaning-giving notions are tacit, unexpressed and private. Sometimes the 'meaning' is tacit and yet public in the sense that most individuals in the society concerned believe in the 'meaning' though they have not formulated their beliefs into an articulated system of propositions. Whatever the shape of the 'meaning' may be, public or private, expressed or silent, individual or collective, a 'meaning' always exists in every society, and the characteristic that these 'meanings' have in common whether they be scientific, religious or philosophical, is that they involve faith in propositions that are beyond proof or disproof, and that they never rest on empirical evidence alone or are, in the end, defensible on purely logical grounds. All 'meanings' in this sense are ideologies (2).

What are the factors in a social situation that bring about changes in the content of an ideology, that lead to the replacement of one ideology by another? Or, we may ask, what new ideological features materially alter the social situation or what social situations are there that can be attributed to ideological changes? Why do certain ideas about the nature of man and society become acceptable and how are the values contained within such notions transmitted from individual to individual? These are proper questions for us to ask and for us to try to answer.

The classic attempt to carry out such a sociological enterprise was Max Weber's demonstration of an *elective affinity* between the 'Protestant Ethic' of Calvinism and the 'Spirit of Capitalism' (3). Is it possible to attempt something along the lines of Weber's analysis today? Can an affinity be shown to exist between certain aspects of contemporary Western societies and the psychotherapeutic ideology that is becoming gradually stronger and more pervasive? The ideology has been named by Paul Halmos 'the faith of the counsellors' and he has designated the society to which it is leading us 'the personal service society' (4). The phenomenon has been observed by others and the name they have given to the end product is different but in substance it is identical. Thomas Szasz refers to it as the 'psychotherapeutic state' (5), while Peter Berger prefers the 'psychological society' (6). Whatever the name may be, it denotes the same thing: a society in which the prevailing philosophy is psychotherapeutic and the basic ideas are derived from Freudian theories of the unconscious, of psychoanalysis, and the nature of man and society.

On the surface, Freudian ideas would seem to have about as much connection with industrialized society as the religious doctrines of Calvin had to do with sixteenth century manifestations of capitalism. Certain contemporary social thinkers such as Peter Berger (7), Arnold Gehlen (8), and Thomas Luckmann (9) to name but a few, have indicated in their works that some affinity might lie in this theory of man and the processes of advanced industrialization; there might be an interrelationship that could account for the immense and growing success of the psychotherapeutic values in what, superficially, looks like a rather unpromising environment.

Industrialization is the major structuring force in contemporary Western societies. During the past hundred years or so, it has succeeded in rationalizing and bureaucratizing the processes of

production while at the same time the economic sector of society
has become autonomous. With the disenchantment of the world,
i.e. the process by which man explains the natural and human
world without invoking a deity and his laws, and the adoption of
methods based on science and engineering as its concomitants,
this autonomous economic field has become progressively segre-
gated from political and religious institutions and the family; thus
the unity of pre-industrial Western society based on the overriding influence of religious notions has given place to a dichotomized society, the sectors of which, in their turn, have become
fragmented, so that one part of the divided whole is the economic,
while the other part has split into pieces only tenuously related.
One important consequence of this process has been that the
separation of the economic area of activity from the family has
created a new dimension of social life: the private sphere. More
than by any other trait, modern industrialized society is characterized by the differentiation between the public and private
spheres (10).

This dichotomization is directly experienced by the individual
members of our society as a psychological reality as well as a
principle that structures everyday life. The perception by the
individual of this state of affairs leads him to an internal dichotomization, that is he becomes the possessor of a public and a private
self, that is to say, he has a minimum of at least two identities. The
individual becomes confused by this plurality, for his identity, the
realization of the self, is uncertain and unstable. Typically, people
living in a society like our own do not know for certain who they
are, and do not know to which of a number of selves that they
experience they should attach paramount importance. This situation has already been defined in a number of ways, Viktor Frankl
calls it the *existential vacuum* (11), others prefer *identity crisis*, both
of these terms being akin to the more familiar and popular concept
of alienation.

Not every individual in our society experiences this effect to
such a marked degree and some are fortunate enough to escape its
consequences, or at least the worst of them. A relatively small
number are able to solve their personal problems of self by identifying primarily in terms of their public selves. This is, however,
in the main only possible for those whose public roles bring

rewards and successes such as to give scope and significance for such identification. Such roles are generally occupational, but where the roles are of such a nature that they are not conducive to this kind of identification, the individual is forced into identifying with his private self. Because of the nature of the work that most people have to do in our society, this unhappy situation is the one in which most people find themselves. The private sphere of life becomes for most of us the location of the 'real me'. An enormous number of ancillary factors assist in this process of splitting the individual into his conflicting and uncertain selves, among the most influential being the mass media, and marketing techniques.

This 'privatization' of identity has an ideological and a psychological aspect. If the 'real me' is located in the private sphere, then the activities of this sector of life must be legitimate for the discovery of the self. In other words, the search for the self in this area is justified because this view of the nature of society demands that it be so. This is the basis for attributing supreme importance to sexuality. Sexuality becomes not an adjunct of procreation, something enjoyable in itself or one of a number of competing human activities but the source of the 'real me'; the self discovered in sexuality is the only valid self. You might be a minor cog in some economic machine or an unimportant clerk in an anonymous organization but only in the sexual context, does the 'real you' manifest itself. Sexuality is the final illusion of an independence and self-determination that have virtually disappeared for most of us in contemporary industrialized society. The critical will observe, and rightly, that for the majority in all cultures of any complexity, independence and self-determination were illusions; but in such cultures, religion gave the individual the assurance of present and future reality.

In our culture the only significant personal discoveries are those made in sexual behaviour. This is the foundation for two contemporary variations on the theme of sexuality: familial sexuality and non-familial sexuality. The first relies upon the proposition that the only satisfactory and durable sexual relationship is that found in marriage, and marriage is given stability and guaranteed against failure by having children. This is the 'myth' (12) promulgated in the women's magazines, 'family serials' on television, in 'family doctor' magazines, by advertising, and innumerable popular novels. It is in competition and conflict with its rival: 'sex-as-the-ultimate-aim-of-living', a theme that is reflected in 'girlie' magazines, magazines for men, sex journals such as *Forum* and that could well be termed the '*Penthouse* or *Playboy* version of life'. Sometimes the two themes merge uneasily as in the experiments in communal living, and 'wife-swapping'. But whether the belief takes the form of 'sex with everything' or 'happy sex within the nuclear family', the fundamental ideology is the same: the 'real self' is within the private sphere and its most significant activities are sexual, thus potency becomes a major source of personal anxiety, even though it may express itself in disguised forms such as a preoccupation with baldness or flatulence. The discovery of the real self in sexual behaviour is the dominant theme in the entertainment offered by the mass media, and has reduced all other plots in the contemporary novel to minor status.

With the decline in the influence of organized religion and the moral codes associated with them, there is now a scarcity of firm social controls, of imperatives, in the private sphere and this has created psychological difficulties for the individual. He, seeking his supposedly 'real self' in his non-public life, must make do with the assistance of only weak and limited identity-confirming processes. Agencies for identity-maintenance exist in the private sphere but the most important of them, the family, has been greatly weakened by the complex series of interacting influences that we describe variously as industrialization or modernization. Social life seems in the urbanized culture of the West to be inhospitable towards the family and it has been transformed from a stable institution into one that is, in individual instances of great number, a fragile and transient thing. Other institutions have had to come into existence to fill the gap or undergo a metamorphosis to meet new demands. Some of these are old institutions that have adopted new functions, the churches for example, whose pastoral care has, in many cases, changed from a concern for spiritual welfare to a concentration on material amenities. Others, such as counselling agencies, are new arrivals. All reflect what Berger calls the characteristics of the 'private identity market' and, if we are to believe Thomas Luckmann, even the churches reflect them today by permitting and sometimes encouraging (except for the Roman

Catholic Church) a personal faith that he designates the 'invisible religion', i.e. a personal brand of faith peculiar to the individual holding it (13). The degree of permissiveness in matters of belief has reached such a point in some of the Christian churches that one can safely repeat the late Dean Inge's comment that 'they interfere neither with one's politics, morals, nor religion'. These identity-marketing agencies are voluntary and competitive, and those that operate in the private sphere only are also consumer-oriented. On the whole, they tend to be highly permissive, in the sense of offering no firm moral commands, and thus they exhibit in their values the absence of social controls that is a trait of the society in which they are situated.

Identity-marketing agencies play a big part in the public sphere too. One of the concomitants of recent industrialization has been the growth of bureaucracy, a form of public control that creates an order not by crude coercion but by legal authority and manipulative and persuasive skills and techniques. It has come, in societies like ours, to replace the kinship systems that played such a great part in simpler and traditional societies, says Ernest Gellner (14). Unlike political movements and parties and the churches, that have remained outside industry and government departments, psychotherapeutic agencies, including counselling ones, play a part in the public bureaucratic sphere as well as in the private sphere; they are, in fact, the links between the two, straddling both worlds. In the private sphere, they supply anxious consumers with a variety of services for the building, maintenance and repair of private identities; in the public sphere they provide with practitioners political and industrial organizations in need of non-violent forms of social control. The same or similar practitioner (psychiatrist, social worker, clinical psychologist, industrial relations consultant) plays two roles: in the private sphere, he assists the individual to recover or repair his identity while in the public sphere he smooths out difficulties and assists in dealing, without violence, with actual or potential troublemakers within the organization. They also have another part to play in industry and commerce: they use their knowledge to assist in the actual processes of selling; as Jules Henry observes: 'a further factor that gives big business increasing advantage over the new (business) and the little man is the capacity of big business, aided by social psychology and psychoanalysis, to channel unconscious cravings into consumption' (15).

The psychotherapeutic ideology has partly succeeded in doing what organized religion has mostly failed to do in contemporary society, that is, it has gone far to help the individual towards reconciling himself to his dichotomized existence (16).

How do the beliefs of the psychotherapies show an affinity with the dichotomized world of modern industrialized urbanized society? It is possible to summarize the essentials of these beliefs into a few propositions. At the basis of all psychotherapeutic ideologies lies the belief that only a small area of the total self is presented to consciousness. This conscious self performs activities, i.e. 'does things', 'thinks things', the drives for which stem from the unconscious part of the self, hence the true meanings of these actions are unknown to the conscious self. All the mental processes that are decisive derive from unconscious sources. Thus individuals are ignorant of their own motives and incapable of interpreting their own symbolizations as expressed in dreams, errors of behaviour, and rationalizations. Interpretation can only come from certain procedures applied by a practitioner, and these procedures are claimed to be scientific and alleged to be scientifically verifiable. Interpretation depends, in great part, upon the uncovering of the phase of infancy, for this period is the most formative and significant in any individual's life; and in assessing the individual's actions in the area of behaviour denoted by sexuality, for this area is of paramount significance for the individual. The continuing activity of the self can be interpreted only in terms of certain psychological mechanisms, of which repression and projection are the most important. Society, or culture if one prefers that term, is understandable only as the scene of the interaction between unconscious driving forces and norms of individual and social behaviour that have been consciously established, i.e. society is the stage of the irreconcilable conflict between the unconscious self and the conscious norms that we call culture. This ideology is deterministic as well as reductionist, and without the reassurances provided by psychotherapy, it would be profoundly pessimistic (17).

The concept that is essential to this ideology is that of the unconscious; it is also that which provides the affinial connection with the contemporary social structure. The complexity and fragmentation of our society are such that they do not permit the individual to perceive his society either as a whole or in its totality. Part, the major part is, like the individual unconscious, hidden and inaccessible; in Berger's phrase 'society is opaque'. The opaqueness of the Freudian model of man reflects an opaqueness similar to that of modern society.

The impulses, the motor forces, the societal drives of our society are likewise incomprehensible to the individual. He can no longer attribute them to God's will manifesting itself in mysterious ways; the best he can manage in the way of explanation is to postulate daemonic urges emanating from the depths of the human collectivity or reify certain human institutions such as 'industry', 'the economic system' and endow them with self-determination and motor power. Whatever the motivating forces of society may be, they are as deeply hidden as the drives in the individual's unconscious. The outer world confirms, in its overpowering and menacing obscurity, in its sinister potential, the individual's experience of his own inner being.

The theme of sexuality that dominates the psychological version of man is at one with the social situation in which the 'real me' is located in the private sphere. Sexuality in our Judeo-Christian culture has for so long been encompassed with taboos, so long the source of deviance, both open and secret, that it would have been the choice for the location of identity-confirmation even without the added strength given to it by its becoming virtually the only area in which both masculinity and femininity can be demonstrated today. The mythology of sex is the religion of industrialized society.

Sexuality establishes the primacy of the private sphere and the theme of childhood strengthens this; the 'real me' is formed in infancy and given self expression in later life in sexuality. The period of infancy and childhood is passed within the family, i.e. the fortress of the private sphere, and this serves to sustain the important corollary of 'familism', i.e. that the family is the most 'healthy' locale of identity affirmation (18).

Moreover, understanding the self to be an assembly of psychological mechanisms, permits the individual, and the organization, to deal with himself or be dealt with along 'technological' lines that reproduce in a different context, the processes that are characteristic of contemporary industrial production. Technical or scientific experts can tinker with the individual mechanisms in a manner analogous to the way in which 'social engineers' are assumed to be able to make adjustments to the mechanisms of the social structure (19).

The interpretation of society (or on a world-historical scale, of all culture) as a kind of drama between the needs of the individual and the demands of the collectivity without which he could not survive, mirrors the fulfilments and frustrations of daily life in a consumer-oriented society. The absence of moral imperatives and certitudes in such a society emphasizes the conflict between individual needs and social constraints. The psychotherapeutic ideology provides the bases for those skills in adjustment without which the conflict would get out of hand and without which such a society would be unable to survive (20).

The psychotherapeutic ideology is a combination of myth and sobriety that embodies the hopes and fantasies of people living in a disenchanted world in which the very rationality and scientific method that achieved disenchantment have paradoxically reenchanted great areas of it again. It presents itself as a science and as a technique of rational control, but it is actually a form of inverted transcendence, a neo-mysticism in which the 'real self' is discoverable not by an ascent to heaven but by a descent into the depths with a guide. It is not without significance that only one person has, apparently, been able to make this descent unaided and alone and that was the Founder of the original psychotherapeutic ideology himself, Freud (21). The other-worldly religions have always sought the mysteries at some transcendental level, but what they localized above, the psychotherapists situate within and below. The other world is now the other self, the healthier, more mature and thus more 'real me' just as the other world was more real than the world of vanities and illusions in which man lived below. It is the discovery of the 'real me' that is the grail of the psychotherapeutic quest and, in spite of its trouble-shooting aspects and its services to all manner of dubious industrial and state enterprises, it is an altogether kindlier, more humane approach than that of its nearest psychological rival, the learning-theory-behaviouristic ideology; at their worst, the

25

psychotherapists treat their fellowmen as cases, at their best the learning-theorists treat theirs as things.

This strange reversal of the disenchantment of the world, this re-mythologizing of the demythologized has, in Durkheim's meaning of the phrase, succeeded in making the symbols of psychoanalytic thought the 'collective representations' of our society. It is also not surprising that sociology might demonstrate an affinity between this ideology and the contemporary in-dustrialized society that we inhabit when we bear in mind Berger's observation that sociology is a form of collective introspection, at least it can be when it is not concentrating on trivialities. A sociology of sociology would probably demonstrate the affinity of sociology with the divided and fragmented social world just as great as the affinity between that world and depth psychology.

The medieval world of Christendom and the essentially similar social worlds of traditional societies were distinguished by certitude in moral matters and an individual sense of belonging to a moral order, which if not 'natural' was at least divine. After years of disruption, the traditional order has ended and the individual is left in an enduring position of personal and moral uncertainty. The associates of uncertainty are an instrumental attitude to work and the privatization of most of the erstwhile public areas of life, and in this situation, the psychotherapeutic ideology offers a substitute certitude and with its increasing acceptance by a growing number of individuals, a considerable degree of power passes into the hands of the psychotherapist because the ultimate in power is to define reality. In the acceptance of a given definition of reality lies collective solidarity that in its turn implies a psychological solidarity.

Notes and References

1 Frankl, Viktor E., *The Doctor and the Soul*, Knopf, New York, 2nd ed., 1965, p. x (Souvenir Press, London, 1969).
2 'Ideology: a system of interdependent ideas (beliefs, traditions, principles, and myths) held by a social group or society, which reflects, rationalizes, and defends its particular social, moral, religious, political and economic institutional interests and commitments.

Ideologies serve as logical and philosophical justifications for a group's pattern of behaviour, as well as its attitudes, goals, and general life situation. The ideology of any population involves an interpretation (and usually a repudiation) of alternative ideological frames of reference. The elements of an ideology tend to be accepted as truth or dogma rather than as tentative philosophical or theoretical formulations. . . .' Theodorson, George A. and Achilles G., *A Modern Dictionary of Sociology*, Methuen, London, 1970, p. 195.

3 Weber, Max, *The Protestant Ethic and the Spirit of Capitalism*, translated by Talcott Parsons, George Allen & Unwin, London, 1930, pp. 55 ff. The best critique to date of the Weberian thesis and the discussion of alternative theses is still Amintore Fanfani's *Catholicism, Protestantism and Capitalism*, Sheed and Ward, London, 1935.

4 Halmos, Paul, *The Faith of the Counsellors*, Constable, London, 1965, and *The Personal Service Society*, University of Wales Press, Cardiff, 1966.

5 Szasz, Thomas S., *Law, Liberty and Psychiatry*, The Macmillan Co., New York, 1963.

6 Berger, Peter L., 'Towards a Sociological Understanding of Psychoanalysis', *Social Research*, Spring 1965, pp. 26–41.

7 Berger, Peter L., *The Sacred Canopy*, Doubleday, New York, 1967; *Invitation to Sociology*, Pelican Books, Harmondsworth, 1967; and his article 'Religious Institutions' in *Sociology: An Introduction*, edited by N. J. Smelser, Wiley, New York, 1967, pp. 369–78 (Wiley, London, 1967).

8 Gehlen, Arnold, *Der Mensch, seine Natur und seine Stellung in der Welt*, 1940 and 1962; *Urmensch und Spätkultur*, Athenaeum, Bonn, 1956 and 1964; *Die Seele im technischen Zeitalter*, Rowohlt, Hamburg, 1957; *Anthropologische Forschung*, Rowohlt, Hamburg, 1961.

9 Luckmann, Thomas, 'On Religion in Modern Society', *Journal for the Scientific Study of Religion*, Spring 1963, pp. 147–62.

10 Gehlen, *op. cit.*, pp. 94–103; Luckmann, *op. cit.*, p. 158. Habermas, Jürgen, *Toward a Rational Society*, translated by J. J. Shapiro, Heinemann, London, 1971, pp. 50–122.

11 The phrase is ascribed to Viktor E. Frankl in Koestler, Arthur and Smythies, J. R. (eds), *Beyond Reductionism*, Hutchinson, London, 1969, p. 410. For a view of alienation by a Neo-Freudian psychoanalyst: 'The facts are, however, that the modern, alienated individual has opinions and prejudices but no convictions, has likes and dislikes, but no will. His opinions and prejudices, likes and dislikes, are manipulated in the same way as his taste is, by powerful propaganda machines—which might not be effective were he not already conditioned to such influences by advertising and his whole alienated way of life.' Fromm, Erich, *The Sane Society*, Holt, Rinehart and Winston, New York, 1956, p. 339 (Routledge, London, 1956).

12 Luckmann, *op. cit.*, p. 161; Sagarin, Edward, 'Taking Stock of Studies of Sex', *The Annals of the American Academy of Political and*

Social Sciences, Vol. 376, p. 1 and pp. 4–5. I am using 'myth' in its equivocal contemporary sense, i.e. not as 'sacred tradition' or 'primordial revelation' but as a 'fiction', 'illusion' and also as an 'exemplary model'; see Eliade, Mircea, *Myth and Reality*, George Allen & Unwin, London, 1964, p. 1.

13 Luckmann, Thomas, *The Invisible Religion*, Macmillan, New York, 1967 (Collier-Macmillan, London, 1971).

14 Gellner, Ernest, *Thought and Change*, Weidenfeld and Nicolson, London, 1964, p. 154.

15 Henry, Jules, *Culture against Man*, Tavistock, London, 1966, p. 40. For a humanized version of the technological approach to social life, see Gans, Herbert J., *People and Plans—Essays in Urban Problems and Solutions*, Basic Books, New York, 1968. For a less humanized approach see Gellerman, S. W., *The Uses of Psychology in Management*, Collier-Macmillan, London, 1970. For an attack on the 'troubleshooting' role of social workers see Wootton, Barbara, *Social Science and Social Pathology*, George Allen & Unwin, London, 1959.

16 The confusion that this sometimes engenders is reflected in books such as Mays, John Barron, *Crime and the Social Structure*, Faber, London, 1967, pp. 207–7. The topic, under various guises, figures frequently in the report of the 'Interprofessional Conference' edited by Paul Halmos entitled *Moral Issues in the Training of Teachers and Social Workers*, The Sociological Review Monograph No. 3, Keele, August 1960, especially the 'Comment' by Marjorie A. Brown, pp. 55–63, and that by G. H. Bantock, pp. 65–73.

17 These propositions can be found scattered throughout the works of Freud, and in Jones, Ernest, *The Life and Work of Sigmund Freud*, Basic Books, New York, 3 vols, 1953, 1955, 1957 (Hogarth Press, London, 1953); and in the invaluable work by Birnbach, Martin *Neo-Freudian Social Philosophy*, Stanford University Press, Stanford, 1962, pp. 1–43 (Stanford University Press, London, 1962). For Neo-Freudian interpretations see Thompson, Clara, *Psychoanalysis: Evolution and Development*, Hermitage House, New York, 1950, as well as Birnbach, *op. cit.* The contrast between optimistic and pessimistic modes comes from Albert Schweitzer.

18 Luckmann, *op. cit.*, p. 161.

19 Gans, *op. cit.*, for this 'technological' or 'social engineering' approach.

20 Schelsky, Helmut, *Soziologie der Sexualität*, Rowohlt, Hamburg, 1955, especially the section 'Sexualität als Konsum', pp. 118–27; and Henry, Jules, *op. cit.*, pp. 3–99.

21 Rieff, Philip, *Freud: The Mind of the Moralist*, Methuen, London, 1960, pp. 65–9; and Jones, *op. cit.*, vol. 1, p. 319. Karen Horney, who was a Freudian heretic, differed on this point and even went so far as to let the side down by writing a little book, *Self-Analysis*, Norton, New York, 1942 (Routledge, London, 1942).

Chapter 2

The Transmission of Values

On 17 May 1966, Paul Halmos delivered his inaugural lecture as professor of sociology to an audience at University College, Cardiff; its title was *The Personal Service Society*, and the lecture was then and still is, the most optimistic version of the presumed trend towards 'the psychotherapeutic state'.

Halmos's argument seems to be roughly as follows (1): a group of what he terms 'professional' workers, and in this category he includes psychiatrists, psychotherapists, social caseworkers, and counsellors, possess common assumptions about the nature of man and society. Occupationally, they 'administer help to others through the medium of intimate personal relationships'. In addition to their techniques, they hold certain 'metaphysical beliefs and moral affirmations' which, he says, add up to 'a creed, a faith, an ideology'.

In its essentials, this ideology advocates concern, sympathy, and even affection for those who are to be helped by the professional practitioners. The creed also assumes the continued extension of knowledge and skill on the part of the professionals and yet he admits that it cannot explain in terms of its own 'positivistic' theory of human behaviour the central significance of this concern and personal involvement on the part of its practitioners, i.e. its theory of human nature cannot account for what is, apparently, a major element in the social action of those who believe in it.

Professor Halmos then goes on to claim that the 'counsellors' (a generic term for the group as already defined) have exerted a great moral influence on the *personal service professions* of our time. He defines these professions as those 'whose principal function is to bring about changes in the physical or psychosocial personality of the client' (2). This group includes, among others, doctors, nurses, teachers, social workers of all kinds, and the clergy. The other professions of our day do not possess this particular characteristic and he terms them the *impersonal service professions*, among which we find the lawyers, architects, engineers, and accountants. He continues, 'No doubt the two classes of the professions have certain basic allegiances in common but these allegiances are elaborated, enriched and refined only in the personal service professions and this is at the very root of the distinction I am trying to make. To understand the ideological orientations of the personal service professions we must bear in mind that these professions are nowadays being trained in socio-psychological theory, and indoctrinated with moral principles which—in spite of all protestations by the more rigorous scientists of behaviour—are fundamentally Freudian in origin. Kindness, tolerance, acceptance, permissiveness, and a scepticism about strong loves and hates, have received a new lease of life in this psychoanalytical, social psychological, and sociological century. For better or for worse, the psychoanalytical rationale for en-lightened education, for a humane penal system, for better in-formed psychosomatic medicine, for a progressive management of human relations in our corporate enterprises, has been widely influential whatever the subsequent and entirely legitimate scientific criticisms of that rationale' (3).

Halmos concludes his argument with four hypotheses. Firstly, that the personal service professions have grown and will continue to grow in numbers in the immediate future; secondly, the personal service professions are influencing the impersonal service professions so that even they, the engineers, architects, lawyers, and others, are beginning to accept many of the basic assumptions of the personal service ideology; thirdly, the traditional ethical assumptions of professionalism are gradually merging with the ethics of the counselling ideology; fourthly, the growth in number and increasing prestige of the counsellors and their participation in the leadership of society are bringing about not only a trans-formation in that leadership but also 'a major change in the moral climate of society as a whole'.

These are views of a trend that it would be difficult to dispute. The number of counsellors has increased in Britain in recent years and the last two years have witnessed the 'arrival' of the social worker insofar as training and professionalization, salary, and rank in the administration can indicate this. The proliferation of top-level administrative jobs for social workers in local government has put them on an equal footing with the administrative office-holders controlling public medical services and education; theoretically every qualified social worker now has the possibility of achieving high rank in the governing establishment. The process of attaining professional status and recognition has proceeded with great success in the last few years, and the establishment in 1970 of the British Association of Social Workers seems to be consolidating these gains. Not everywhere in the West has the trend been so successful for social work as it has been in Britain; in West Germany, for example, there has been a noticeable setback with the refusal by universities to accept training in social work as part of their programme of courses (4). In Britain, the efforts of more conservative academics to bring about the same kind of 'miscarriage' have been circumvented by such courses having been eagerly accepted by the British alternatives to orthodox universities, the polytechnics, and by many of the newer university foundations.

Government reports on social policy have, in Britain and in spite of party politics and changes in government, maintained, though sometimes in a diluted form, the fundamental tenets of the creed (5). If we can assume W. J. Goode to be substantially correct in his description of the processes involved in and leading to professionalization (6), then we can safely presume that the tendencies hypothesized by Halmos will inevitably be strengthened. As Goode indicates, one of the major tasks of an existing profession, or of an occupation claiming recognition as such, is the socialization of recruits into acceptance of the association's ethos. Thus we can argue that the ethos will be progressively strengthened as the group achieves professional status and consolidates its gains. The ethos will cease to be merely a justification for individual and group action, it will become that which legitimates the very existence of the group as a profession. Goode shows that one of the main objectives of professionalization is the achievement of a graduate recruitment, i.e. a kind of 'closed shop' with a 'graduates only need apply' sign on the door. In Britain this has resulted in a number of courses in the newer universities and the polytechnics leading towards academic degrees, the possession of which permits their holders to enter the social work profession without any

31

further 'outservice' training. This 'direct-entry' system has coincided with the disappearance of most of the training institutions that individual categories of social workers had set up earlier.

Halmos claims that the ideology that he is describing is 'fundamentally Freudian', without denying this, it is, however, possible to contend that it is based on what Schelsky calls a 'vulgarization of Freud' (7), i.e. a version of the Freudian view of man and his nature that ignores the profoundly pessimistic orientation of Freud's thought, as well as its essentially 'bourgeois' scale of values and its absence of permissiveness. A contemporary whose views coincide in many respects with those of Halmos is Philip Rieff, though he emphasizes that much of this ideology, although deriving from certain interpretations of Freudian thought owes even more to the Neo-Freudians. It is almost as if the expulsion of the 'heretics', Jung and Adler, by Freud himself has been re-enacted in the manner in which the Neo-Freudians have modified his thought and given it both an optimistic and public face that it never had in the mind of the Master. If it is possible to classify social thinkers into those with an optimistic orientation and those with a pessimistic, then Freud clearly comes within the latter category.

Without offering any empirical evidence, and within the context of the United States only, Philip Rieff seems to have come to conclusions regarding trends which are very similar to those advanced by Halmos (8). When allowances are made for the differences in the cultural contexts, there emerges a viewpoint that differs from Halmos's only in the two respects of the absence of that optimism that characterizes the latter's and the reservations about the degree to which its development and growth can be attributed to Freud. As Rieff does concern himself with the 'vile simplifiers' whose popularization of a debased Freudian ethic plays the major part in the psychotherapeutic ideology, his analysis of 'the triumph of the therapeutic' tends also to be a little less warm. He stresses the 'anti-communal' nature of Freudian doctrine, and argues that it cannot be put to use in the general service of the community without drastic modification, and it cannot be entirely 'remissive' without ceasing to be analytic, but he says, 'Americans, in particular, have managed to use the

32

Freudian doctrine in ways more remissive than he intended, as a counter-authority against any fresh access of communal purpose' (9). He adds, 'By mid-century, the controls and the remissions from those controls have grown so nearly equal that the one works no better than the other. More precisely, the old established controls are enunciated so vacuously, and in such hollow voices, that they sound like remissions; and the remissions have become so elaborately stated, by some of the most charming voices in our culture, that they seem rather like controls.' In addition, he notes that even Freud expected 'new devices of control and release to succeed our failing ones' (10). He continues with what can only be described as a sad version of the Halmos thesis, 'on the other hand, a heavily remissive psychotherapy may become a permanent institutional fixture of modern culture—a kind of secular method- ism for those who remain obstinately uncomfortable in their pleasures. Structurally induced conditions, such as the decline of an ethic of work, may, like individual neuroses, seek their own pathological resolution. The new saving symbolic may never arrive, *although from time to time, in various places, its arrival has been announced* (not italicized in the original) and new remissions experimentally tried. What appears now fairly certain is that the control-release system inherited from an older, mainly agrarian, culture into our technologically advanced, urban one cannot renew itself' (11). Rieff claims that when men's 'secondary needs' are automatically satisfied, they may no longer need to love a communal purpose as an end; and 'the organization of indif- ference may well succeed the organization of love', a point of view in which those priests of the psychotherapeutic ideology who have moved further away from Freud would hardly share. The Freudian doctrine, undebased by the modifications of some of its contemporary adherents would, other things being equal, no doubt lead to a 'permanent disestablishment of any deeply inter- nalized moral demands' (12). This might have occurred if, Rieff remarks, ours was 'the first cultural revolution fought to no other purpose than the greater amplitude and richness of living itself' (13). If the 'revolution of rising expectations' was not accompanied by the concomitant of relative deprivation, this would be an acceptable supposition. It might even look acceptable from the high-cost residential areas and the stockbroker belt or even from the observation post from which Herbert Marcuse views Western society, but it seems premature to say the least when account is taken of the widespread poverty still existing in the 'affluent' societies of the Western world (14). The objective of the cultural revolution is probably as Rieff indicates, but in not attaining its objective, its ideology has undergone some drastic modifications. The psychotherapeutic ideology has had to become a meliorative one that has had to accommodate itself to the exigencies imposed by alienation and relative deprivation on the one hand, and to the task of providing an ethic and justification for rescue operations which, if the crude dogma of affluence were true, would not be required.

It is not essential that a consideration of the concept of the psychotherapeutic society and its present ethic should concern itself with the extent to which it is Freudian in origin. In the first place, the degree of orthodoxy or heresy is largely irrelevant to its contemporary manifestation, and in the second place, it is the ethic of adjustment as expressed in the simplistic literature in which the converted declare themselves or from which they derive their ideology, it is the vulgarization of Freud, that is the concern of this enterprise rather than Freud's own ideas.

There is, however, a point of interest in this problem of origins. It might be suggested that the Freudian doctrines are to developed Western type industrialized society what Calvin's doctrines were to the evolution of capitalism in the West in the sixteenth and seventeenth centuries. As the religious element gradually disappeared from the secularized ethic of capitalism in the nineteenth and twentieth centuries, so the origins became of purely historical interest. Western type capitalism has become an exportable commodity, as its present world-wide distribution confirms. As Weber clearly indicated, once capitalism had become a regime with its own built-in forces of preservation and continuity, its religious affinity ceased to be necessary for its further expansion. The spread of the psychotherapeutic ideology and its manifestation in the 'the personal service society' no more require the *original* Freudian doctrines than Western capitalism requires the Protestant Ethic in order to root itself in Singapore or Hong Kong. As capitalism has been able, as an on-going 'system' to dispense with Puritanism, so the psychotherapeutic ideologists of the West have been able to adapt the essentially Puritan and stoic doctrines of Freud into the ethic of social adjustment.

Although it is not essential to examine the implications of Freudian doctrines in the present study of the relationship between the psychotherapeutic ideology and industrialized society, they do light up some of the more obscure areas of that ideology and strengthen the contention that the psychotherapeutic ideology is a vulgarization of Freud.

'Freud, like other innovators, started as a minority of one'—so said David Riesman (15), and the discovery that he had predecessors does not diminish his significance any more than does his vulgarization reduce his importance as an original thinker (16). No matter how modified, adapted or debased his ideas have become with the passage of time and innumerable 'interpretations', these ideas are the Gogol's *Cloak* for the contemporary psychotherapeutic ideologies of the West, but it is well to remember that the versions presented in textbooks, the mass media and popular works of self-enlightenment owe little of their social content to Freud. The ethic of social adjustment is essentially a political, or rather a politico-economic, ideology even though it has its roots in the thought of a man who probably never conceived of his ideas having a wide political implication. In spite of much ambivalence in Freud's thought, there are certain features that are quite clear: socially and politically Freud was authoritarian, élitist, and conservative. The liberator of man's individual psyche was oddly right-wing in his attitudes to public life (17). He referred to the working-classes as 'trash' while at the same time displaying a disconcerting egalitarianism in demonstrating that fundamentally all men, rich and poor, aristocrat and commoner are similar and are driven by the same inherent biological urges. Beneath the superficialities of class and status all men are the same, was clearly a view held by Freud and implicit in his psychology, but it is equally clear that he considered the lower classes inferior, just as he apparently thought women were. There was also a marked absence of that care, or even affection for his patients that Halmos says is one of the features of the personal service professions. Those who have adapted and interpreted his thought might well have been correct in creating a social philosophy of passive apolitical acceptance of an existing social, political and

35

economic order, because this is certainly the direction towards which his doctrines lead when applied to public life, but the widespread adaptation of people to their environment undertaken by professional workers out of some kind of spiritual commitment, that Halmos himself admits, cannot be validated by the philosophical and 'scientific' theory of human nature they believe in, is certainly an extension of Freudian thought for which there is no adequate mandate in the writings of the Master.

More than ten years before Halmos advanced his hypotheses concerning the advent of the personal service society, David Riesman hinted at the possibility of social change along basically similar lines, and argued that in part these tendencies derived from neo-Freudian modifications with which Freud himself would probably have shown little sympathy (18). The Protestant Ethic exalted the value of work and Freud seems to have accepted this evaluation, but the psychotherapeutic ideology has, in great part, abandoned this, but it has not yet been replaced by a purely hedonistic approach to the ideal job (19), i.e. that which brings in the largest income for the least work, but by the halfway house of the 'right job', the kind of blend of leisure and satisfaction that provides a salvation for the self in doing something other than merely providing the means for a higher material standard of living or making a profit for the company. Riesman saw signs of this gradual and complex reorientation of the aims of work in the disappearance of salesmen. Few people wanted to be commercial travellers or to go into direct selling anymore; and when they did, they preferred the new field of 'marketing' in which the nature of the activity tended to be masked, or they were, in the USA, recruits from ethnic groups not yet 'acculturated to the newer American values' or from Texas or Oklahoma where the 'frontier spirit' was still strong. This reorientation had not so much led to the 'Death of a Salesman' as to the *death of salesmen*. He emphasized as far back as 1953 how much difficulty American corporations were having in attracting salesmen into their organizations, 'college graduates today want jobs in personnel work or other service occupations, rather than in the exposed and isolated position of the salesman' (20). Much of this attitude, he admitted, stemmed from a reluctance to take risks, but it can be argued that these reservations about jobs also owe much to those influences that Halmos claims are at work at various levels in our kind of society and that will eventually lead to the triumph of the ethic of the personal service professions. Riesman, without attributing any of this directly, or even indirectly, to Freudian doctrines, wrote that the managerial climate is becoming determined by 'men who take courses which deal with human relations in order that they will be able to get along with their colleagues in the office, or at least to discuss problems of human relations at American Management Association meetings'. He drew attention to two aspects of this new concern for other people's feelings (or perhaps a tenderness towards one's own conscience) in examples drawn from two aspects of dealing with ageing. The first was provided by those firms and organizations that dealt with the problems posed by ageing employees and colleagues by creating 'make-work' posts for them; the second was supplied by firms having compulsory retirement at a certain age. These two apparently opposed resolutions of similar problems were actually two aspects of the same state of mind, i.e. that which resulted in reluctance to dismiss or retire someone. The first subterfuge allowed the superannuated to continue in employment in a non-job, while the second facilitated dismissal by remote control. Both devices saved somebody from feeling bad about having to sack an employee or colleague. Another facet of this reorientation towards work and ultimately towards social life itself, Riesman found in the changed emphasis placed on family life which, he argued, became apparent when 'occupational achievement' was played down and the 'family scene, with its pastoral virtues, was played up' (21). Businessmen and organization men tended to devalue individual success when talking: 'children are a kind of unequivocal good in a world of changing values, and we can lavish on children the care and emotions we would now feel it egotistical to lavish on ourselves. The young age at which people are marrying today is a further factor; having started to go steady at fourteen, they want to settle down at twenty. Whereas a generation ago a career man and a career girl would have considered marriage an obstacle to their work aims, today marriage and children are in a way part of the leisure and consumption sphere, the side of life currently emphasized' (22). So the twin themes of the cult of posterity and familism, both attributes of the psychotherapeutic ideology, appear in the world of the organization man. But Riesman does not lay the blame for all this on Freud. If an origin has to be found for this new tenderness of mind, then it might be better to assume, as did the late Morris Ginsberg, that there was detectable in the course of human history, a gradual and progressive social evolution towards altruism and neighbourliness, a true, if imperceptible, moral progress, or as Binswinger has it, the growth of the feeling of 'togetherness' (23). The decline in influence of the Protestant Ethic with its gospel of work may also have contributed to the growth of tender-mindedness or the decline might itself be related to, or even a product of, the growth of altruism; about these riddles we know next to nothing.

The paradigm of the psychotherapeutic society under its diverse names, i.e. of a society moving inexorably towards the goals contained within the notion, informs most of contemporary British social thought. I use this vague term advisedly because it enables me to include under this rubric a great part of the sociology produced in this country, much of what is termed 'social administration' (that is, the academic writing and teaching that deals with social policy), and a goodly portion of the literature upon which the teaching and practice of social work is based. Of course, not all social workers would subscribe to all the assumptions and implications of the paradigm—not every social worker wishes 'to pose as a miniature psychoanalyst or psychiatrist' (24)—though the most influential groups of social workers such as psychiatric social workers and other types of caseworkers certainly would because, among other things, they have been 'professionalized' to do so. Sociology in Britain has tended to show a marked leaning towards the left, whether in the form of the radicalism of the non-conformist conscience or in the form of Fabian socialism. The impulses towards the left have rarely been Marxist, rather have they been those deriving directly from a Christian origin or from that conglomeration of attitudes and opinions, that amalgam of altruism and philanthropy which defies definition, but characterized a great deal of sociological writing between the 1890s and the 1940s (25). The British Labour Party and British sociology have much in common in their origins: both derive their dominant themes from non-Marxist socialisms and radical nonconformity. To some extent, the therapeutic society is more of a paradigm of social thought in Britain than anywhere else in the world; it has by no means a comparable standing in Western Europe, and only in the United States does its support approach anything like the significance that it has in this country.

By 'paradigm' I mean figuratively what Thomas Kuhn means literally when he used this term to refer to ways of thought in the natural sciences (26). The term has become an 'in word' among sociologists, though it has only recently been used with any precision in sociological discussion (27). A paradigm is a term that communicates what is usually meant by a 'model' without the physical attributes that seem inseparable from the latter. It is a linguistic device or example that serves as a common frame of reference, a means of orientation, and a basis for defining the situation relative to a scientific discipline or humane study. Examples in sociology are: the paradigm of society as being constituted of interlocking and interacting systems; another paradigm is that of 'homo sociologicus', that is, social man as role player, the world as a stage upon which players perform their many roles; yet another familiar paradigm is that of society seen in terms of progress or evolution. When the progress is assumed to be both moral and material the paradigm is referred to by British historians as the 'Whig Interpretation of History' (28) and I suggest that the notion of the personal service society is an interesting variety of this paradigm.

In the last few decades, the paradigm that has dominated American sociology has been that of the functionalist school, whose vision of society is that of a system composed of numerous interacting sub-systems. Society tends towards equilibrium and the cement that holds the whole complex of sub-systems together into a more or less smoothly functioning whole is value-consensus, i.e. agreement on the desirable norms for society by all its members. In so far as there has been a paradigm in British sociology (and the empirical bias in British sociology has militated against the acceptance of an *explicit* paradigm) it has been one based on the functionalist scheme of things and in this respect Britain has been followed in imitation of American sociological orientations by West Germany, Italy, and even France, though in Europe, as in America itself, the enthusiasm of the 1950s for 'system sociology' has taken some severe knocks recently. This paradigm is conformist in essence; a sophisticated equilibrium theory being really nothing more than 'God's in his heaven, all's right with the world', and if something is not all right, then a little tinkering will soon fix that and things will return to balance and stability after the short-lived disfunctioning caused by imbalance. Quite apart from its 'truth', which cannot be proved or disproved, it appeals to defenders and apologists of the status quo. In addition, it has a 'scientific' sound that fits in very nicely with the prevailing interest and admiration for computers, systems-analysis, behaviouristic studies and the other elements of a 'scientific' sociology that have been fashionable since about 1950. The paradigm has not been without rivals, the most important of which is the so-called 'conflict theory of society'. This assumes that human society is the product of the interaction of inevitably conflicting forces and interests (29). These two paradigms lead to two quite diverse attitudes and modes of social action, the *priestly* and the *prophetic*. With a few notable exceptions, the priestly mode has been in the ascendant since the early 1950s, but is now under severe attack from the prophetic.

The priestly mode is, after Calvin's definition of it, concerned with the effort of bringing men into touch with the real through the mediation of its image embodied in the moral community's representation in symbol and ritual—Calvin was an unacknowledged precursor of Durkheim, at least in some respects. The prophetic mode, as expressed in Isaiah 11 : 1–4, is concerned with criticism and change; the prophet is the artist of mistrust, to paraphrase Nietzsche. The prophet says Isaiah 'shall smite the earth with the rod of his mouth, and with the breath of his lips he shall slay the wicked'.

From the point of view of this classification, the ideology of the psychotherapeutic society as declared sociologically by Halmos and others with similar opinions, belongs to the priestly mode. With adjustment to the environment as a main objective it seeks to achieve that 'getting into touch with the real' and the path to this is by salvation from within. Mediation is achieved, for some, by the psychoanalyst or psychiatrist, for others, by the social caseworker.

The prophetic mode has, as yet, manifested itself mainly among sociologists owing allegiance to and in continuity with the grand tradition of revolution and radical political reform; among such the name of C. Wright Mills immediately comes to mind, but others, although not advocating radical political change, give support to this mode by concentrating on the claim that human society is a man-made product and is therefore unlike a physical environment, analogies with which are thus illicit. Sociologists whose work tends to give support to the prophetic mode are not yet large in numbers but the work of some has already gained grudging recognition in certain academic quarters, in particular Peter L. Berger and Thomas Luckmann, both of whom owe much to the phenomenological philosopher cum sociologist, the late Alfred Schütz (30).

Opposition to the priestly mode is already beginning to come from some social workers. In April 1971, fifty-six social workers in Southwark petitioned their local authority to make empty houses available for squatters (31) and many similar examples can be found in the United States, moreover some social work students are beginning to carp at the priestly bias shown in their courses, and one of the social work journals, *Social Work Today*, encouraged discussion of a highly critical nature in the first half of 1971. But this new approach is still relatively weak and is likely to run into considerable difficulties in Britain as social work becomes professionalized and top-ranking social workers become part of the establishment since they will have vested interests in local and central government bureaucracies. As the demand for professionalization grows, and as more and more social workers obtain really well-paid jobs in the bureaucracies of state and municipality, idiosyncratic groups of 'prophets', whose beliefs will inevitably lead them into political action if not even to violence, will be seen as a group of dangerous deviants who will jeopardize the claims and status of the rest. They will, therefore, be subjected in ever increasing degree to the various processes that protect the 'priests', who will either drive the 'prophets' out into the wilderness by declining to appoint them to any but the worst-paid posts and by blocking their chances of promotion, or they will 'talk them out of it' in those time-honoured ways so well known to learned and professional bodies when faced by deviant and divisive views (32).

But it could be that those who detect the coming of the

psychotherapeutic society and those who claim it is already here are both wrong. They fail to take into account the opposition from the conventional conservatives. Those who view society as a functional system have never taken very kindly to psychoanalysis and its creation homo psychologicus. Talcott Parsons, archpriest of the functionalist church, may have accepted psychoanalytic principles, but few are capable of following either the intricacies of his thought or his style and most functionalists show a predilection for learning-theory and behaviouristic schools of psychology which are devoid of the notions of caring and concern. The popularity of ethological works such as Desmond Morris's *Naked Ape* and *The Human Zoo* and of the even more extreme works of Robert Ardrey testify to the survival of a narrower, more positivistic view of the human situation. The personal service society believers might be the unwitting sustainers of the industrialized bureaucracies that govern our societies today, but the emphasis lies on their unwittingness, for better or for worse, they have, with their hearts if not with their heads, always been on the side of the men of good will. Within the very environment to which their ethic of social adjustment calls us to adapt, there are enemies of theirs who rarely speak out loud and clear, but when they do they speak with the confidence and authority of those who have succeeded in the competitive struggle, they speak with the voices not of those who have merely continued to exist but of those who have survived. These voices are the genuine spokesmen of the paradigm of the functionalist-systems society, they are the direct inheritors of the crude mechanistic scientism of the nineteenth century, their intellectual ancestors founded the Eugenics Society, their practical wisdom is based on the pragmatism of the stock-breeder. They are élitist in the crudest sense and attack the foundations of the Halmos thesis on the grounds that it reduces all men to a lowest common denominator. I quote, unfairly perhaps, from an extreme attack on the psychotherapeutic society by Ludwig von Bertalanffy; he is attacking what he calls the 'robot model of man':

'As behaviour and personality essentially are shaped by conditioning in Pavlov's, Skinner's or Freud's sense, there is not much difference between human individuals, and even between pigeons, rats and monkeys on the one hand and human beings on the other. The same principles apply everywhere—and it is a good thing that they do; for this is true democracy. Hence it is only proper that what is outstanding is cut down to size; while the subnormal, abnormal, pathological and even criminal must, by touching concern and care far surpassing that for the healthy, be brought back into the flock of general uniformity. After all, when a child is asocial or fails in school, when a juvenile commits a rape, or a criminal—poor chap that he is—becomes a murderer, it's all the fault of wrong upbringing, sibling rivalry and the like.

'There is, in our society, a veritable fascination with all that is sick, degenerate or substandard. The three per cent of mentally retarded children in the population are in the centre of public concern; the normal 97 per cent must do with teachers far too few in number, ill paid, and working under a system such that adolescents reaching university do not command their mother tongue. The same applies with slight variations, to delinquents and criminals lovingly cared for while "senior citizens" are left to pauperism, and to every sort of scum in society which, for the reason of its degeneracy, hits the headlines' (33).

This is the voice of the authentic 'know-nothing' right. It represents that reality for which the priestly mode has made itself the mediating agency, it is the voice of the authoritarian, data-bank computerized society for which the priestly mode of the psychotherapeutic ideology is the soft hand. The élitists whose views are represented above are apparently ignorant of the yeoman service the counsellors do them, just as the counsellors seem unaware of the environment to which they are asking us to adjust.

To understand the nature of the psychotherapeutic ideology it is necessary to descend from the level of Halmos's lecture to that of the kind of statement that practising social workers occasionally make. The suggestion could be made that the former's views are almost as remote in implication from the rank and file social worker's doctrines, as the thought of Freud is from that of his popularizers. As an example of what social caseworkers are likely to conceive of as their mission, I have chosen an example that came into my hands by chance. It is a document written by two social workers employed as student counsellors in a higher education establishment and is dated January 1971. The counsellors concerned were trying to 'sell' the need for counselling to the academic and administrative staff who, in common with most of their colleagues in Britain, were not aware of the pressing needs for counselling and the benefits to all that could be derived from it. The personal service society is not yet with us, but it is making progress and witness to this is the fact that no one to whom the paper was addressed seriously opposed the views put forward in it or refused to consider them (perhaps this is an exaggeration, I should say that some sections of the paper were challenged but perfunctorily, as happens when people realize that challenge is a waste of time when the battle is already lost).

The paper was entitled *Counselling in a Changing Culture* and contained ideas put forward at the NCSS Conference on the Advancement of Counselling, 1971:

'At a recent conference on the advancement of counselling in this country it was apparent that although the majority of delegates present were very much in sympathy with the aims of the conference, i.e. counselling in all spheres was important whether it be educational, personal or vocational, there was obvious anxiety on the part of a few as to who were counsellors and who were not and what the role of the counsellor was. There seemed to be a fear that trained counsellors would become an élite who would overshadow others working in the education/ social work field who had either not had any formal training in counselling or were otherwise less well qualified, yet had for some years been counselling as part of their work.

'There have been and still are people in the social field who though untrained make good counsellors. They are sympathetic, sensitive people who can listen.

'But, until recently the role of the counsellor has been undefined, informal and even amateur. The rapid acceptance of the benefits of good counselling in the medical, social and educational fields has highlighted the matter of professional as opposed to non-professional counselling.

'The only culture which has clarified and formalized the role of the counsellor is the North American. For over thirty years the counsellor has been part of the educational and community welfare scene and has had the benefit of university training programmes, research and a well-defined career structure.

'This does not mean that we should necessarily follow the American pattern in the same way; the counsellor's role may legitimately vary, both spacially [sic] and temporally from one culture to another.

'Why are we more aware of the need for counselling today than in the past?

'Margaret Mead makes the important point that in all previous societies, there have always been individuals who were cast in the role of guru, philosopher, wise man and oracle to the community. He was accredited with knowing all the answers, or if he did not know them all he knew the most important ones. He was the final authority. But Margaret Mead points out that now there is no final authority in our culture, no society knows all the answers nor [sic] claims to know them.

'Interestingly enough, this is perhaps the first time in history that the adult generation has been prepared to admit that it does not know all the answers. The younger generation may and often does go further and claim that there are no answers anyway. This is perhaps the real source of the "generation gap" which is more akin to cultural conflict, a clash of value systems than a mere chronological difference.

'The primary concern of the young, and which is articulated so militantly in student groups, is the growing importance of values: the values of the person, the values of autonomy and integrity of the person.

'The "transitory" values of the adult generation have their roots in nineteenth century thinking, and have consisted in idolizing such things as security, respectability, conformity and possessions, whereas the younger generation value ideas of exploration, insecurity, honesty, solidarity and communal involvement.

'As yet the change in the value system has not been absorbed into the blood stream of our educational and community policy-makers. In time, possibly over two generations, it will.

'We suggest that this set of changes in our value system is the socio-psychological background which has generated the need for counselling services. It is this change which has accelerated the need for the informal counselling role to become a formal one, from an informal agency of society to a formal agency of society and which is causing considerable anxiety to those who are unsure of the role of counsellor.

'*The individual shows his maturity by his ability to adapt to the changing environment* [not italicized in the original]. The mature person knows his strengths and weaknesses and is able to accept help when it is needed. The immature person feels insecure in a world of changing values and often refuses help when needed most.

'Then who needs counselling?

'Perhaps, at some time in our lives, all of us. We may benefit from counselling as part of an ongoing, continual growth process (development counselling) or at crisis points in our life (fire-brigade counselling). Yet, we suggest that none of us is as mature as we might become, just as we are all culturally-deprived to some extent. Nobody is wholly endowed to the limit of his capacity in terms of culture. Finally, everyone is to some extent handicapped though not to the degree of those we normally think of as "the handicapped". If so, then there is another factor which generates the need for help.

'The provision of a counselling service must primarily be for those in the greatest need, but it is likely to become a vital element for those living into the changed culture of the twenty-first century.

'It is often thought that counselling is only for the tiny minority of psychopathologically disturbed. We suggest on the contrary, that the counselling role can benefit the vast majority of "normal" people who are to some extent immature, inadequate or culturally deprived and the special skills of the psychiatrist, the psychotherapist and the psychiatric social worker to be called in for the more deeply disturbed members of the community.

'What relevance has this to the staff, students and counsellors at an institution of higher education? We would suggest that the following points are of relevance to us and can act as a spring-board for discussion:
    i. What is the role of a counsellor in such an establishment

and where does it differ from or overlap with the role of, e.g. the personal tutor? Should non-counsellors counsel?

ii. The conflict of value systems makes its effect felt in such a place as much as anywhere. We as counsellors and you as staff are inevitably involved in this conflict at various times.

iii. The counselling service is not concerned with only the tiny minority of psychologically disturbed students but with the vast majority of healthy students and staff, who may be to some extent immature, handicapped or culturally deprived.

iv. If cultural change is taking place in our society, are we, counsellors and academics, agents of this change?' (34).

When an occupational group makes its bid for recognition as a profession, one of the first moves it takes is to claim an expertise. It cannot be denied that the authors of the above manifesto were certainly doing just that. What is this field of competence they allege they possess?

They mention sympathy and sensitivity as being attributes of untrained counsellors so presumably these must also be qualities found in trained personnel. They mention 'maturity' so it is assumed they possess this to a high degree, and apparently they command some techniques that enable them to assist people to 'adapt to the changing environment' in addition to being able to guide people somewhere through the maze of 'changing values' and 'the conflict of value systems'; furthermore they make assumptions about the values of the adult generation and even more speculative assertions about the values held by the whole mass of 'the young' and their 'primary concern'. It is not necessary to quibble over what they might mean by 'culturally-deprived' because the basis of their expertise seems to reside in some seer-like qualities that they express in the language of the priestly mode. As Helge Peters indicates in his article on the professionalization of social work, it is not possible to reduce social work to a set of generalizations; practice is based on the *ad hoc* treatment of each case and the expertise is only describable in the language of mysticism.

But it is unfair to confine quotation solely to one paper by practising social workers; so let us turn to a more distinguished practitioner, Helen Harris Perlman. Helen Perlman is professor of social work in the School of Social Service Administration at the University of Chicago and, to quote her publishers, 'author of the best-selling textbook, *Social Casework: A Problem-Solving Process*'. Her theory and her practice do not stem directly from Freud, but from the 'developmental psychology' of E. H. Erikson and an adaptation of the sociological theory of roles and role-playing. But all non-behaviourist and non-learning theory psychologies derive from Freud, and Erikson makes full acknowledgment to his debt to the former. What Mrs Perlman's actual practice owes to Freud only she and her clients know; from her writings, Freudian doctrines appear to be reduced to nothing much more than introspection and 'know thyself' which comes about through 'working with' the client, i.e. discussion with a 'caring' and 'empathic' caseworker; but I shall let her speak for herself.

Her basic view is expressed in what she means by the 'ongoing relationship' between the social (case) worker and the client: the 'wanting' or drive in the client, combined with the help the social worker can offer him, is what makes their being together have a purpose. The caseworker takes the client as he is, in his *being*, but their business together is his *becoming* (35). She attributes the difficulties of clients to uncertainties about roles, damaged or deficient identities as well as deep-seated personality disorders but she gives full allowance to the societal factors involved and seems inclined to accept prevailing notions about alienation and anomie. The caseworker's task she sees as an attempt to remedy through the client's own resources these deficiencies. Discussing these weakened identities, she writes. 'There are no ways yet known to undo the frail substructure caused by these psychic vitamin deficiencies. But there are ways by which to shore it up, to compensate for it, to bulwark whatever certainty and confidence remains. These lie in the tangible, immediate-present opportunities to exercise one's powers and find one's purpose in vital life roles. When a caseworker helps his client to find himself and to feel himself adequate to love and work tasks, he reinforces that person's sense and affirmation of identity' (36).

She outlines her position in a paragraph that is the quintessence of the psychotherapeutic philosophy:

'For many years the theoretical basis for the social work method called "casework" has been that of dynamic psychiatry. In sketch, the pervading belief has been that the maladjustments and frustrations in people's lives were the result of the personality disturbances or deficits they brought to their life circumstances, and that these were the product of an inexorable chain of earlier hurts and frustrations and errors of response. The treatment focus followed logically from this. It was upon the person's subjective self-expression, his emotions, his self-awareness and knowledge, interpretations of his past and present reality, his understanding of what forces in his life-experience had shaped him, and so on. The treatment assumptions were that as he gained confidence in his helper's support and caring for and belief in him, he would be freed to know himself more truly, more open to examine and realistically to appraise his own feelings and behaviour. He would feel less impelled to repeat old behaviour patterns; he would find tensional release and surcease in the therapeutic permission; he would be able more correctly to understand his impulses and compulsions and to assess what feelings and behaviour were realistically called for at a given time and place and thus with greater ease and success would manage himself accordingly' (37).

On the actual methods, she has this to say,

'The basic methods (sometimes called "techniques") of influencing human behaviour are common to all helping processes. They have grown out of solid repeated observations of what actions in person-to-person or person-to-group transactions seem to spark and sustain human motivation, to nurture and expand human potentials, either to block people or to release them, and make them either anxious or free. These ways of relating to and influencing people will be variously played out depending upon what an individual case calls for and upon the style and skill and special function of the helper. But except for the actual provision of tangible goods and services which social work frequently offers, these helping techniques are all forms of communication that have their roots in the dynamics of spontaneous or learned exchange. They consist, in the main, of attitudes and verbal communications that seek to reach into the help-needing person's feelings and thought process. They are generally held to include the helper's demonstrated empathy and caring for his client; his respect-fulness; his affirmation of the client's social worth; the inquiries by which he and his client establish the problem; receptivity and attentiveness; clarifications and explanation; counsel and advice when called for; confrontation and comments that stimulate self-and-situation exploration and interpretation; planning and rehearsal of actions to be taken—and so forth.'

To this she also adds: 'the nature of the working relationship', i.e. the clarification of the roles of 'client' and 'helper' that forms the 'contract' for the relationship (38).

Perlman is aware of the accusation made against social workers by critics such as Barbara Wootton, that they are not concerned with remedying the remediable defects in the client's situation, and she writes in a footnote, 'I omit here (from the discussion quoted above) what social casework does *not* omit: the recognition that there are circumstances that impinge upon people from the outside that are in no sense attributable to personality faults and that are the result of social and economic lacks and deficits' (39). She also recognizes the two modes that I have already mentioned and speaks of the reaction among some social workers to the 'personality cult' by which she means concentrating 'upon the individual personality either as a source of problems in social functioning or as a treatment locus'. She constrasts this with the 'sick society' approach characterized by 'the belief and averment that it is in *society* that sickness lies, not in the individual, and that a sick society offers the individual only sick means by which to express his normal drives and meet his normal needs. This theory stance results in a considerable shake-up of ideas about what helping troubled people should consist of' (40).

She admits that there are clients whose situations are such as to make introspective reflection and self-examination implausible and who are more the victims than the creators of their social circumstances. She appears, however, to be quite unaware of the difficulties that the premises of her psychology create for the contention that one could be the creator of one's own social circumstances.

The 'personality cult' is clearly, in the contemporary context of the above discussion, the priestly mode; but is the 'sick society' approach to be considered as an example of the prophetic mode? I think not. Firstly, the concept of sickness is not treated metaphorically but literally by those social workers holding this stance; that is, they are using the idea of sickness in the physical sense as being an appropriate way of thinking about societies. If, as some people (41) suggest, the notions of sickness, illness, disease and pathology are mere 'myths' when applied to the mental states of individuals, then these notions are even more misplaced when applied to collectivities of individuals, i.e. societies. Secondly, the whole concept of mental sickness, individual or collective, stems from the same sources as the 'personality cult', and the treatment for the condition is not much different from the treatment of individuals except that it is applied to groups or is based on the gradual absorption of psychotherapeutic ideas by the 'sick' collectivity. In the hands of social workers and psychotherapists, with some notable exceptions, the 'sick society' approach falls short of the prophetic mode as it lacks that commitment to radical changes in the political and economic spheres; it tends, at its best, to be but 'piecemeal ocial engineering' rather than a variety of the revolutionary tradit n.

Her book does have s ne interesting things to say about the spread of the 'personality cult' or casework approach. She argues that those who have experienced help, patients or clients, tend to become 'true believers'. 'The y tend to accept and make their own their helper's interpretations of their problems and their helper's conceptions of how they need to cope with them. Indeed their "treatability" is marked by their capacity so to attach themselves to their helper, so to "relate", "identify", "feel at one with", that they take in his attitudes, appraisals, judgments, and come to possess or to be possessed by them. What happens, then, is that a system of thought about what is good, mature, desirable, allowable, healthy, to-be-valued for the individual and his person-to-person and person-to-task encounters moves out from helper to be absorbed as an emotionally freighted conviction by those whom he helps. The client or patient comes to express this as *his* belief,

51

his guide to his behaviour' (42). It is this phenomenon of value transmission from caseworker (or psychotherapist) to clients that spreads out 'into widening circles of influence to become part of the spirit of the times'. Thus, in addition to the influences that Halmos's hypotheses assume must be added the influence exerted by satisfied customers in the spread of the psychotherapeutic ideology.

A factor that facilitates the transmission of values from the professional to his client and then on into the society itself, is the absence of any uniformly accepted set of moral values in most western societies today. The processes of socialization that take place in the family and the school are often inadequate and partial, and are frequently without the support of general public agreement, thus the opinion of the professional or expert in every sphere of activity takes on a priestly quality that transcends the narrow field of competence that is properly its own. The professional has become almost the only readily listened-to arbiter in controversies that are essentially over moral issues. The more closely the professional is concerned with those areas of life held today to be especially significant, e.g. sex, family, child-rearing, personal health, self-fulfilment, the more imperative his voice becomes and the greater the attention and obedience to his views.

In addition to the absence of wid ly accepted standards of conduct being conducive to the dissem lation of their own views by professionals, it also helps to account for two other related phenomena; the first is the strength of the organized opinion of scientific and academic communities as it expresses itself in the suppression of idiosyncratic views, and the second is the prevalence and success of 'comparison literature'. By 'comparison literature' I mean books, magazines, and journal and newspaper articles the appeal of which is directly to those who have doubts about their own performances. This literature either reassures them or consoles them or does both. They are, I suggest, unwitting means of bolstering up shaky identities. The reader finds in such literary material a standard, usually set up by an expert or professional, against which he can measure his own performance, and in the absence of any other convincing standards, he can reassure himself of his own ability in an area of living that is immensely important to him. With the tendency to find ultimate satisfaction in the private rather than the public sectors of life that is so characteristic of our time, these areas tend to be predominantly sexual. A careful examination of much of the literature that is described as 'permissive' and a lot that is considered pornographic will show that it really belongs to the category that I am describing (real pornography does not sell very well, at least not relatively to comparison literature). From magazines such as *Forum* to best-sellers such as *The Games People Play*, the main motivation for reading them is, I suggest, to find an answer to the question, 'How do I rate compared with the performances described here?' It is true that there is a kind of mild voyeurism in this readership as well, but it is relatively unimportant in comparison with the desire of the reader to compare his own performance with the norm set out in the book he is reading. The performances that such comparison literature mainly deals with are sexual, marital, and the upbringing of children, three of the most important identity-confining areas of contemporary living. The literature is permissive (remissive in Rieff's terminology), and comforting. It is permissive insofar as a wide latitude in sexual performances is encouraged, and comforting in the sense that if there is something nasty going on, it is not because of degeneracy or a 'weakening of the moral fibres' (43) but because of faults and errors in upbringing, parents, and familial environment dating back to infancy, and for which the individual has no moral responsibility. He is, moreover, reassured about his performance becoming more 'normal' if only he takes the advice of the expert about how he can achieve this, and, of course, it is his moral duty to do so.

As examples of what I mean by the 'am-I-like-them, as-good-as, better than?' kind of article, I cite the magazine *Living* sold in supermarkets. The issue for April 1971 contained an article on 'frigidity' written by a doctor; almost any woman could read the article, compare herself with the norms set out in it and come away reassured. The first issue of a new BMA sponsored monthly entitled *You—the magazine about your life today* appeared in May 1971 to the accompaniment of a sizeable dose of commercial TV publicity. The contents of this first issue contained among articles on slimming, pregnancy, and body odours (three other facets of life that are productive of intense anxieties) an equally

53

reassuring article on male impotence by which almost any short-coming in performance could be legitimated (44). I am not suggesting that such comparison literature is not a good thing but only that it contains an implicit ideology that is fundamentally related to the ideology of the psychotherapeutic society, which is not really surprising as the authors are mostly drawn from the ranks of the personal service professions that are most imbued with it.

It has long been a conviction of teachers and others that if you want to produce a certain kind of adult, the best thing to do is to start working on the child as early as possible. So counselling has spread from students to schoolchildren and as another example of the attempt to transmit psychotherapeutic values to the as yet uncommitted, who are not 'patients' or clients is a book by Alick Holden entitled *Teachers as Counsellors* (45). Holden is a deputy headmaster, teacher of biology, a JP, and a marriage guidance counsellor. In his book, he clearly indicates that he has no doubt of the need for counselling and he is equally convinced of the counsellor's function as well as his expertise. His basic assumption seems to be that the individual contains in-built therapeutic mechanisms which come properly into action only when certain personal relationships of a face-to-face order have been established, and it is the business of the counsellor to establish such a personal relationship with his client. He describes counselling as 'an experience through which one person, the counsellor, concerns himself with the life and affairs of another, the client, without becoming emotionally involved and seeking to impose his wishes upon the client. This demands that the counsellor accept the client and his situation as it is to start with, so that he can begin to help the client to find solutions to his own problems, and then prescribe them for him' (46). He attempts to answer the question 'Why personal counselling in schools?' by demonstrating a need for it in the following propositions. The intellectual bias of our schools, often expressed in an authoritarian fashion, can cause rejection of the pupil by the school, i.e. the school writes the pupil off as being no good, or the pupil rejects the school; the bad effects of these can be mitigated by counselling. The declining moral influences of organized religions can be offset 'in certain undefined respects' (47). Counselling might also compensate for 'apparent changes' in the structure and significance of the family. Counselling may also have some effect in combating the consequences brought about by the intrusion of television upon social value judgments. Teaching methods that are semi-automated can, according to this view, and it is no doubt correct, gravely affect the relationship between teacher and pupil and this might be remedied by counselling. Finally, he gives the answer of all answers, some pupils 'think that a counselling service is necessary'.

The psychotherapeutic ideology has spread recently into what would seem, at first, a very unpromising area: organized religion. In the United States, organized religious institutions, the churches, have already gone a long way towards consumer-orientation in the sense of 'marketing' their services (48), and among these services 'pastoral counselling' has figured for many years. In the last twenty years or so, 'pastoral counselling' has appeared high on the programmes of many churches in the United Kingdom. In a recently published book by Kathleen Heasman (49), the author distinguishes between 'pastoral counselling' and 'pastoral care'. Pastoral care has been, of course, one of the principal functions of the Christian priest or minister since the Church came into existence and she defines it as '. . . concerned with the giving of spiritual help, as in the case of the priest or pastor when he makes available the spiritual resources of the church to which the person belongs. This would include the benefits of the sacraments and the help which can be derived from the reading of the scriptures or from prayer' (50), in other words, ghostly counsel. Pastoral counselling she regards as 'the process of caring for the human being as a person in all the aspects of his nature and endeavouring to help him become a whole and mature person' (51). It seems that pastoral counselling is only another name for general counselling and, in fact, some schoolteachers refer to their school counselling as pastoral, but what is significant here is that the churches have jumped onto the bandwagon as the values of the psychotherapists have been transmitted to the clergy. It is no doubt true that a common Judeo-Christian background informs both the 'faith of the counsellors' and the faiths of the clergy, as Halmos points out, but this does not alter the fact that the churches have entered the 'repair of damaged identities' market on the only terms available to them in industrialized society: 'if you can't beat them, join them', a device of expediency the consequences of which are not always likely to be those initially desired.

The counsellors have managed to gain in Britain and the USA a status that, if not yet quite 'professional', is within sight of being accepted as such. They have established their expertise, even if not to everyone's satisfaction, and they have an ideology that is both an ethos and an ethic. What of the alternative ideology, the prophetic mode?

If we ignore radical and revolutionary movements in politics, sociology, literature, etc. and concentrate our attention only on the field of social work, then the prophetic mode is scarcely represented. The fifty-six Southwark social workers and the psychotherapists who speak of a 'sick society', and whose counterparts among social workers are to be found among those (relatively) few who reject casework for what they call 'community work', are not so far removed from the orthodox psychotherapeutic stance as they would have us believe. They hold the same fundamental views on the nature of man and society, although their interest in collectivities as well as individuals serves to conceal this basic agreement. Social work teachers such as Robert Bessell refer to this particular posture as 'social action' (52) and the latter says this about it:

'The form of social work that is currently receiving a great deal of attention is social action, when instead of seeking to help individuals, groups or communities adjust to particular situations, the social worker decides that it is the situation itself which ought to be changed. All sorts of methods to achieve this aim have been suggested, ranging from persuasive lobbying to public protests and violence. Not unnaturally, resorting to such extreme measures by no means has the support of even a majority of social workers in the British context, but there can be hardly any long-serving social worker who has not had experience of working to adjust a situation for the benefit of his clients. Even if the social worker disowns violence in any situation, he is surely bound to admit the use of persuasion to bring about change or else he would be guilty of using social work as a means of reinforcing an unjust situation' (53)

These remarks seem to give support to the comment on social workers made by Peters when he asks, 'On whose side are they on?' Dissatisfaction over specific injustices, indignation about individual cases, even demonstrations and violence do not indicate the prophetic mode unless the underlying desire and motive is to change the whole social order, and there is little sign of this in the sporadic manifestations by social workers of dissatisfaction with their job situations or in the irritation of some social work students with their teachers who concentrate on a casework approach.

Bessel indicates that even the 'social action' approach is not held by the majority of social workers in Britain, and their growing status as 'professionals' within an 'establishment' setting must surely deter many who might otherwise be inclined towards such an approach, but the approach of such activists is, anyhow, much less radical than it seems to be (54).

The values of the psychotherapeutic ideology appear to be gaining ground; the process of their transmission is well under way, and this ideology, in spite of its humanity and compassion, leaves untouched the essential nature of our industrialized, dichotomized society. Perhaps it is because of its humanity and compassion that it leads to a modern and secular form of quietism that both supports and condones the kind of society that creates most of the individual problems that it seeks to relieve.

Notes and References

1 Halmos, Paul, *The Personal Service Society*, University of Wales Press, Cardiff, 1966.
2 *Ibid.*, p. 5.
3 *Ibid.*, p. 6.
4 Peters, Helge, 'Die misslungene Professionalisierung der Sozialarbeit. Das Verhältnis von Rolle, Handlungsfeld und Methodik in der Fürsorge', *Kölner Zeitschrift für Soziologie und Sozialpsychologie*, Köln, Vol. 22, Juni, 1970, pp. 335–53. Dr Peters cites as the criteria needed by an occupation seeking professionalization as its ideal achievement: prerequisities (educational certificates) so that the person desiring to enter the profession must decide to do so relatively early in life; a body to accredit training schools and specify their curricula; the establishment of such courses of study and their attachment to universities; devices to define sharply who is and who is not properly in the profession.

He then asks why it is that this attempt at professionalization by social workers has not succeeded in West Germany. He suggests the following as partial explanations. Social work was recognized in Germany from about 1900 but was for many years predominantly an occupation for women concerned with problems of poverty and social welfare (it had a 'do-gooding', Victorian-material-help ethos). Professionalization began successfully enough in 1905 with the first school for social work training, and by 1919 there were twenty-six such schools and their final certifying examinations were set and approved by the state. The minimum entrance requirement for such courses was the 'mittlere Reife' (something akin to GCE at O level). In the 1920s these schools were opened to men and with their arrival came the demand for some kind of 'objective', 'scientific' approach to social work methods, but Nazism put a temporary stop to this, as well as stultifying the schools themselves. After 1945, social work became once more a focus of public interest and the pre-1933 tendencies for a more 'rigorous' scientific basis for the 'discipline' reappeared. Basing his views on those of Otto Lingesleben, Dr Peters argues that it was the increase in the post-war years of male entrants that stimulated more than anything else the demand for professional status. Unlike most of the women social workers, the men came mostly from the upper levels of the working-class and saw the occupation of social worker as a step-up-the-ladder-job. But this demand for professional standing stimulated inquiry into the nature and the methodology, if any, of social work.

According to Dr Peters, it has proved virtually impossible to find a 'scientific' (objective) basis for what are really *ad hoc* solutions to specific problems, solutions based not on theory but on administrative regulations, and the exigencies of individual cases considered from the viewpoint of altruism. He argues that although the search for a basic methodology persists, it is proving fruitless. Furthermore, the routinization of practice has not materially altered the situation; social work is not a 'science', it is a social philosophy. It cannot be 'objective' he argues, because its practice does not depend on objective, empirical data, but relies on diffuse notions of need. The social worker has no skills and expertise comparable with those of the physician, lawyer, or even the teacher, and it is because of this lack, plus the ambiguous role of the social worker, that he has not succeeded in gaining the support of the universities in Germany—yet.

On the subject of role ambiguity, he argues that the social worker always works for an organization (state or private) and to put it crudely, the social worker is a legitimating agent (he legitimates 'hand-outs' or other forms of help) but at the same time, one wonders, 'Whose side is he on ?' Social workers appear to have done a better job in Britain and the USA in persuading the influential elements in society that there is a need for their expertise and that they actually possess the latter. They have managed, in Dr Peters' words, 'to develop a professional self'. Academically, their success has been in marked contrast to that achieved in Germany; while they have not managed to obtain degree courses in social work at Oxbridge, they have not only managed to do so in the newer 'plate glass' universities and the polytechnics, but they have succeeded on several occasions in compelling academic bodies to agree that such degree courses will only run if they meet the requirements and stipulations of the professional social work associations; thus they have, in Britain, succeeded in an apparent reversal of the traditional process of professionalization.

5 Examples are *Community Work and Social Change* (Gulbenkian Report)—report of a study group on training set up by the Calouste Gulbenkian Foundation, Longmans, London, 1968. The 'Seebohm Report', *Report of the Committee on Local Authority and Allied Personal Social Services*, HMSO, London, 1968, Cmnd 3703. The 'Skeffington Report', *People and Planning: Report of the Committee on Public Pariticpation in Planning*, HMSO, London, 1969.

6 Goode, William J., 'Community within a Community: the Professions', *American Sociological Review*, 22 (1957), pp. 194–200.

7 Schelsky, Helmut, *Soziologie der Sexualität*, Rowohlt, Hamburg, 1955, p. 111.

8 Rieff, Philip, *The Triumph of the Therapeutic—the Uses of Faith after Freud*, Chatto and Windus, London, 1966.

9 *Ibid.*, p. 238.

10 *Ibid.*, p. 238.

11 *Ibid.*, pp. 238–9.

12 *Ibid.*, p. 240.

13 *Ibid.*, p. 241.

14 The United States Government has, on many occasions during recent years, admitted to widespread poverty within its borders. The West German Federal Republic Government admitted to five millions living in poverty within the BRD (ZDF, Mainz, 5 February 1971).

15 Riesman, David, *Individualism Reconsidered*, Doubleday, New York, 1954 (Collier-Macmillan, London, 1964).

16 Whyte, Lancelot Law, *The Unconscious before Freud*, Basic Books, New York, 1960 (Tavistock Publications, London, 1967).

17 For Freud's élitism, see Birnbach, *op. cit.*, p. 28; Rieff, *op. cit.*, p. 228; Roazen, Paul, *Freud: Political and Social Thought*, Hogarth, London, 1968, p. 272. On his 'reactionary conservatism' as well as his 'liberalism', see Riesman, David, 'The Themes of Work and Play in the Structure of Freud's Thought', *Psychiatry*, Vol. 13, No. 3, 1950, and 'The Themes of Heroism and Weakness in the Structure of Freud's Thought', *Psychiatry*, Vol. 13, No. 3, 1950. This last article also contains some observations on Freud's attitudes towards his patients. For the authoritarian element in his nature, see Riesman, David, 'Authority and Liberty in the Structure of Freud's

Thought', *Psychiatry*, Vol. 13, No. 2, 1950, and for his attitudes towards the 'lower classes'; also Rieff, *op. cit.*, p. 228 and 310 for the same and the masses.

18 Riesman, David, *Individualism Reconsidered*, Doubleday, New York, 1954 (Collier-Macmillan, London, 1964); 'New Standards for Old: from Conspicuous Consumption to Conspicuous Production' (1953), pp. 148–63.

19 See the concept of the 'happy alienated worker' as developed by David Riesman and William Stephenson (1967).

20 Riesman, *op. cit.*, p. 152.

21 *Ibid.*, p. 158.

22 *Ibid.*, p. 159.

23 Binswinger, Ludwig, *Being-in-the-World: Selected Papers*, translated by J. Needleman, Basic Books, New York, 1963.

24 Wootton, Barbara, *Social Science and Social Pathology*, George Allen & Unwin, London, 1959.

25 Abrams, Philip, *The Origins of British Sociology*, Chicago University Press, Chicago, 1968, pp. 31–52 (London, Chicago University Press, 1969).

26 Kuhn, Thomas S., *The Structure of Scientific Revolutions*, Chicago University Press, Chicago, 1962. 'Paradigm' is a grammatical term: *The Concise Oxford Dictionary* defines it as 'example, pattern, especially of inflexion of noun, verb, etc.' See also Boudon, Raymond, 'Notes sur la notion de théorie dans les sciences sociales', *European Journal of Sociology*, XI, 2, 1970, pp. 201–51, especially pp. 203–4.

27 Friedrichs, Robert W., *A Sociology of Sociology*, Free Press, New York, 1970, pp. 4–10 (Collier-Macmillan, London, 1970). The distinction between the priestly and the prophetic is to be found in this book, but an earlier formulation is in Chambers, Clarke, A., 'An Historical Perspective on Political Action versus Individualized Treatment', *Current Issues in Social Work Seen in Perspective*, Council on Social Work Education, New York, 1962, pp. 51–64.

28 Butterfield, Herbert, *The Whig Interpretation of History*, Bell, London, 1931, pp. 9–63.

29 Dahrendorf, Ralf, 'Out of Utopia: Towards a Reorientation of Sociological Analysis', *The American Journal of Sociology*, LXIV, pp. 115–27. A little book in the series 'Library of Social Work' entitled *Sociology in Social Work* by Peter Leonard, Routledge and Kegan Paul, London, 1966, mentions 'conflict theory' but the bias in the work is towards the 'functionalist' approach, and on p. 31, the author says in reference to his book: 'We shall be drawing primarily upon the structural-functional approach'.

30 Mills, C. Wright, 'The Professional Ideology of Social Pathologists', *Power, Politics and People—The Collected Essays of C. Wright Mills*, edited by I. L. Horowitz, Oxford University Press, London, 1963.

31 Raison, Timothy, 'When social workers go political', *Sunday Telegraph*, London, 2 May 1971, p. 16.
32 Polanyi, Michael, *Knowing and Being*, Routledge and Kegan Paul, London, 1969, Ch. 5; 'The Growth of Science in Society', pp. 73–86 and 94 for influence of colleagues and external examiners on idiosyncratic academic views; Grazia, A. de (ed.), *The Velikovsky Affair*, University Books, New York, 1964 (Sidgwick & Jackson, London, 1966), for an account of how contemporary cosmologists deal with a deviant opinion; Mulkay, M., 'Some Aspects of Cultural Growth in the Natural Sciences', *Social Research*, Vol. 36, No. 1, Spring 1969, pp. 22–52 for a general overview of how the scientific community treats aberrants; Cicourel, Aaron V., *Method and Measurement in Sociology*, Free Press, New York, 1964 (Collier-Macmillan, London, 1964), has relevant comments scattered throughout its pages. Publishers and producers deal with deviance by 'rewriting'.
33 Bertalanffy, Ludwig von, *Robots, Men and Minds*, Braziller, New York, 1967, pp. 8–9.
34 The document quoted is reproduced here in its original form, save for such minor alterations as were required in order to preserve the anonymity of its authors and of the institution to which it referred.
35 Perlman, Helen Harris, *Persona—Social Role and Personality*, Chicago University Press, Chicago, 1968, p. 140 (italics in the original) (Chicago University Press, London, 1968).
36 *Ibid.*, p. 192.
37 *Ibid.*, p. 195.
38 *Ibid.*, pp. 216–17.
39 *Ibid.*, p. 240.
40 *Ibid.*, p. 196.
41 Szasz, Thomas S., *The Myth of Mental Illness*, Harper and Row, New York, 1961; Scheff, T. J., *Being Mentally Ill—A Sociological Theory*, Weidenfeld and Nicolson, London, 1966.
42 Perlman, *op. cit.*, pp. 194–5. For similar views on the transmission of values by professionals of all kinds, see the article by Everett C. Hughes, 'The Humble and the Proud: The Comparative Study of Occupations', *The Sociological Quarterly*, Spring 1970, pp. 147–56, especially p. 152.
43 That moral fibres still exist in the 1970s may come as a surprise to some but not to all. The press reported on 16 May 1971 the alleged comment by Mr Oliver Wilson, manager of the student residences at Horsham of the University of East Anglia, that 'One can tell people who are taking drugs because their rooms are untidy, and their appearance suggests a general deterioration of moral fibre.'
44 Mortimer, Arthur, 'Men who can't', *You—the magazine about your life today*, British Medical Association Family Doctor Publications, London, May 1971, pp. 79–81.
45 Some lay (not medically qualified) psychotherapists refer to their 'clients' as 'patients'.

46 Holden, Alick, *Teachers as Counsellers*, Constable, London, 1969, pp. 57–8.
47 *Ibid.*, p. 69.
48 Berger, Peter L. in Smelser, *op. cit.*, pp. 374–6.
49 Heasman, Kathleen, *An Introduction to Pastoral Counselling—for social workers, the clergy, and others*, Constable, London, 1969.
50 *Ibid.*, pp. 18–19.
51 *Ibid.*, p. 18.
52 Bessell, Robert, *Introduction to Social Work*, Batsford, London, 1970. 'Social action' in this book is not used in the sense that I have used the term earlier in Chapter 1 and this chapter. I have used it in the Weberian sense, i.e. as designating those acts of men that are charged with meaning for themselves and others, e.g. a knee jerk is not a social action, but writing a letter is, and so is shaking hands. Bessell uses it as synonymous with 'political action'. For the more extreme American interpreation of 'social action' see Terrell, Paul, 'The Social Worker as Radical: Roles of Advocacy', *New Perspectives: The Berkeley Journal of Social Welfare*, Vol. 1, Spring 1967, pp. 83–8.
53 *Ibid.*, pp. 132–3.
54 For the views of some British social workers on 'social action' see 'Social action—Working Party's discussion paper for Branch consideration' in *BASW News;* Newsletter of the British Association of Social Workers' in *Social Work Today*, Vol. 2, No. 13, 7 October 1971.

Chapter 3

The Mystique of Counselling

A modified form of psychoanalysis is fundamental to all social casework. The method of social casework is reducible to a one-to-one, face-to-face relationship, of which type counselling is the classic example.

What is this method and what is the training required? What is it that the counsellor–social worker possesses in the way of special qualities and skills that enables him 'to assume responsibility for other people's lives and happiness'? (1). Some idea may be obtained from examining the specifications of training courses and their aims. The University of Aston in Birmingham runs a one-year postgraduate full-time course 'specifically designed to train graduates wishing to qualify for professional counselling roles in universities, polytechnics, colleges of education, colleges of further education, sixth-form colleges and other educational settings' (2). In the material with which this course is marketed, there are some pertinent statements.

A definition of academic counselling is given:

'Counselling is an educative process in which a professionally trained person helps a student marshall his own resources in such a way that he may find an appropriate resolution to an academic, vocational, or personal decision or problem. The way in which counsellors approach problems varies according to the nature of the problem and also according to the counselling "school" to which they adhere. The main tool of the counsellor is the one-to-one interview, though group counselling is also favoured by some' (3).

The reference to 'schools' of counselling is an admission of the existence of the directive minority, but as will be appreciated from what follows, the course is based on non-directed psychotherapy of the depth or psychoanalytic form.

The functions of the academic counsellor are also set out in some detail: '. . . to prevent students underachieving or dropping out of higher education . . . to help students who have marked problems with examination stress' (4). But much more space is devoted to a rationale for academic counselling:

'Counsellors are also concerned with the personal and social development of students. Common developmental tasks among students include the need to define the self well enough to make necessary academic, occupational, and personal decisions, emancipation from parents, integration of sexuality into the personality and the development of the capacity for intimacy. It is likely that a number of relatively stable students will want to see counsellors to find out a little more about themselves, to obtain emotional support in time of crisis, or to discuss some developmental problem. Some students may have moderate to severe personality problems. The symptoms include apathy, depression, lack of identity, autonomy conflicts, loneliness, lack of concentration, obsessive compulsive thought patterns and behaviour, underconfidence, feelings of social (including social class) inadequacy, and difficulty in handling their own and others' aggressiveness. In instances of moderate to severe neurotic problems medium or long-term counselling may be appropriate—in some instances referral for more intensive help may be necessary' (5).

The content of the course consists of the following studies: 'Human growth and development; abnormal psychology; statistics and human assessment; individual and group counselling theory; counselling—research findings and methods; academic counselling; occupational counselling; behavioural counselling; social contexts of counselling; supervised practical work in counselling; opportunities for individual and group discussion.'

The reason for this choice is made clear thus:

'The course content is based on the belief that there are three main components, albeit interrelated which should form the core of counsellor training. First, there is the academic component, which introduces the trainee to general developmental, abnormal, psychosomatic, behavioural, occupational and social psychology. The academic component of the course also includes work in individual and group counselling theory, testing and other forms of human assessment, counselling research findings and methods of conducting counselling research, social contexts of counselling and methods of improving reading and study skills. Second, there is the experiential component of supervised practical work in live and simulated counselling settings. Use will be made of film, audio and video tape, and a two-way screen interview room in teaching these performance skills. Practical experience is regarded as the central and integrating component of the course. Third, and perhaps most difficult, is the whole area of personal development of counsellor trainees—increasing awareness of their own behaviour patterns, eliminating or modifying unwanted behaviours [sic], and improving their sense of basic security and self-esteem. To this end opportunities for personal and group discussion will be provided as part of the tutoring and teaching of the course' (6).

From a study of introductory texts on counselling, it is possible to isolate a number of the basic assumptions underlying the training of psychotherapeutic workers and counsellors in Britain and the USA and to generalize about the skills that they are expected to develop. These assumptions and requirements can be expressed in the form of a number of propositions, thus:

(a) The problem presented by the client is usually a symptom of some personality difficulty or difficulty in personal relationships.
(b) To treat the problem symptomatically might merely change its form and the symptom will probably reappear (this is but a restatement of a basic Freudian position, i.e. that the treatment of psychological symptoms by hypnotism, chemotherapy or other non-verbal methods is bound ultimately to fail because they do not remove the underlying cause of the symptom).
(c) What such clients need is a deeper understanding of themselves and of the causes of their behaviour, and this is just what counselling seeks to give them.
(d) To achieve this, it is necessary to gain an insight into the feelings and thoughts of the client and thus discover his real self. A 'sensitive awareness' of the kind of person the client is becomes apparent to the counsellor after a time.

c   65

(e) The essence of this process lies in the relationship between two people—it is a continuous one through which one human being tries to help another 'by the methods which underlie the production of good relations' (7). It is not just a giving of interest, friendship and understanding but one that leads to a response from the client, leading to a new response from the counsellor, i.e. a dynamic interaction with changing responsive attitudes and emotions. It does not really resemble friendship because the counsellor gives help and the client receives it (8). Unlike friendship it is a temporary state, as it is terminated when the client's need goes. The characteristic quality of this relationship has been variously described as 'sympathy', 'rapport', and 'empathy'. 'Sympathy' does not meet with much approval from counsellors because it emphasizes the emotional component in the situation; 'rapport' they consider too vague; 'empathy' is the vogue word with them. This word, derived from the German and originally associated with art appreciation, has come to mean, in the psychotherapeutic usage, as indicating a relatively detached but profound sharing of another's feeling (9). Empathy is always for the benefit of the client, and this leads onto the next proposition.

(f) The dynamic relationship between counsellor and client must always be accompanied by the expression of feeling, but the counsellor's emotional involvement must be 'controlled' and this control is closely linked to the requirement that the counselling situation ought to take place in a permissive atmosphere.

(g) The client should be able to express his thoughts in his own way without having the feeling that the counsellor will not understand, be shocked or condemn him for what he says. The counsellor commences with a wish to help another human being in trouble but as the relationship develops the desire to help becomes expressed emotionally, in feeling, and in order to complete his task, the counsellor must control this emotional involvement so that he does not get carried away by it.

(h) The counsellor responds but his response only has value insofar as it gives psychological support by empathic listening, strengthens the client's security in expressing his feelings, and helps him to show progressively deeper feelings and encourages their expression.

(i) 'Transference' occurs if the process is developing properly

(10). The past is revived and relived in the present; feelings formerly experienced in relationships with people important to the client in his early life are relived in the counselling situation, and the feelings are transferred to the counsellor. The counsellor does not always have 'to work through' this phase psychoanalytically but needs to be able to recognize and understand transference and its inevitability.

(*j*) The counsellor has to be able to see his client as a whole person and respect and accept him as he really is; but this does not mean approval of deviant behaviour, only understanding it.

(*k*) The counsellor must have a good knowledge of himself. If he has not resolved his own conflicts, he will find it hard, if not impossible, to help another person resolve his. Furthermore, he must not impute his own feelings to his client because if he does this, then he cannot perceive reality, and this is a kind of rejection of the client.

(*l*) The counsellor must not 'over-identify'. Over-identification is when the counsellor responds emotionally to something that he recognizes in his client as being like something in himself.

(*m*) The client must not lose his sense of dignity and worth by the counsellor's adverse reactions to his revelations.

(*n*) The last seven propositions together add up to 'acceptance'. Acceptance enables the client to feel freer from tension and anxiety and thus less needful of protecting himself from acknowledging his deeper feelings and attitudes; so he is less inhibited and permits himself self-revelation, even when it is profoundly disturbing to him, in the security of their relationship without loss of his inner sense of dignity.

(*o*) It is necessary for the client to be able to see his problem or need clearly and 'in perspective', and it is the counsellor's task to help him to do so and 'to work through' the emotional disturbance which surrounds the problem and which impedes him from fully appreciating it and what it entails.

(*p*) The counsellor must not impose his solution to the problem or his choice of alternatives on his client, and so manipulate him into playing a subordinate role. He must not make his client subordinate by hurrying him along at a pace that is not the client's.

(*q*) A major part of the counsellor's task is to make the client aware of the social constraints and limitations on his (the client's) self-determination, i.e. he must make the client aware of the social reality of his situation.

These seventeen propositions, more or less, are the basic ingredients of the counselling mix. The approach indicated by them is, on the whole, a Neo-Freudian one, i.e. one based on so-called ego psychology. While the techniques of psychotherapy have altered very little, the orientations have. In the Neo-Freudian process of 'dropping the pilot', the Freudian orientation towards a psychology of the id and instinctual impulses has given way to a more technological view of the mechanism of the mind. The ego is now viewed as an integrative mechanism less concerned with defending itself against the id (still seen as the reservoir of primitive impulses) than with dealing with anxiety and finding means of satisfying the needs of the organism. When faced with conflict, the ego's main function is to find a solution, rather than defend itself against recognition of the conflict or having to struggle with it. From this point of view, the client already has a built-in device that enables him to find solutions within himself: his ego is his own personal problem-solver and it is assumed that he possesses the latent ability to make use of it. The counsellor has to assist the client to realize his potentials and in doing this, he strengthens the ego.

All textbooks on counselling stress the virtues of discussion, which is not surprising as counselling is almost one hundred per cent verbal therapy. In the 'on-going process' of discussion, the need for repression is diminished and the feelings of anxiety, inadequacy and defeat are reduced as they achieve verbalization. The counsellor aids this strengthening procedure by reassurances and suggesting things to do in which the client is likely to succeed. In this manner, and often without any great degree of awareness, the client gains a mastery over his own life that he did not have before. But before this can be achieved to any notable degree, the counsellor has to help the client to see with some measure of clarity the nature of the external social reality that surrounds him, and his relationship to it. It is claimed that 'unrealistic outlooks and attitudes' are often at the root of his difficulties and when he appreciates this fact, then he can be helped to adapt or change his attitudes to the 'needs' of reality. But the client must achieve this for himself; just being told and giving his assent will not result in the required adaptation. This is at the very heart of the doctrine of the ethic of social adjustment, and its resemblance to faith through genuine conversion is very striking; the missionary does not want 'rice Christians' and the counsellor does not want their equivalents either. Consideration of this 'reality' must be left to later; here, it is only necessary to mention that the textbooks carry a warning to the counsellor not to over-reach himself at this point. Often the counsellor would like to explore the psychological roots of his client's emotional maladjustment, but it is rarely the case that he has the time to do this, and most textbooks warn him that in addition he probably has insufficient skill to achieve it as well. His function remains to carry the client through a period of crisis rather than to 'strengthen his basic character structure', though many counsellors have such ambitions and many think them quite legitimate. 'The counsellor's job is to do what he can to further the process of adjustment and to create greater freedom for the person to gain a truer perception of the outside world and of his powers for relating to it' (11). The final stage of any counselling process is therefore seen as one in which the client has reached some sort of solution to his problem as he has grown in self-knowledge and self-realization of his potentialities; a development that is accompanied by a lessening of strain, a diminution of anxiety, a decrease in defensiveness, a greater acceptance of himself as he works in close co-operation with his counsellor. Towards the conclusion of the relationship the counsellor can introduce some 're-educative ideas' towards meeting the client's situation in a more constructive manner.

To what extent the counsellor imposes his own values and his own version of what constitutes external social reality on his client and so influences the whole course of the counselling process in an ideological fashion, is the question that is at the core of all criticism of the mystique. The exponents of counselling practice and the authors of training manuals and courses for counsellors deny that the counsellor wants to 'play God', but even if this were to be true in the sense that individual counsellors do not want to tell clients what to do and how to do it, it is very likely still to be true in the narrower sense of easing the client into a position from which he perceives the external world metaphorically through the counsellor's eyes. B. F. Skinner (12) says that because they cannot help it, they will be compelled to 'play God' anyway, but Carl Rogers denies this (13). If any reliance is to be placed on recent psychological experiments and research into learning, then Skinner seems more likely to be correct than Carl Rogers, *even assuming no desire on the part of the counsellor to persuade*. Although the textbooks are aware of the gross effects of deliberate reinforcement by vocal expressions, body movements, facial expression, direction and intensity of gaze, and verbal comments as well as of the processes of projecting biases into the thinking of the client, they are reticent, when not apparently quite unaware of the subtler and finer forms of influence that, to use the language and assumptions of psychotherapy itself, are unconscious on the part of the counsellor. Counsellors have a set of values and it moulds their reactions to their clients and the inevitability of this is what Skinner means when he says they cannot help 'playing God'. 'Social workers desire neither conformity with their opinions nor uniformity in cultural and individual patterns of behaviour; writes Gordon Hamilton (14) in her textbook of social casework that was reprinted ten times between 1951 and 1965; a claim that puts them not so much on the side of the angels as among the angels.

The interpretation of outer reality is quite a different problem to that of the interpretation of inner reality, that is, of motivation. It is true, as Hamilton says (15) that interpretation at the level of motivation is not usually attempted in the limited kind of therapy that is properly counselling—as the technique required, she says modestly, is within the sphere of psychoanalysis and thus beyond the counsellor's competence. But, she argues, most caseworkers would consider it possible and desirable to interpret the attitudes and feelings that the client offers and is only either aware or partly aware of. She warns that actions and feelings determined by unconscious motivations must be understood but 'often left alone'. The experienced social worker shows caution that is a response to the client. He has to gauge the extent to which the client wishes understanding or is ready to comprehend the meaning of what he says. 'Premature reality testing', to use Hamilton's phrase, can be ineffective and can also lead the client to dismiss the interpretation, especially when he is projecting his difficulties upon other people or things, in which case his defences take the shape of resistance. How the caseworker knows this is part of the mystique. The well-trained caseworker, without probing the client or arousing resistance will, because of the assumptions implicit in his training, perceive the underlying motivations and the requirements of each case situation and will determine for himself the extent to which the client may also have to share this knowledge. Hamilton stresses the need for caution and emphasizes that appropriate forms of interpretation should take the form of explanations of practical external current problems and conscious feelings and behaviour. She makes a sharp distinction between counselling and casework therapy and psychoanalysis, and claims that 'moderate changes may be effected by situational adjustments, counselling on a conscious level, clarification of real issues, without the goal of "insight", which may be gained only in a special sort of emotional experience' (16). The 'reintegration of the personality through insight' is the aim of psychoanalysis, and she argues that counselling sessions in which stimulated rather than free association takes place are not conducive to such a fundamental reorganization. Stimulated association is, however, sufficient, in her opinion, to provide the grounds for indicating to the client current patterns of behaviour 'both in a heightened use of and the control of the transference possibilities in the relationship' (17).

Is this statement one that really fits the practice of social casework? Later in her book, Hamilton says that the termination of treatment is related to the original request and 'its shared reformulation with the client' and then goes on to make, in the context of the treatability of clients, the following give-away observation, 'from the outset one must realize that the modification of character, so commonly the concern of social work, may be even more difficult than the relinquishment of neurotic symptoms' (18). Unless she is using characer in a quite unusual sense, this sounds remarkably like the 'reintegration of personality' that is, according to her, the concern of psychoanalysis alone. The essential difference between the techniques of psychoanalysis and that of casework counselling appears to lie in the absence of free association from the latter and its concentration on interviewing at a conscious level. Hamilton defines insight in the psychoanalytical sense as 'the understanding of unconscious repressed material which repeated interpretation may induce' through free association and the use of symbolic material and fantasies. In his paper, 'Distinguishing between Psychotherapy and Casework', Jules Coleman writes:

'In psychotherapy, the appeal is again to the conscious ego, but as an aid in the process of dealing with painful intra-psychic conflicts. It is also a useful device in reducing tension levels in the therapeutic relationship. In short-term psychotherapy, insight into historical genesis or ego patterning is avoided as far as possible but it does find its place in cases of longer duration, although it may here lend itself to intellectual defence, and thus prolong treatment. The reality aspects of intellectualization may make the seeking of insight more useful in casework than in psychotherapy' (19).

Hamilton claims that only a limited use is made of interpretation in social casework and that the worker does not usually seek to break through the client's defences (intellectualizations) save when his resistance is unduly difficult and negative, or when a markedly negative transference is taking place. The various defences against treatment that are summed up in the term 'resistance' have to be discussed and hostility and aggressive feelings may have to achieve verbal expression, but this does not mean that the counsellor has to undertake a plunge into the deeply repressed.

The notion of 'caring' that plays such an important role in 'client-centred non-directive' counselling is essentially one drawn from Heidegger, Jaspers, and Buber via Carl Rogers, from whom the whole concept of the non-directive client-oriented approach also stems. These ideas are certainly not Freudian and they are but one of the two major elements in the counselling mystique. However, the omission of free association, the interpretation of dreams and fantasies as well as other aspects of depth analysis does not deprive fundamental Freudian concepts of their importance as the other main component of the mystique. The hypothesis that ideas, feelings, fears, and wishes are rooted in the unconscious and that their intellectualizations or rationalizations are defensive strategems is the very basis of the intellectual standing of psychoanalysis; it is of the greatest possible significance, for without the assumptions of the unconscious and the process of rationalization, the therapeutic techniques of psychoanalysis would have no foundations. 'Things are not what they seem' is the philosophical basis of Freudian therapy and it is a very considerable element in non-directive counselling. It is the key concept with which the counsellor shows the client a glimpse, or more depending on how far he goes with the process, of his 'real' self, and by virtue of this and his special capacity for 'caring' for his client, reconciles him, more or less successfully depending on the individual circumstances, with the 'real' external social world. So two 'realities' are disclosed, and in making them apparent, the counsellor does not, it is claimed, impose his own views, values, opinions, and solutions on his client.

So far the authorities and authors quoted have taken up a stand that could be described as that of modified or not extreme adherence to the non-directive approach, that is, the counsellor is still much concerned about the genesis of the client's problem and a specific solution to it as well as about the psychic changes that occur during the counselling sessions and so they have tended to play down the 'modification of character' aspect. Carl Rogers has gone a long way to setting counsellors on a road that leads to a far more extreme approach and in which the main objective is 'constructive personality change'. Given that the premisses of counselling and the need for it are accepted, Rogers' approach seems a more reasonable one; if the skill and time are available, it seems sensible to do the job properly rather than be content to leave it partly completed.

Rogers believes that when an individual aware of a problem or difficulty and suffering tension because of it and seeking help to resolve it enters into a face-to-face relationship with another person sufficiently accepting and permissive to allow him to express his emotions and feelings freely, then through this catharsis he gains insight into the dynamics of his behaviour and sufficient relaxation to allow the constructive and integrative factors in his personality to effect a curative change. Rogers stipulates six conditions necessary for personality transformation:

'For constructive personality change to occur, it is necessary that these conditions exist and continue over a period of time:
1. Two persons are in psychological contact.

73

2. The first, whom we shall term the client, is in a state of incongruence, being vulnerable or anxious.
3. The second person, whom we shall term the therapist, is congruent or integrated in the relationship.
4. The therapist experiences unconditional positive regard for the client.
5. The therapist experiences an empathic understanding of the client's internal frame of reference and endeavours to communicate this experience to the client.
6. The communication to the client of the therapist's empathic understanding and unconditional positive regard is to a minimal degree achieved.

No other conditions are necessary. If these six conditions exist, and continue over a period of time, this is sufficient. The process of constructive personality change will follow' (20).

One of the main areas in which this controversy over the extent of the use of 'insight' flourishes is that of marriage guidance counselling. To what extent they are or are not psychotherapists in the rather narrower sense of the term, appears to disturb some of the experts. Albert Ellis (21) says that in the United States most reputable marriage counsellors have had their basic training in some branch of the clinical or social sciences or in theology, but a new group is coming into existence whose basic training is in the novel expertise of marriage counselling. Both groups agree that marriage counsellors ought to be trained in their own field provided that they are aware of and recognize their limitations, i.e. that they are not fully trained psychoanalysts or psychiatrists. There is, however, according to Ellis, a tendency for those trained in other disciplines to be guarded in their approval of those trained specifically in marriage counselling on the grounds that marriage counselling (guidance is the preferred term in Britain) is essentially a clinical or psychotherapeutic procedure, and they would prefer its practitioners to be recruited from one of the clinical disciplines. Marriage counselling, both in Britain and America, contains a considerable element of information and education, and is often directive in its approach. In addition, it tends to be concerned with the conscious or ego levels of the client, a trait that it shares with most other forms of counselling, and like them it often makes an attempt to gain access to under-lying or unconscious personality factors in the emotional dis-turbance that is the raw material of the counselling process. A growing body of opinion (in which we find Albert Ellis) seems to be adopting the view that marriage counselling is not really different from psychotherapy, and is indeed a specific form of psychotherapy. They claim that the clients of marriage counsellors are as severely disturbed as any client of any other branch of psychotherapy and that the main sources of premarital and marital difficulties are due to personality disturbances that raise problems that cannot be resolved until the counsellor reaches the underlying unconscious or repressed thoughts and emotions that are troubling the client. Some go so far as to accuse their colleagues of trying to do just this without being aware of what they are doing or without the requisite training that would enable them to do it skilfully—and the sooner they learn the better, is the implica-tion. There is a tendency to confuse the issue because some marriage counsellors reify the marriage; after all, they do often counsel two people instead of the usual single client, and it is the specific relationship between their two clients that is the focus of the procedure. Such counsellors speak of a 'sick marriage' and such a phrase is at one with much similar contemporary American jargon that is travelling across the Atlantic to Britain, and implies a style of thought in which marriage is never viewed as an institution or an intimate personal connection but as a mechanism, and so there is talk of 'making the marriage work' or of 'the marriage breaking-down'. Whether the metaphor is one of reification or a simple mechanical analogy is not important; what is relevant is that sooner or later, all metaphors are taken literally. Others manage to avoid the 'technological' approach and stress the fact that marriages consist only of 'role-playing' individuals, but this has its difficulties too and tends to lead them along the unilluminated path to the stage upon which their players perform. It is probable that the majority of American marriage counsellors consider their clients as individuals in a particular kind of setting, in spite of the jargon with which they describe their activities.

The training of American marriage counsellors emphasizes the clinical approach:

'. . . the counsellor's qualifications ought to include a knowledge of human growth and development, and of the dynamics of human behaviour and human motivations; a capacity to differentiate between normal and abnormal behaviour mechanisms; and some understanding of the everyday give-and-take problems of family living and relationships within the family group. In addition the marriage counsellor needs to be skilled in basic counselling techniques, and to have developed an awareness and disciplined control of his own biases, prejudices, attitudes and needs as these may affect his work with his clients' (22).

One of the best short accounts of the counselling process, and one that unintentionally stresses all the features that make it a mystique, is to be found in a book by a British marriage guidance counsellor, J. H. Wallis. He says that the marriage counsellor is concerned with what people feel about themselves and with their personal life rather than with their overt behaviour and he makes the orthodox psychotherapeutic claim that they cannot solve the mysteries of their inner selves by theorizing about how they feel because this 'leads to self-deception, self-justification or self-accusation' (23) and thus elucidation can only come about in the relationship with the counsellor or with the group that he is leading. 'He (the client) discovers these facets of his own personality not by theorizing but by actually experiencing them in his discussions with the counsellor (or with the group led by the counsellor)' (24). He dismisses the widespread popular belief that common sense is all that is required:

'Marriage conflict cannot be solved by common sense; if it could, the partners could resolve it without the aid of a counsellor' (25), a quite remarkable *non sequitur*. He argues that 'this therapeutic process is very difficult to understand (or perhaps even believe) unless one has had experience of it. It is very different from conventional methods by which one person tries to help another' (26). This is the rejoinder made rather testily by Freud himself (27), and exemplified in the joke about the psychiatrist who, on diagnosing a patient as paranoid, is asked how he knows, and replies, 'because he is like the other paranoids I've treated' and on being pressed as to how he knew they were paranoid, is led into an infinite regression or circularity. Such problems as marital conflict cannot be solved by common sense; this is the point of no return: the opacity of contemporary life is reflected in the tortuous and oblique approach of the psychotherapist. He alone, the master of the mysteries, can raise the lid on that which lies inside the participants in even the most everyday of everyday occurrences in personal life in our society. The therapeutic process cannot be described save in mystical terms, and the mystic can never 'explain'; he can only attempt to communicate his feelings to someone who has had similar experiences, or by his communication try to induce such experiences; but how does the other person 'know' that he has had or is having similar experiences? This is not an attack on mysticism or an attempt to demonstrate that it is a worthless mode, but merely an attempt to indicate that these experiences are of essentially the same nature as that of the religious mystic. It is, after all, the psychotherapists who have attempted to devalue mystical experiences but are, unfortunately from their point of view, as unable to explain the nature of the psychotherapeutic experience as the mystics are at a loss to present their experience of God in common sense terms.

Finally Wallis comes to the point where he asks,

'. . . whether the work we are describing is to be regarded as a form of psychotherapy. This is relevant for two reasons. First, the concept of therapy is not exact and even the term psychotherapy is not precise so it is all the more important to see where counselling fits in with these general terms. Secondly, some indication of the counsellor's role within the general field of personal therapy is necessary if we are to understand the methods used in selection, training and supervision.'

He then describes other forms, older ones, of helping people by practical acts to ease or change their material circumstances and argues that these have their proper place and are not 'inferior' to counselling. The counsellor is midway between the extremes of psychotherapy and 'the hand-out', 'meals on wheels' approach.

'The psychotherapist (if analytically trained) is primarily concerned with the irrational, unconscious aspects of his client's or patient's difficulties. He approaches the seemingly impossible task of helping his patient to become aware of those aspects of his personal life that are hidden most deeply—not only from others, but from himself. He has his own highly specialised training to enable him to go a little farther and a little more deeply into the hidden aspects of the patient's problems, the submerged part of his personal conflict—the very aspects that the patient cannot recognize and which he unconsciously strives to keep concealed because of the pain of recognition and the pain which originally led to the split between the conscious and the hidden sides of his conflict . . .' (28).

Subsequently he distinguishes between the psychotherapist and the marriage counsellor:

'In psychotherapy, the therapeutic use of the patient's unconscious reactions to the therapist is central to the process, whereas a counsellor observes the client's reactions and uses them as indications of what may be troubling him in his marriage. The area within which the counsellor is working is primarily a greater self-understanding in the client in relation to his wife (or husband, of course) rather than in relation to the counsellor, whereas in psychotherapy it tends to be the other way round' (29).

According to this argument, the marriage counsellor is concerned with the client's reactions and the unconscious elements in them only in so far as they can be used to assist in understanding the client's marriage. Wallis adds a rider to the effect that the distinction between psychotherapy and counselling is not as clear as it might seem from the literature. After discussing this point for about a page and a half, he concludes that the terms are not quite interchangeable and the reason for this seems to derive from two sources: firstly, the lack of relevant psychotherapeutic training among counsellors and secondly, the resolution of a specific practical problem being the main concern of the counsellor. He concludes with a modest statement that it is the counsellor himself who benefits most from receiving psychotherapy in tutorial sessions with his psychotherapist, because this helps him to understand himself and thus be a more effective counsellor; he returns periodically to his psychotherapist-tutor for what might be termed a 'fresh laying-on of hands' and he can then go forth as Wallis most aptly describes him, 'in a very real sense, midway between his client and his own therapist or training tutor' (30). After this description of what could appropriately be described as a priestly function, Wallis disclaims that either counsellors or psychotherapists are paragons with no matrimonial or personal conflicts of their own; 'they are both of them people who have been trained to help in particular ways' (31).

This last observation is not the only indication in Wallis's book that he is aware of some of the criticisms that have been levelled at counsellors of all kinds, and marriage counsellors in particular. His first chapter starts off with 'objections to marriage guidance' and among these are the by now standard criticisms of counselling in general. It would be appropriate to look at some of these in conjunction with the contention that psychotherapeutic treatments, including counselling, have an ideological affinity with highly industrialized bureaucratized society. The first objection is that counselling is unscientific, and so marriage counselling is also unscientific. As the scientific standing of psychotherapies is not at issue here, this objection is not relevant to us and we can ignore the enormous literature that has grown up around this topic (32). Next comes the objection that marriage is such a personal, private matter that no outsider should concern himself with it. This objection would apply to all forms of counselling in which the sexual side of the client's personality was under consideration and could equally well include every intimate aspect of his life, and as, by its premises, the psychotherapeutic ideology assumes that most, if not all, personal problems and difficulties stem from these areas of the personality, then the objection applies to all forms of counselling, but as it is a moral proposition, we need discuss it no further here. The third objection is that counselling is not a job for amateurs; the definition of counselling by counsellors makes this proposition self-evident: counselling is an expert and pro-fessionalized skill, therefore counsellors must be expert and cannot be amateurs (they can, of course, be unpaid volunteers as are some marriage guidance counsellors, and they can be part-time as well). Long discussions about people's feelings make them morbid and introspective is the fourth objection, and therefore should not be pursued as it is a bad thing to make people morbid and introspective. Even if we admit the moral argument that to do so is a bad thing (and we are not here concerned with moral arguments), there is no empirical evidence to show that this effect results or does not result and the objection, in its non-moral aspects, is merely intuitive speculation (it is hard to conceive of any empirical research that could 'prove' or 'disprove' the claim). Fifthly, counselling tends to be morally permissive, whereas it ought to offer moral leadership, and this is again the kind of value judgment that is not our concern here. For good measure we can add to the foregoing the accusation made by Barbara Wootton that counsellors 'suffer from the peculiar repulsiveness of those who dabble their fingers self-approvingly in the stuff of other people's souls' (33). This again is an objection that does not concern us here, though there is a facet of psychotherapeutic social casework and counselling closely related to this trait that is relevant and that is to be found in the objection mentioned by Wallis that has up to now been omitted: people who do counselling are suspect; one should be suspicious of the motives of those who do it.

In discussing this point in the context of psychoanalysis and related forms of psychotherapy, Charles Rycroft writes,

'The idea that neurosis is caused by lack of love in childhood can also lead analysts into priggishness. If neurosis is the result of parental deprivation then perhaps analysis is a form of replacement-therapy and the effective agent in treatment is the analyst's concern, devotion and love. But this view of the matter leaves unexplained why the analyst should consider himself to be the possessor of a store of *agape* or *caritas* so much greater than that of his patient's parents. Analysts who hold that their capacity to help patients derives from their ability to understand them, and that this ability depends on their knowledge of the language of the unconscious, are really being more modest. The claim to possess professional expertise does not contain a concealed claim to moral superiority over the laity' (34).

Whether or not the last part of Rycroft's statement is valid, it still only answers part of the problem because the counsellor and social caseworker claim that the therapy resides in the relationship between themselves and their clients. Why are they so strongly motivated to hand our their psychic benefits in much the same way as earlier do-gooders and altruists handed out money, clothes and soup? The professional analyst is, in most cases, handsomely paid for his services, and is sometimes cynical about the lucrative nature of this branch of medicine (35). But the social worker is relatively poorly paid, and some are even unpaid voluntary workers. Present-day psychotherapeutic social workers consider themselves above the earlier directive social workers and philanthropists who are all condemned sweepingly as moral snobs: 'The Victorian and Edwardian social worker gave material and financial aid to the poor man and his family, having first ascertained that they were worthy to receive it' (36). This is, of course, a generalization that cannot be substantiated, but even were it true, in what way would it differ from the contemporary social worker's psychic hand-out? It could perhaps be claimed that some moral advance has been made because the contemporary social worker gives his psychic counsel to all comers, but this is only because the premisses of his faith assume that all clients are in need of it and it is within his power and that of his colleagues to give it; and this stricture is not an unprovable generalization like the comment on Victorian social workers, but a statement of what is implicit and explicit in the faith of the counsellors.

The distinction between psychotherapy and counselling is a feeble one; both operate on the psyche. The psychotherapist uses the whole range of procedures, while the counsellor uses conscious-level techniques plus a hefty dose of the kind of understanding that the *Psychopathology of Everyday Life*, *The Forgotten Language* and similar works give him and which supply him, backed up by an oral tutorial tradition, with his 'insight' into his clients. The therapy of counselling resides, so the counsellors claim, in the peculiar nature of the relationship between them and their clients (37).

The counsellors' contention contains an element of moral superiority fully as great as that alleged of Victorian social workers. They may not offer money and food to those worthy of receiving it, but they offer their own special brand of sanctimoniousness which accrues to them by virtue of the fact that they know how to live better than their clients do, or indeed, judging by the claims made in the paper mentioned earlier, better than anybody else save their colleagues and other psychotherapists, and what claim could be more arrogant than that? But they do, in fact, make an even more arrogant one. Not only do they know the secrets of the client's innermost being and can thus produce the 'real' self as a conjuror pulls a rabbit from a hat, but they also 'understand, permit, and appreciate' from their store of empathy and because they possess a specially developed ability to understand without condoning or condemning, an attribute that W. B. Yeats observed was possessed solely by God: 'Only God can love you for yourself alone' (38). The counsellors deny this and claim that their knowledge and understanding comes from their expertise and their professionalism; their emotional involvement is controlled. To put it all in simple and crude phrases, they cannot explain from whence comes this impersonal love of their fellowmen. Most priests, missionaries and saints love their fellowmen on behalf of a god, or for his greater glory, or as a moral duty, or even for the benefit of their own souls, but the counsellor does none of these things for he is on a plane very much closer to that of a god, not only is he a member of a secular priesthood but his own godhead lies within himself. The most arrogant 'holier than thou' attitude of all is the Olympian one of understanding and not judging, if true it is a usurpation of a god's prerogative. The priest forgives and understands, not because he possesses personal qualities that make these possible, but because he is acting as the agent of the divine. The lady bountiful, the philanthropist, the reformist, and the do-gooder hand out their charity or help, and the bread may be bitter to eat, but the counsellor hands out acceptance, empathic understanding to those who have failed in the process of living: counselling is an interminable but silent moral harangue. The client who has failed in an adjustment to external 'reality', who has not achieved emotional maturity, or who has failed to achieve intimate relations with others might not be 'responsible' in the sense that these defects might be traceable to faulty upbringing, bad parents, or a number of other factors quite outside the control of the client; but he is still morally inferior, he is still a 'client' in the ancient and original meaning of the term. The counsellor may not condemn his client's deviancy or the botch that he is making of his life, but he categorizes him as one who requires his help in the art of living and this reduces the client to a childish state of dependence, to that of a pupil. Traditional moral teachers have usually claimed to do just that, namely 'live better' but the unique characteristic of the counsellor is that he claims not to be doing this, but assisting his client to do it for himself. Furthermore, counsellors cannot account for their possession of an overdose of affection for their fellowmen; on the one hand, they deny any claim to sainthood; on the other, they deny, with even more fervour, that they obtain a satisfaction from 'dabbling their fingers in the stuff of other people's souls' or from being morally superior. It is pertinent to inquire if their claim to controlled emotional involvement is what it is said to be; is it, perhaps, really nothing more than a profound indifference, a kind of asexual Don Juanism, a promiscuity of intimate but transitory relationships? Maybe the actual reward for the work they do really does come from 'assuming responsibility for other people's lives and happiness'.

The view that there is a moral or value judgment implicit in counselling and related therapists should come as no surprise save to those who are unaware that there is one in all medical treatment. The concept of health is basically a moral tenet, and the affirmation of the desirability of health is certainly another. But there is a difference between the practice of physical medicine and that of psychotherapy. The physician or surgeon who practises physical treatments can take this value as a self-evident truth and one that he hardly need think about, let alone have to justify. It is, after all, 'society' (the reification is here merely a form of shorthand) that puts him in his position for the purpose of preserving the health or, more commonly, regaining the health of his patient. Furthermore, the criteria of physical health belong to that common sense, taken-for-granted area of life without which social existence would be impossible. A broken leg is a broken leg in Western Europe, the USA, the USSR, and the Andaman Islands; a fever might be caused by germs, devils, or magic but its physical manifestations are always bad things. The notion of 'psychic' or 'mental' health or whatever other phrase is currently preferred, is neither so self-evident nor so universal. A concern with the niceties of political liberty, the self-determination of national or cultural minorities, and freedom to express political opinions might be considered in

83

some Western countries as indications of a sane, non-authoritarian state of mind and, at the least, of political 'maturity', whereas in the USSR they might be construed as signs of mental disorder.

In what way can counselling be said to have an affinity with contemporary industrialized and bureaucratized society? Counselling is confused; it is a mixture of alleged scientific findings and procedures (39) and personal factors that operate in inexplicable fashion; the motivations of its practitioners are not always clear or unambiguous; the practice is a mystique. It reflects the doubts and uncertainties of contemporary views of man and his nature, we cannot decide whether we are machines, animals, or some species *sui generis*; so we compromise with a mixture of all three. We cannot measure or even perceive directly the human soul, so we content ourselves with the equally elusive mind (unless we assume only an electronic device as some biologists would have us believe); we have little of 'caring', *caritas*, or intimacy in our public lives and probably not much more in our private ones, but we cannot deny the need for these things so we have to institutionalize them by feeding them into our institutions in the form of techniques to improve human relations and create the illusion of 'caring'. The obscurity that surrounds the mystical relationship between client and psychotherapist is not unlike the opacity that pervades our public and economic life in which nothing is what it seems to be. Politicians are devious and untrustworthy; to regard them with respect or deference betokens a naivety unbecoming to an adult or a cynical pretence that cloaks personal or vested interest. The day-to-day functioning of business and industrial enterprises offers the same opacity: the functioning of industrial enterprises bears little relationship to the formulations of academic economics; businessmen pursue a line of mysticism all their own, they make a profit yet are devoted to the good of the community; they produce for the national interest and not for personal pecuniary aims and they make of production an end in itself, yet they apparently derive great pleasure from commercial intrigue and the attainment of prestige even when it is at the expense of the national interest (or whatever is currently considered desirable). This is even more important a facet of human life than previously because the economic sector dominated by industrial criteria has invaded large areas of public life and expanded within

the private sphere to a degree that would have seemed incon-
ceivable in traditional societies and even in developing societies
two hundred years ago. Public life, in all its aspects including the
industrial, is dominated by bureaucracies and they impinge on
and penetrate the private sphere too. The bureaucracy is ostensibly
devoted to efficiently serving the goals of the organization of which
it is a part, while at the same time it may lose sight of these goals
and even 'forget' them; it may cease to be a part and become the
whole, and become efficient only at preserving itself: bureaucracy
can become rule by nobody and result in total irresponsibility (40).
A public world and a private world in both of which rationality
flourishes only in its minor and trivial aspects; a world in which
environmental pollution, the destruction of irreplaceable natural
resources, unrestricted population increase and the toleration of
disease and remediable physical suffering exist side-by-side with
feats of rationality such as space exploration and organ transplants,
a world in which, deprived of the consolations of traditional
philosophies and orthodox religious faiths, the individual finds
recourse only within the self liberated by a mystic interaction and
communication with another.

To use, as Frankl suggests, a psychological approach to the
understanding of psychotherapy leads to the conclusion that
psychotherapy of the Freudian-Adlerian variety is essentially a
process of 'devaluation'. He asks, 'What are the motives which
underlie it? What is its hidden basic attitude, its secret tendency?
Our reply is a tendency toward devaluation. In every given case
its efforts to evaluate the intellectual content of psychic acts are in
truth efforts to devaluate. It is always trying to unmask. It evades
all questions of validity—in the religious, artistic, or even scientific
fields—by escaping from the realm of content to the realm of the
act. Thus it shies away from the complexity of questions requiring
knowledge and tasks demanding decisions; it is in flight from the
realities and possibilities of existence' (41).

According to Frankl, the psychotherapist sees his fellowmen in
the form of masks and behind these lie only neurotic motives. The
psychotherapist claims that art is only a flight from life or love,
while religion is nothing more than a primitive reaction to the
fear engendered by cosmic forces; all spiritual creations are mere
sublimations of the libido or compensations for inferiority feelings

or the means whereby security is achieved. This is a process of 'debunking' that accepts nothing for what it claims to be or seems to be and thus permits of no defence because it is not possible to prove the debunker wrong. Additionally, the debunker gains support from our kind of society because it is one in which its members possess no strongly held or unchallengeable convictions about it or themselves. The strength that exists in devaluation lies in the support it gives to doubts about the reality of things: nothing is what it really seems to be. We are unfree or rather freedom is an illusion for we are at the mercy of the hidden part of us, the id, the unconscious, the 'it'. For our peace of mind and satisfactory mode of living we must accept this inner constraint. It is, argues the psychotherapeutic ideologist, better to realize this and accept knowingly this psychological determinism than to pursue illusions of freedom. It is necessary to make the best of a bad job and admit that we are not only constrained by our impulses from the depths but those impulses are in their turn constrained by the fact of society. Contemporary sociology and very often the literary and visual arts also emphasize the constraining nature of social institutions, and the contemporary view of society that appears to us to have most validity is that put before us by Kafka. Unfreedom and the impracticability of exercising responsibility are key issues in contemporary rebellion (rebellion, not revolution, because few of the rebels have any alternative society to put in the place of the one they are protesting about). Psychological determinism, 'psychologism', the ideology of the psychotherapeutic all mitigate against revolution; it is, after all, ultimately pointless, but the individual rebel can be consoled and comforted, his ideals and protests devalued, by the reassurances of the counsellor—this might be cruel to be kind, but what mother is not?

Frankl's 'devaluation' means more, however, than just the denigration of the arts, religion, and other manifestations of high culture. It means, finally, the denial of the notion that people are morally responsible agents who in most cases, means what they say and do, and who deserve to be treated as if they do. The process of devaluation that Frankl says lies at the heart of the psychotherapeutic ideology is the antithesis of the liberal bourgeois rationalism of developing industrialized society.

Some social workers are aware of the anomalies in their work situation and also of the ambiguous nature of some of their activities, but a reading of their literature does not indicate that they appreciate the passive character of the role they play as troubleshooters for the major bureaucratic and industrial organizational forces in our society. They seem to consider themselves as active participants rather than as the instruments by which their clients are reconciled to the unsatisfactory conditions of their lives. Whether this activity is good or bad, desirable or undesirable is not here at question; what is of concern here is the unwitting support that non-directive, client-centred social casework gives to the dominant forces in our society by directing the client inward towards himself rather than outward towards radical change.

Alfred J. Kahn, in an article published in 1965, appears fully aware of the influence of the giant bureaucracies and organizations in American society; he is also alive to the progressive reduction in the influence of primary groups and of the decrease in the number of primary groups with which the individual comes into contact. He stresses the harmful influence of the 'rat race', not only for adults but also for schoolchildren. He deplores the abdication of choice by individuals in favour of organizations and groups that set themselves up as 'decision-makers' for others, such as 'Book-of-the-Month' clubs and similar bodies. He is aware of the unsatisfactory nature of such a society and of the need to do something about it, and he intends that something should be done. What he proposes puts him in the camp of the optimistic professionalized American social workers, eclectic and not averse to giving material as well as psychic aid. He believes firmly that the modern social worker is an expert and his expertise is greatly improved by infusions of knowledge drawn from the 'behavioural and social' sciences. Modern social work is more than administrative altruism on the one hand and diluted psychoanalysis on the other. The altruism has been modified by knowledge drawn from cultural anthropology, role and stratification theory, small group theory, organizational theory, theory of planned change, urban sociology, and economics among other 'sciences'. As for the psychiatric-psychoanalytical approach, this has been modified by the ego psychologies. This is the familiar mishmash expressed in contemporary fashionable verbiage (42).

Kahn sees the present and future tasks of social workers of all types and persuasions as clustered about new 'social roles' and the 'social supports' for such roles:

'The first-line challenge is the invention of those social institutions, arrangements, and services that meet the new circumstances and support the child-rearing, socialization, and interpersonal experience patterns deemed essential. If primary group relationships are valued, these social inventions should concentrate on them.

'These are not theoretical abstractions; they are generalizations referring to a process in which social work is engaged but needs to go further—group programmes for adolescents, new camping and cultural activities for family units and adolescents, new forms of day care or nursery service, informal kaffeeklatsch and baby-sitting centres in deprived areas, many services for senior citizens, from Friendly Visitors and home helps to "meals on wheels", and so on.'

He then goes on to argue that there must be two elements in the response: The gradual development of *new social roles* appropriate to the responsibility and status of primary groups, and the parallel invention of *social supports* for such roles' (43).

He goes on to claim that the contemporary 'urban-suburban-industrial environment' is, in many ways, unsuitable for man's physical and social nature and needs 'humanization' and it is this that will provide the 'social supports' for the social workers' new roles. These humanization activities include a vast range of citizens' advice bureaux, camp services, nurseries, etc., but in addition to all this material aid, 'therapeutic-rehabilitative case services' (or 'intrapsychically oriented helping strategies' as he sometimes calls them) will continue to be essential 'and may be better understood by many now too deprived to care whether they are adjusted' (44). Kahn ends with two claims as to how social workers can bring about the amelioration of these contemporary conditions that are not conducive to the nature of man: social workers ought to participate 'as experts, technical consultants, and process "facilitators" in planning coalitions for the development of policies and programmes to implement the new possibilities in such social welfare domains as income maintenance, housing, youth services, services to the aged—to illustrate with only a few possibilities'. Furthermore, they should participate as 'enablers, technicians, and leaders in local, city-wide, statewide, and national efforts to design and promote needed institutional change' (45).

Kahn's proposals do not really sound much like a radical programme, but rather the conventional 'social engineering' approach basically concerned with making minor ameliorative adjustments to the functioning machinery of urban living in a highly industrialized society. He sees his programme as a good thing and envisages his band of social engineers, fully equipped with the latest from their 'new relationships with behavioural and social science' going into their new roles and armed with their new supports. But these roles and supports are essentially reconciliatory, not radical, they are the therapies for a 'sickness' or 'malfunctioning' in a social system that is taken as given, they are the social work counterpart to what Marcuse calls 'repressive tolerance' in political life.

Some American social workers have not been so sanguine about the encouraging nature of these trends that Kahn welcomes. In particular, the emphasis on professionalization and expertise has disturbed social workers such as Bertha Reynolds who claims that 'professions are shaped in important ways by their clients' and she looks rather pessimistically at the way things seem to be shaping. She argues that in the process of professionalization, American social work has adopted the 'dominant ideology as well as the "upper class" definition of its proper function' (46). She views this with concern because the achievement of social prestige via professionalization has had to be at the expense of abandoning 'militant social action' while at the same time the identification with the poor and disadvantaged is being lost. The two indicators of this trend, she finds, are 'the concentration on casework, to the relative neglect of social action', and 'the move on the part of private agencies to attract a different "class" of clientele'. These two are followed by a concentration on 'disturbances in interpersonal relations' and the kind of sweeping claims made in the paper quoted above (47), in which a preoccupation with the poor and disadvantaged is replaced by the doctrine that the services of social workers ought to be a regular and constituent part of 'a community's planned provision for the broad needs of all its people'; it is, in other words, a claim on behalf of a secular priesthood. She says, 'Most agencies do not intentionally make it their policy to avoid serious social problems, but it is easy to refine one's techniques to the point where only relatively refined people can make use of them'. Herbert Bisno makes these criticisms even more incisively when he says, quoting Abraham J. Simon, that 'There is the implicit belief that the professional advancement of social work is correlated with the general welfare of society. Again and again in the literature of social work we find this assumption of an "automatic harmony" between the status aspirations of the profession and the effective performance of a truly "socialized function" that will take into account ends as well as means. Here we seem to have an "invisible hand" theory in modern dress; a theory which fits in neatly with the organic unity assumptions of our modern corporate society.' He adds:

'Three consequences are likely to follow (from the process of professionalization): first, a continuing de-emphasis on controversial social action, which has broad moral implications; second, a related lessening of attempts to influence social policy and the acceptance of the role of technician-implementer; and third, change in the ideology of social work that will lessen the gap between its system of ideas and that of the dominant groups in society' (48).

(The ideology mentioned that is liable to change is not the psychotherapeutic one, but that of the 'muck-raking' social reformers and moral entrepreneurs of the early years of the twentieth century) (49).

It can be said, in summary, that the mystique of counselling is based on the assumption of an inexplicable process that takes place during and in the relationship between counsellor and client, and that leads to the uncovering of hitherto concealed and latent capacities in the latter. The motivation of the counsellor is assumed to be self-evidently worthy and not to require further elucidation or examination beyond the negative claims that it does not derive from the wish to be considered a saint or from some diffuse and suspect desire to help; it is not based on sentimental altruism or philanthropy, but is motivated by the actual possession of skill and expertise and is a by-product of professionalism. In some form or another the mystique has pervaded all the areas of social work, though it was originally confined to social casework in the narrow sense of the term. Its intellecutal bases are a vulgarization or heresy of Freudian psychoanalysis with borrowings from Adler and others, and its emphasis has been altered so that its present formulations concentrate more on the ego than on the classical aspects of Freudian psychology. Its techniques are essentially verbal, its most important being one of interpreting the client's verbal statements and overt behaviour by devaluation. The mystique has gained strength as the ideology of social work has changed from philanthropic reform bordering on radical change to one of social engineering and psychic welfare of every member of society. The ideological change has been a concomitant of the struggle for professionalization with its attendant increase in social prestige and social status.

The penultimate word on the mystique can be left, appropriately, with Father Felix P. Biestek, S.J., the leading American Catholic apologist for counselling whose book *The Casework Relationship* is a widely used students' textbook in Britain and America:

'The casework relationship reveals the exalted professional ideals that beckon a social worker. He is expected to be both a firm-footed realist and a clear-eyed idealist. As a realist the caseworker is expected to see, understand, and help with the hard, sometimes ugly and repulsive, realities in the lives of his clients. As an idealist the caseworker is expected to recognize in a practical way the dignity and nobility of people who, in some instances, may have lost respect for themselves.

'As an idealist the caseworker is the champion of the rights of individuals; as a realist he is aware that individual rights are limited by the rights of other individuals and by the common good of society.

'As a realist he understands the importance of the emotional component in the lives of people who are in trouble; as an idealist he knows that emotional needs and problems, important as they may be, are not the most important considerations in human living. Without imposing his own standards and values upon clients, he tries to help them remain within objective social, legal, and moral boundaries . . .' (50).

He is, in other words, the ambiguous agent of the equivocal forces that dominate our society, an ambivalent creature stepping out of the opacity that is our society: he is opaque as our society is opaque; his mystique derives from the mystery that is the social world we inhabit.

But he also claims to be a professional and like all aspirants to professional status and the rewards attendant upon it, the social worker has to meet the minimum criteria upon which a claim to professionalization are based: he must demonstrate a demand for his services; he must show that he possesses an expertise that is peculiar to his occupation, i.e. a specific skill in meeting the demand; and finally, a readiness to do more for his client than the fee (or salary) paid for his services warrants alone, that is, the need of his client must be the only limitation on the extent of his service. It is not unknown in the history of professionalization for aspirants to create a demand that they can then fulfil; there are also precedents for the claim to doubtful expertise being successfully pursued. Part of the success achieved by the psychotherapeutic ideology lies in the excellent marketing campaign that the psychotherapists and social caseworkers have carried out on their own behalf, a degree of success only equalled by advertising agents and management consultants, both of which are byproducts of advanced industrialization in a market economy (51).

Notes and References

1 Referring to the value of holiday work in social work agencies for intending social work students, Professor Howard Jones writes in the 'Foreword' to Bessell's *Introduction to Social Work:* 'What you can certainly acquire by such means is the "feel" of the work: what it is like to be in the position of having to assume responsibility for other people's lives and happiness, and to conduct your daily work through a face-to-face relationship with distressed individuals without being overwhelmed and immobilized yourself'. Bessell, *op. cit.,* p. 4.
2 Department of Education, University of Aston in Birmingham, 1971.
3 *Ibid.*
4 *Ibid.*
5 *Ibid.*

6 *Ibid.* The course given at Aston is very much like the course proposed in Wrenn, C. Gilbert, *The Counsellor in a Changing World*, American Personnel and Guidance Association, Washington, 1962. The syllabus is similar save for 'Introduction to the problems of ethical relationships and legal responsibilities in counselling' (pp. 166–8), the omission of which from the British course is, perhaps, not without significance. The other major difference between the courses is that the American proposal is for a *minimal two year course* for graduates (italics in original). This book by Professor Wrenn ran to 75,000 copies betwen 1962 and 1968.

7 Heasman, *op. cit.*, p. 55.

8 *Ibid.*, pp. 55–6.

9 Rycroft, Charles, *A Critical Dictionary of Psychoanalysis*, Nelson, London, 1968, pp. 42–3.

10 *Ibid.*, pp. 168–9. 'Transference: (1) The process by which a patient displaces on to his analyst feelings, ideas, etc., which derive from previous figures in his life; by which he relates to his analyst as though he were some former object in his life; by which he projects on to his analyst object-representations acquired by earlier introjections; by which he endows the analyst with the significance of another, usually prior object. (2) The state of mind produced by (1) in the patient. (3) Loosely, the patient's emotional attitude towards his analyst.

11 Heasman, *op. cit.*, p. 66.

12 Skinner, B. F., *Science and Human Behaviour*, Macmillan, New York, 1953 (Free Press, London, 1965).

13 Rogers, Carl R., *On Becoming a Person*, Houghton Mifflin, New York, 1961 (Constable, London, 1967).

14 Hamilton, Gordon, *Theory and Practice of Social Case Work*, Columbia University Press, New York; published for the New York School of Social Work, Columbia University, 2nd ed., Revised 1951 (tenth printing 1965), p. 21.

15 *Ibid.*, p. 77.

16 *Ibid.*, p. 78.

17 *Ibid.*, p. 79.

18 *Ibid.*, p. 79.

19 Coleman, Jules V., 'Distinguishing between Psychotherapy and Casework', *Journal of Social Casework*, XXX (June 1949), p. 250. Hamilton sums up her views thus: '. . . the interview is designed to stimulate and elicit feelings, to which end the worker-client relationship, essential to the casework process, is deepened by transference elements which must be carefully controlled interview by interview. The treatment situation is used to release feeling, to support the ego, and to increase the person's self-awareness by bringing to his attention his attitudes and patterns of behaviour both in the life experience and in the interviewing treatment situation (although usually more of the former), the caseworker tending to use the transference to

redirect the psychological energies into reality channels. The client's use of defences must be understood, but in general, constructive defences and adequate, even if neurotically balanced, family relationships are left undisturbed, unless the effect on children is marked. If more radical therapy is indicated the client would be prepared for and referred to psychoanalysis. In fact, preparation for referral to therapeutic procedures elsewhere has been highly developed within casework practice, and calls for as much skill in therapeutic management as in other areas. As we have repeatedly indicated, evidence of disease processes always suggests medical responsibility and collaboration.' *Op. cit.*, pp. 269–70. The above refers to American practice and that some six years ago, but the situation is still much as Professor Hamilton describes it. In Britain, referral today means, more often than not, a relatively short series of chats with a psychiatrist, sometimes only one chat, at a hospital outpatients' clinic followed by chemotherapy, unless, of course, the patient needs hospitalization, or is able to afford private psychoanalytic treatment.

20 Rogers, Carl R., 'The Necessary and Sufficient Conditions of Therapeutic Personality Change', *Journal of Consulting Psychology*, 21, 1957, pp. 93–103.

21 Ellis, Albert, in Harms, Ernest and Schreiber, Paul (eds), *Handbook of Counselling Techniques*, Pergamon Press, London and New York, 1963, pp. 147–51.

22 American Association of Marriage Counsellors, Committee on Standards for Training: *Report on Standards for Training*, American Association of Marriage Counsellors, Inc., New York, 1958.

23 Wallis, J. H., *Marriage Guidance, A New Introduction*, Routledge and Kegan Paul, London, 1968, p. 122.

24 *Ibid.*, p. 122.

25 *Ibid.*, p. 125.

26 *Ibid.*, 130.

27 Freud, Sigmund, *The Standard Edition of the Complete Psychological Works of Sigmund Freud*, The Hogarth Press and The Institute of Psycho-analysis, London, 1964; Vol. XXIII, 'Preface' to *An Outline of Psycho-analysis:* 'The teachings of psycho-analysis are based on an incalculable number of observations and experiences, and only someone who has repeated those observations on himself and on others is in a position to arrive at a judgment of his own upon it', p. 144.

28 Wallis, *op. cit.*, pp. 135–6.

29 *Ibid.*, p. 137.

30 *Ibid.*, p. 138.

31 *Ibid.*, p. 138.

32 For the controversy over the scientific status of psycho-analysis, see Rycroft, Charles (ed.), *Psychoanalysis Observed*, Penguin Books, Harmondsworth, 1968, the 'Introduction: Causes and Meaning' by Charles Rycroft, pp. 7–21, and the bibliography; also Martin,

Michael, 'An examination of the operationists' critique of psycho-analysis', *Social Science Information*, VIII (4), August 1969, pp. 65–85.

33 Wootton, Barbara, *op. cit.*, p. 279.

34 Rycroft, *op. cit.*, p. 17.

35 Verbal communication by a psychoanalyst (who must perforce remain anonymous) to the author: 'You know, my patients pay seven guineas an hour just to buy a friend'.

36 Brown, Marjorie A. in Halmos, Paul (ed.), *Moral Issues in the Training of Teachers and Social Workers*, *The Sociological Review*, Monograph No. 3, August 1960, Kraus Reprint, Nendeln, Liechtenstein, 1967, p. 56.

37 '. . . the fundamental therapeutic factor in psychotherapy is more akin to religion than to science, since it is a matter of personal relationship . . .'. Guntrip, Harry, *Personality Structure and Human Interaction*, Hogarth, London, 1961, p. 256.

38 Yeats, W. B., *Collected Poems of W. B. Yeats*, Macmillan, London, 1950. 'For Anne Gregory', p. 277:

> 'I heard an old religious man
> But yesternight declare
> That he had found a text to prove
> That only God, my dear,
> Could love you for yourself aïone
> And not your yellow hair.'

39 Brown, Marjorie A. in Halmos (ed.), *op. cit.*: 'Social work practice cannot progress more rapidly than the social sciences on which it depends', p. 56. This approach to social work is the opposite to that taken by writers such as Dr Peters, who ask in what way the social sciences are pertinent to the practice of social work. The two approaches are irreconcilably opposed, the one claiming that social work is based on 'science', the other that it is not.

40 Arendt, Hannah, *On Violence*, Allan Lane, The Penguin Press, London, 1970, p. 38.

41 Frankl, *op. cit.*, pp. 18–22.

42 Role theory is one aspect of sociology and social psychology that certain caseworkers emphasize, viz. Professor Perlman. That some sociologists have found it important is clear from even a brief review of recent sociological writings. Professor Worsley goes so far as to say that: 'The concept of rôle is the central concept in the social sciences. Its analytical utility is immediately obvious: it distinguishes between the idiosyncratic attributes of the personal occupant of a position and the behaviour normatively enjoined upon him by virtue of that occupancy. As in the theatre—from whence the metaphor is borrowed—the script is written for the actor: he does not invent the rôle. Yet it is at precisely this point that the limits of the analogy reveal themselves. Too often, the "social" rôle is conceived of as absolutely fixed. Moreover, in functionalist schemes, rôles are com-

monly seen as forming part of an interdigitated, holistic system. The individual is a passive *tabula rasa*, who receives impressions from the outside (culture) which shape his personality. Men are "socialized" into rôle-playing: in the end, they appear entirely determined. (This would, of course, only be true if culture was fixed and unambiguous, and if the process of communication of culture were 100 per cent efficient.)': Worsley, Peter, 'The Distribution of Power in Industrial Society' in Halmos, *op. cit.*, p. 15. Role theory has distinguished forebears: Shakespeare, William James, G. H. Mead, to name but three. Although its usefulness is widely accepted by sociologists, cogent criticism of the theory has come from diverse sources. Two of the leading critics, Ralf Dahrendorf in his *Homo Sociologicus* (1959) and Peter L. Berger in his *The Precarious Vision* (1961) attack its determinism and deny that role-playing excludes the possibility of human freedom. The theory is, naturally, most popular with the functionalist-system building kind of sociologist and it is therefore not surprising that it should appeal to social caseworkers. It is rather less than a theory and more of a description of how individuals are alleged to react to one another in institutionalized (or structured) social situations. As a set of descriptive and analytic postulates, it possesses much that is meaningful and enlightening, but beyond these thoroughly worthy features, it is difficult to see in what way it could be of any practical aid to a social worker (case or any other variety) in any actual situation in which his help is required. At its best, the theory can do no more than tell him what he already knows from his common sense knowledge of the social world.

43 Kahn, Alfred J., 'The societal context of social work practice', *Social Work*, Vol. 10, No. 4 (October 1965), pp. 145–55 (italics in the original).

44 *Ibid.*, p. 154.

45 *Ibid.*, p. 158.

46 Reynolds, Bertha Capen, *Social Work and Social Living*, Citadel Press, New York, 1951, pp. 3–4.

47 Chapter 2, p. 44.

48 Bisno, Herbert, 'How social will social work be?', *Social Work*, Vol. 1, No. 2 (April 1956), pp. 12–18.

49 For this particular ideology and its historical setting see Hofstadter, Richard, *The Age of Reform*, Knopf, New York, 1955 (Cape, London, 1962).

50 Biestek, Felix P., *The Casework Relationship*, introduction by Eileen Younghusband, Allen & Unwin, London, 1961, pp. 136–7.

51 On the elements of stigmatization and exchange as well as dependency that enter into the practice of social welfare work, see Pinker, Robert, *Social Theory and Social Policy*, Heinemann, London, 1971, pp. 153–73.

Chapter 4

The Doctrine of Maturity

'Immature' as a term of abuse is widespread in popular usage. It implies that someone's behaviour, social or sexual, is that which would be expected of a person younger than the individual in question. 'Mature' in the same usage implies a set of qualities that the speaker finds becoming to the age of the individual under discussion, and that he approves. In popular use, and also in the mouths of social workers and psychotherapists, there is always this element of value judgment: maturity is something good immaturity is bad; the former is approved, the latter is disapproved. 'Maturity appears often in the statements of aims of youth workers and many teachers, either as the overriding aim or as one in a list of qualities which it is hoped to develop in members' (1), so write Davies and Gibson, authors of a book for youth workers that advocates a 'client-centred practice for youth club leaders and youth workers' and is a modified social casework approach, i.e. modified to meet the special conditions of youth club work. The paper already mentioned above, *Counselling in a Changing Culture*, makes frequent mention of maturity', e.g. 'the individual shows his maturity by his ability to adapt to the changing environment. The mature person knows his strengths and weaknesses and is able to accept help when needed most. . . . None of us is as mature as we might become . . . counselling can benefit the vast majority of "normal" people who are to some extent immature.' Carl Rogers offers a justification for psychotherapy in terms of maturity: 'In general then the conclusion appears justified that where client-centred therapy has been judged to show progress or movement, there is a significant observable change in the client's everyday behaviour in the direction of greater maturity' (2).

Most of those who use 'maturity' and 'immaturity' with easy familiarity do so without ever explaining what they mean by it,

D   97 though they apparently mean (*a*) 'mature' describes behaviour befitting a certain age and status, and (*b*) it also indicates an ability to adapt or adjust to the situation in which the individual finds himself. 'Immature' indicates (*c*) childish or infantile behaviour unbecoming to a certain age and status, and (*d*) an inability to adjust to the situation that shows itself in rebelliousness and violence that is unproductive and ineffective in bringing about a betterment in the individual's situation. But on the whole there is very little serious attempt in the literature of social work and psychotherapy to define what is meant with any precision. For example, Holden uses the term 'maturity' as if its meaning were self-evident and he nowhere defines or clarifies it but he makes statements such as 'personal development and maturity are often keys which unlock the door to unexpected intellectual ability' (3). In reference to the selection of teacher-counsellors, he refers to entrants to teaching as being young and 'this emergence into full occupational and private independence and responsibility and all its corollaries is part of his as yet incomplete maturation, of coming to terms with himself . . .'. Later he writes, 'If this repetitious emphasis on the maturity of the whole person seems tedious and unfair, it is wise to bear in mind that many of the intending counsellor's clients may know more about the hard truths of life than the counsellor himself . . .' (4).

As a biological term 'mature' has a fairly precise meaning (we shall return to this later when discussing 'development') but when applied to psychological states or human social behaviour it always implies comparisons with norms that are themselves far from clear The psychotherapist's use of the concept of maturity, and also that of the social worker, is essentially based on norms that are derived from the psychiatrist's consulting-room. They appertain to the sphere of the pathological and are derived mainly from psychoanalytic practice. No matter how valid such practice may be in dealing with 'diseased states', it gives no warrant for transferring its findings, hypotheses and nomenclature into the field of 'normality', that is to say, psychoanalysis is a specific form of 'abnormal psychology' not a general psychology and its classifications cannot be extended generally without considerable modification. Much of the abusive significance of 'immature' probably stems from 'devaluation' taken to the extreme where it is transformed into what Farber describes as 'character assassination' (5). This is the process of interpreting a person's behaviour and statements in pejorative terms derived from psychoanalysis; it is an abuse of psychoanalysis whereby a person's character and motives are disparaged and impugned, and one of its most typical and everyday occurrences lies in imputing infantile, and thus immature, motives to an adult.

Apart from 'character assassination' of this kind, which one must not always assume is the result of some personal animosity on the part of the assassin but a consequence of his general stance, there is a large range of explicit definitions of the concept of maturity and the only factor they seem to have in common, apart from their diversity, is some very vague notion of development. A classification of the formulations of 'maturity' would result in three categories of theories: biological, relativistic, and developmental. There is, however, an overlap in the sense that developmental theories are usually associated with the biological concept, and relativistic theories contain an element of the developmental. For example, Carl Rogers writes of 'psychological maturity' which seems to mean a measurement of one's own growth in terms of the extent to which one can help others to grow, i.e. help them to achieve a satisfactory identity; 'the degree to which I can create relationships which facilitate the growth of others as separate persons is a measure of the growth I have achieved in myself' (6). In client-centred therapy, he argues, self-perception increases and the 'ideal-self' (the fantasy version that everybody has of what he is and how he ought to be, a 'living super-ego') becomes less demanding and this permits the 'self-picture' to become better 'adjusted'. The emerging self that results from this perception possesses a higher degree of inner comfort, of self-understanding, self-acceptance, and self-responsibility and finds greater satisfaction and comfort in relationships with others. It results in behaviour that is less defensive, is more socialized and has a greater acceptance of the 'reality in himself' and in his social environment, and results in the possession by the individual of a 'more socialized system of values'. Rogers says, 'he will, in short, behave in ways which are regarded as more mature, and infantile ways of behaving will tend to decrease' (7). Successful psychotherapy results in an increase in maturity, and when Rogers describes someone as behaving 'in a more mature way' he assumes the following ten characteristics to have developed in the individual: he sees himself differently compared with his pre-therapy self-picture; he accepts himself and his feelings more fully; he becomes more self-confident and self-directing; he becomes more the person he would like to be; his perceptions become more flexible, less rigid; he adopts more realistic goals for himself; he changes maladjustive forms of behaviour, such as gambling and alcoholism; he accepts other people more easily; he 'becomes more open to the evidence, both to what is going on outside of himself, and to what is going on inside of himself; he changes his basic personality traits in constructive ways '(8). All these add up to 'psychological maturity'.

This view of maturity is not unlike Freud's own beliefs. The first was that man's instincts were constrained by society (culture) and that the constraint was always resented and the instincts could only be subject to fluctuating and unstable control because of the strength of these impulses; the second was that the opposing views that life was meaningful and that life was meaningless had to be given up. Instead, man (almost Aristotelian) had to follow a middle course, mediating between the hostile forces of instinct and culture, negotiating a *modus vivendi* for himself while aware of the limits to his own ability to affect his impulses and his culture. For Freud, maturity resided in the developed capacity to carry out negotiations that gained the individual a little here even at the cost of losing a little there. As Roazen puts it, 'Freud looks at the hatred that exists beneath the social order in terms of its potential fusion with the more social drives as the individual matures' (9). Maturity is a 'tenuous achievement' (10) because it consists of integrating various human needs and is always subject to regression. The conflict that exists between the individual and the social order exerts a pressure on the former to return to earlier stages in his life when conflict was less. Later Freudians such as Kris and Menninger (11) argue that one of the functions of the ego is to regulate this regression, and in the mature individual the ego has an integrating capacity to use this regression constructively instead of allowing the unconscious impulses to drive the individual back to an earlier stage. Jung describes this as 'the descent into the unconscious' and when it is subject to ego control it results in artistic expression. 'Men cannot remain children forever; they must in the end go out into "hostile life" ' (12) and the ability to do this without suffering too great a damage constitutes psychic maturity. Maturity in the Freudian sense is the capacity to suffer and be depressed and to tolerate frustration, delay, ambiguity, and separation; it is not a state of personal happiness or contentment in which anxiety and despair have disappeared, but one in which meaninglessness has been accepted. The extent to which this Freudian view of maturity has been debased and vulgarized can be appreciated whenever one turns to popular literature. Here is an extract from the writings of the popular American columnist, Ann Landers: '. . . each of us, of course, possesses large—or small —pockets of immaturity; the totally mature individual does not exist. Nor does one grow up all at once. Like physical growth, emotional growth is achieved one day at a time:

'Maturity is the ability to control anger, and settle differences without violence or destruction.

'Maturity is patience, the willingness to give up immediate pleasure in favour of the long-term gain.

'Maturity is perseverance, sweating out a project despite setbacks.

'Maturity is unselfishness, responding to the needs of others.

'Maturity is the capacity to face unpleasantness and disappointment without becoming bitter.

'Maturity is humility. A mature person is able to say, "I was wrong". And when he is proved right, he does not have to say, "I told you so".

'Maturity means dependability, integrity, keeping one's word.

'Maturity is the ability to live in peace with things we cannot change' (13).

She finishes with the statement that when she is asked to deal with an immature sweetheart, teenager, husband or wife, the best advice she can give is to tell them to grow up.

Freud and Rogers provide us with theories that are developmental and though there is an implied connection between stages of psychological development and stages of biological growth, the connection is not over-emphasized. In purely biological terms, maturation refers to the process in which the organic potentials of the organism develop and unfold. It is not synonymous with growth. Jersild distinguishes between the two concepts: 'Growth and maturation have a meaning in common. However, maturation denotes not solely a change in the physical equipment of the organism but also a change in function, in *capacity to perform* through the use of this equipment' (14). The process describable as the maturation of a structure is not one of an automatic development of capacities, but one that depends partly upon the appropriate stimulation by the environment. The latter includes diet, affection, education, and exercise, all of which can facilitate, retard, modify or even destroy the ultimate unfolding of innate structural potentials. But the kind of behaviour that the organism finally displays depends upon its physical structure. Education, training, exercise, indeed all the environmental factors are effective only in so far as the organism has an innate capacity to respond to such stimuli. There is a reciprocal relationship between innate structural potentials and environmental influences.

The process described as maturation of the physical structure proceeds in the human infant in an orderly and predictable (other things being equal) progression. The maturation sequence is roughly comparable from infant to infant to such an extent that norms of growth and behaviour appropriate to such growth have been postulated and widely accepted by pediatricians from Gesell to Spock. In the case of physical growth and motor skills there do not even seem to be important differences discernible in widely diverse cultures. There are, however, wide individual differences of growth within the ranges set by the norms, and differences in the rate of physical development, it has been suggested, could have significant consequences in the social life of individuals whose differential rates of growth are marked (15).

Although biological, physiological, and anatomical maturation seem to occur within certain clearly discernible limits irrespective of the culture in which the individual grows up, the designation of behaviour as being appropriate to any given stage presents no such uniformity. From the sociological and anthropological point of view, it has to be conceded that what one society considers 'psychologically' or 'socially' mature behaviour appropriate to a given age, another society might treat as 'infantile' or 'immature'. When we come to consider the concept of maturity from the standpoints of sociology and anthropology we are compelled to adopt a tentatively relativistic approach; the most we can say is that within a given society and at a *given time* certain forms of behaviour are considered appropriate to certain ages and are classed as 'mature', while other forms of behaviour are considered inappropriate to certain ages and are classified as 'immature'. The further one goes from tradition-dominated societies, the less the consensus within the society becomes as to what is or is not mature behaviour. In contemporary British society some sections might consider backing horses as a daily occurrence even to the extent of losing a considerable portion of one's income to the bookmakers, an 'adult' thing to do, something that becomes a 'real' red-blooded man, while others might construe it as denoting that those who do such things are fixated at an infantile stage of psychological or social maturity; both opinions tend to ignore the fact that for the sub-culture to which the individuals in question belong, such behaviour is socially approved and sanctioned, whatever other sub-cultures within the same society might think. Of course, it could be argued that sub-cultures notwithstanding, the criterion of rationality would lead adult individuals to abandon such gambling as unprofitable, but this view omits to take into account the fact that some sub-cultures do not instil clearly defined and formulated concepts of rationality into their members. A similar approach is discerned in the evaluation of individuals of differing sub-cultures who come together in, let us say, an undergraduate university course; students who do not dress like 'students' or do not leave their parental homes are often viewed with suspicion, and doubts about their maturity are entertained. There is little sense in laying down absolutes such as 'fledgings must leave the nest' or 'it is normal to indicate one's membership of a group by wearing the group's costume' because, apart from cultural differences, an individual might be creating an identity by not conforming to the established pattern, and this might well be more 'mature' than mere conformity (16).

The theory that can be most justifiably labelled 'developmental' and the one that is the most closely related to biological growth is that advanced by Erikson, and it is the one most widely accepted by client-centred non-directive social caseworkers and by those others who adhere to the psychotherapeutic ideology. It derives from Freud but emphasizes the ego at the expense of the Freudian stress laid on the id and the instinctual impulses which provide the built-in material for the conflict between man and society. The chapter entitled 'Eight Ages of Man' in his book *Childhood and Society* has exerted an influence of such strength over social workers and their teachers as to have led to their treating it almost as a divine revelation.

Erikson (17) claims that there are eight stages in the life of man, and during each stage the individual displays, or fails to, certain qualities that the author calls 'ego-qualities' and which he defines as criteria 'by which the individual demonstrates that his ego, at a given stage, is strong enough to integrate the timetable of the organism with the structure of social institutions' (18). The eight ages of man are: 'trust versus basic mistrust; autonomy versus shame and doubt; initiative versus guilt; industry versus inferiority; identity versus role diffusion; intimacy versus isolation; generativity versus stagnation; ego integrity versus despair'.

These eight 'ages of man' are stages of biological growth as well as of ego development. Each of the growth stages is accompanied by societal concomitants and the individual, in order to achieve a satisfactory adaptation to the demands made upon him at any given stage by his fellows in his society and to bring to fruition the potentials that are present in his biological growth, has to develop 'ego-qualities' which lead him to behave in ways that his society considers appropriate to the 'age' which he has reached. The theory is thus biological, psychological and sociological. Failure to display the appropriate responses at a given age indicates that the development has ceased, regressed or become diverted into less appropriate responses, i.e. the behaviour is, if the development has proceeded along the lines indicated, 'mature' in the common sense use of the word, and 'immature' if the development has deviated. For each stage there is a limited range of appropriate behaviour; outside this range, the adjustment is less than satisfactory. As a psychoanalyst with training and experience in anthropology, Erikson is aware of an element of relativity in the behaviour that is considered appropriate in any given society, but despite this, his scheme is basically applicable to any and every society, both simple and developed.

The first stage, 'trust versus basic mistrust' is that of early infancy; the infant has to learn to feel at home in the world and to accept the existence of goodness in others and in himself, i.e. to learn not to mistrust his environment. In this the influence of the mother (or mother substitute) is paramount. Failure to develop along these lines leads to feeling that the world about is evil, and malevolence rather than goodness is characteristic of himself and others.

'Autonomy versus shame and doubt' is the second stage of infancy and is marked by the achievement of sphincter-control (the anal phase of classical Freudian theory). It is that stage of development at which the child learns how to control his bodily excretory functions. The impulses leading to defaecation and urination are socialized.

The third stage 'initiative versus guilt' is that of childhood rivalry with those who are prior to the child (father, elder siblings) and have a favoured position with regard to his mother. The child learns that in this rivalry he must inevitably lose and this leads to resignation, guilt and anxiety. If the development progresses, the child gains an insight into the nature of familial life, and thus ultimately of a larger social life, and a sense of moral responsibility. This stage is marked by the discovery of the pleasures and pains of manipulating things (including the child's own body) and in 'attacking' the world around. Successes and failures lead to a sense of guilt and anxiety, particularly over the destructive powers that the child has, but if things go well, the child is left tolerably well socialized, that is without a crippling super-ego.

Between eight and thirteen years, the child enters the fourth stage, 'industry versus inferiority'. Here he discovers and acquires skills and develops a 'technological' approach in his use of tools and weapons. This is the time at which the child is instructed in the arts of social life and comes into contact with a wider world in his school, the culture of which tends to assume an autonomous role in the life of the child. The danger at this stage is that the child might acquire a sense of inadequacy and inferiority if his performances fall short and he attempts to emulate adult achievement. If this 'inferiority' does manifest itself, then he is likely to regress to an earlier stage and thus his development will be on the way to becoming less than satisfactory.

Youth begins at the fifth stage, 'identity versus role confusion' and the process takes the individual through adolescence into early adulthood. His relationships with his parents are redefined as he grows away from them into society. The stage is characterized by a search for identity which leads to much confusion and sometimes to 'over-identification' with the significant others of cliques and crowds to the point at which individual identity seems to have disappeared. Erikson describes this stage as one in which the young person tests and tries on the ideologies, value systems, creeds and beliefs of his time together with explorations into the relationship with others, particularly of the opposite sex; this is the age at which the individual 'falls in love'. Erikson says that 'to a considerable extent adolescent love is an attempt to arrive at a definition of one's identity by projecting one's diffused egoimage on another and by seeing it reflected and gradually clarified. This is why so much of young love is conversation' (19).

From the early twenties to early middle-age is the stage of 'intimacy versus isolation'; if successful, the individual achieves a capability for intimate and concrete affiliations and partnerships as well as the moral strength to abide such commitments even though they call for sacrifices and compromises. Additionally, he is capable of creative work. Erikson quotes Freud's famous dictum about *lieben und arbeiten* as the distinguishing achievements of this stage.

Middle-age is the stage of 'generativity versus stagnation'. Development leads to a concern with establising and guiding the next generation, or whatever may become the absorbing object of a parental kind of responsibility.

The final stage is that of old age, 'ego integrity versus despair'. The individual comes to accept his own death as natural and as a part of the general order of things.

The above summary does less than justice to this masterly theory of human development, but there is no reason to expand it here. It has been criticized on the grounds that it involves too simplistic a dichotomy: every stage is marked by its 'good' development which can be diverted into its 'bad' counterpart; it is, say some critics, altogether too neat. Others have commented that it is the kind of theory that has been beloved of some thinkers since the ancient Greeks and implies that something innate is

working itself out in this process of development; it is a version of
the 'being as becoming' thesis that Lucretius expresses in the
words: '. . . a human being, all of whose capacities are wrapped up
in the embryo before birth. Ere the child has seen light, the principle of beard and grey hairs is innate'. The latter objection is not
one that many would support today when the notion of natural
growth has become one of the axioms that most of us accept. The
former objection, i.e. that the dual and antagonistic classifications
are too simple is a more tenable criticism. Here, the truth or
falsity of the theory is not in question, only the extent to which, in
the use made of it in the training of social caseworkers, it can lead
to a passivity in social life and an undue concentration on one's
own development. It tends to take the environment (social and
political as well as economic) for granted, but this is no valid
criticism; it is, after all, a psychological theory and as such
perforce takes the environment as given. Nothing in the theory
itself would lead one to assume that adjustment to the given
environment of our society at all stages is the only satisfactory way
of living, though this is the tacit conclusion reached by many
admirers of Erikson, but more of this when the last of the 'maturity'
theories popular with the psychotherapeutic ideologists has been
considered.

In recent years, youth club leaders and other kinds of youth
workers have been introduced in their training courses to a
'client-centred practice', that is a modified form of counselling.
This approach is now widely accepted though it has not displaced
the 'activist' ideology that was at one time dominant. The 'activist'
approach is briefly one of fulfilment through 'worthwhile' activities such as sports, camping, canoeing, swimming, as well as
handicrafts and artistic pursuits; it is closely associated with
values derived from the Victorian middle-classes and the Protestant Ethic. It assumes that good citizens as well as contented
citizens can be produced by hard work, team games and thrift.
The 'activist' approach still seeks to inculcate 'manly' and gentle-
manly virtues and stresses initiative, self-discipline, and high
moral tone. Its basic tenet is that people grow and develop by
doing worthwhile things together. Clearly such an approach is
compatible with middle-class aspirations and ideals and it is
therefore not surprising that it is still strong in the Scout and

Guide movement, in the lower-middle class Boys' Brigade, and in church sponsored youth clubs as well as in the youth clubs run as ancillary by certain grammar schools (20).

Outside the youth clubs and centres that are middle-class in orientation (Scouts, church clubs, etc.) the majority of youth clubs managed by committees under the ultimate control of local authorities cater for the working-class adolescent, especially on those evenings when he has no money available to go elsewhere, or to those who have not found any more satisfactory means of filling in their leisure hours (rather let us say their non-work hours). Some of such clubs make a practice of catering for gangs and groups of teenagers engaged in various activities that put the members on the periphery of 'respectable' society: they may be gangs of motor-bike fetishists whose irresponsible riding puts them into the category of delinquents or potential delinquents, but apart from these 'greasers' there are various other teenage deviates such as 'aggros', 'mods' and 'rockers' and the rest of the hotchpotch of whatever is fashionable in this contra-culture of relative deprivation to whom the middle-class values of 'activities' make little appeal. Such clubs tend to be a combination of coffee-bar (cheaper than the commercial variety), dance hall (though many of the members do not approve of such middle-class activities as dancing), and a general place to 'muck about' in. The leaders and workers in such clubs are tending more and more to look upon themselves as some form of counsellor rather than the mere managers of places where coffee is cheaper and there is somewhere to sit around. It is not to be supposed that their members require counselling any more than do those who are members of, let us say, church clubs or the Boy Scouts, but they probably show their need more clearly. Anyway, of recent years, the trend among the leaders of such clubs and their teachers has been away from coffee, cakes and ping-pong to individual and group counselling in as much as the club situation facilitates or makes such counselling possible.

The two approaches are not exclusive and they are frequently found intermixed, something that is made easier by the fact that most club leaders and youth workers are in a state of considerable confusion about what they are doing; their roles are not clearly defined and so role ambiguity occurs. An influential book by two teachers of youth leaders is that by Davies and Gibson (21). They advocate the client-centred approach without denying some value to the activities school and they put forward the concept of 'social maturity'. It should be appreciated that to discuss such a theory as theirs in the same chapter as that in which those of Freud and Erikson have been considered is not a question of bad taste but of the necessity of concentrating on what the individual social, youth or community worker is fed. As Ann Landers represents a debasement of Carl Rogers, so Davies and Gibson demonstrate to what lengths the over-simplification and vulgarization of anthropological and sociological thought can lead when to the mixture is added a good measure of the psychotherapeutic ideology.

They discuss the concept of maturity in terms that are far from clear, and they favour paradoxical statements such as 'a sound maturity is built upon many expressions of immaturity' (22). They then launch into their own exposition of what they mean by 'full social maturity'. The concept is based on the following argument: many views of maturity seem to be based on qualities such as 'initiative', 'leadership', and such like and 'maturity' is just such another quality. As the individual can develop 'his' qualities of leadership and initiative, so he can develop his inherent and inalienable quality of maturity. 'Maturity' is a quality that grows as the individual ages until at some point an overall maturity is reached and on this 'plateau' the process ceases. But this view ignores the fact that the behaviour that indicates the possession of such qualities is related to a situation and only displays itself in a situation. They argue that an individual does not attain 'maturity' over the whole area of life simultaneously but only in certain areas. Because the individual has to adjust to new situations, 'maturity' is only an applicable designation to behaviour in each given situation. The argument runs thus: an adult who has spent twenty years in the army and has adjusted to the military life and in that sphere is 'mature' retires and gains a civilian employment. In the new situation, he has to readjust his behaviour and he learns how to do so with more or less speed. During the process of 'settling into' his new job, he will display 'immature' behaviour but as he succeeds in settling in his behaviour will demonstrate greater and greater maturity. During the transitional period of adjusting to the new situation he will show more or less mature behaviour relative to the situation. A boy of eighteen may be a 'mature' school captain but when he goes to university, he will display immaturity as a freshman until he has learned the behaviour appropriate to his new situation. So maturity depends, in great part, on experience in the situation and learning what kinds of behaviour are appropriate; failure to do this indicates 'immaturity'. It will be seen that this notion of 'situational maturity' is not unlike the view that 'maturity is indicated by behaviour appropriate to an age'. Substitute 'situation' for age, or 'role' for age and we have a theory of maturity that is based on the sociological concept of role. Davies and Gibson speak disparagingly of attempts made to equate maturity with 'stability' and to force adolescents to behave in 'adult ways', meaning by this that they are to learn 'tricks of behaviour accepted as indices of maturity a decade or more ago depending on the age of the adult concerned' (23). They seem unaware that their role theory of maturity suffers from the same defect; it is not necessary to be a particularly sophisticated sociologist to appreciate that role expectations vary from time to time and person to person.

Immaturity, then, is the inability to adapt to a given social situation. The mature educated individual in our society will have developed, according to Davies and Gibson, a 'social skill' in which flexibility and versatility figure prominently. This skill indicates 'maturity in the sense of a highly-developed sensitivity to the requirements of others on oneself and a flexibility to express the appropriate aspects of one's individuality to meet the situation. Such maturity does not grow rapidly, and assumes the self-discipline and humility which comes from a careful discernment of one's own social situation and personal potentiality. What is required of social educators today is that they help young people to this self-understanding and self-expression' (24). Aware of the dangers of a role theory approach but uncertain of where the pitfalls are situated, they add: 'Far from being in some way untrue to his "real" self by sensing out for each occasion how he will behave, he is a man of many parts, a many-sided character. He is ready to display whatever side of him is called for by the situation as he finds it . . . He is ready to lead or not . . . to be laughed at or not, to play a servicing role or not as the circumstances seem at the time to call for. He does not determine his course of action because his status in another, temporarily irrelevant, setting is different from that of others present. He does not inherit from past decades or past experiences, when customs suited other environments, stereotypes of what tasks and behaviour are properly his' (25). This sounds very much like the kind of behaviour that Whyte pokes fun at in his *Organization Man*, and clearly owes much to Riesman's concept of 'other-directedness'.

This approach is not a developmental one in the sense of Erikson's, but a relativistic one because 'maturity' or 'immaturity' is always relative to a specific situation. It is not relevant to object that by this theory some individuals may be 'mature' in one set of circumstances but not in another because common sense and everyday observation of our fellows confirms that the appropriateness of an individual's behaviour varies from circumstance to circumstance (appropriate here indicates that the behaviour is deemed so at a given time and place within a given culture). Cogent objections to the theory are: it ignores the fact that the individuals in any circumstances define the situation for themselves, the definition of the situation is not imposed upon them entirely by 'society' or anyone of those taking part or necessarily even by the majority taking part (26). Furthermore, the implication is clearly that man is 'only a coat-hanger for his roles': he just puts on the requisite costume and, like any good actor, gives a creditable performance. But the strongest objection, I submit, is that this notion provides no criteria with which values can be allocated. Skill in adjustment to the demands of the situation is the only criterion and 'mature' or 'immature' are determined only by the quality of the performance. The socially mature individual will be able to play his part well in a gang of criminals or a meeting of churchwardens; in a group of Pakki-bashing aggros, maturity would be exhibited by those members who bashed the most and subscribed most wholeheartedly (although this need only be superficial as role theory does not demand that the role player actually believes in his role) to the mores of the group. It is difficult to escape the conviction that Davies and Gibson are advocating someone akin to Zane Grey's *Lone Star Ranger*, that is the 'goody' who joins the 'baddies' gang and gives such a convincing performance that none of the baddies realize that he has infiltrated to destroy them. Then what about the baddy masquerading as a goody? Many a Hollywood gangster film testifies to the skill with which this role can be played. The final objection is that the authors permit the notion of 'overall maturity', that was earlier excluded, to creep in again as they imply that with experience the socially educated individual can adjust to any situation.

If we ignore the 'social maturity' approach for the moment and refer only to the developmental theories of Freud and Erikson, it would be futile to dispute the meaningfulness of these conceptualizations as guides or indicators for the assessment of individuals faced with unhappy marriages, bereavements, financial or occupational problems. Erikson's 'Eight Ages' indicate where rationality lies and appropriate strategies for the individual within the narrow confines of his personal and intimate life, but what illumination do they provide for an assessment and evaluation of social behaviour in the widest sense of the term? What help are such theories in dealing with political and economic action on the grand scale? Those who would describe political violence as immature behaviour are not in the position of those who would attack it on the grounds that it is ineffective; the latter can rest their case on a selection of historical evidence, the former have nothing save a personal value judgment to support them. Superficially, political violence and demonstrations seem to exhibit regressions and fixations if the developmental approach is assumed to be valid outside the personal aspects of living, but from the point of view of rationality, these methods are very often effective in bringing about social change and in some cases would seem to have been the only effective resource available. It seems reasonable that one should have to adjust to whatever one cannot change, but a great deal of man's environment is only given in the most limited sense of the word. Man's physical environment is capable of being transformed as we are learning to our cost with 'ecocatastrophe' just around the corner; and his social environment has almost none of the limitations on change that the physical environment imposes. Men, both individually and in groups, have brought about vast changes in their social life as the most beginning student of history could demonstrate, and it is not particularly damaging to say that in the end things are much about the same again because firstly 'in the end' has not yet arrived, secondly many people die and institutions disappear in a socio-political revolution, so that the 'same' is never the same because the cast has been changed—*l'orchestra cambia ma la musica è sempre quella* might well be true, but in order to know that the music is the same, one must first change the orchestra.

That strategy which might permit an individual to resolve his marital problems might have no relevance to the problem of a strike or whether or not a demonstration will promote a political objective. Social life is composed of more than marital problems and relationships with parents and a theory of human development or growth or maturation, call it what you will, must do more than reduce social life to a set of personal achievements in the fields of family, marriage and relations with other people of a more or less face-to-face intimate nature. If it does not do so, then it will be conducive to a passive acceptance of the wider world as given and to living only to *lieben und arbeiten*, worthy but limited aims which if consistently followed throughout man's history would have resulted in no history. 'Happy the land that has no history' might be true, but if it were to be considered desirable by people than there would have to be a return to the *Gemeinschaft* way of life, and it is well to remember that after the Second World War, a number of people in the Allied countries blamed that war on the many Germans who had for generations been contented to *lieben und arbeiten* in sleepy little *Gemeinschaften*, while society broke up about them (27).

With a persistence that distresses those who view their fellows as wrongheaded, political change has come about as the result of violence which in the private sphere of life would have indicated puerile attitudes and gross immaturity. The psychotherapeutic ideology inculcates attitudes that turn inwards to the person and away from concern with what lies outside; its concept of psychological maturity is only social in the very narrowest sense; it is sociological because it stresses the significance of relationships with other people and social institutions, but it has little or nothing to say about the wider issues that ultimately shape our individual destinies and determine the social institutions within which we live; it is a psychological version of *laissez faire* and leads inevitably to a passive acceptance of the political and economic status quo.

The doctrine of 'social maturity' as put forward by Davies and Gibson suffers from all the defects mentioned above and in addition provides a notion of maturity that is based on pure adjustment. Erikson's theory does not prevent social change, it merely ignores it by concentrating attention on the personal development and the implication that a satisfactory life is dependent on that alone; it concentrates the gaze inwards and has nothing to say about anything excluded. There is nothing in Erikson that would positively dissuade someone from becoming a revolutionary, only the thought might never enter his mind. But the 'social maturity' theory is one whose implications lead to complete acceptance of and adjustment to whatever is presented, it does not advocate change or stability, it offers only a robot interpretation of man.

Some analysts and psychotherapists have commented on the shortcomings of Freudian theory, and theories based on it, when an attempt is made to apply it to wider social issues than those of individual existence, it then shows its weaknesses and its inability to consider man as anything more than an isolate: 'The metapsychology of Freud, Federn, Rapaport, Hartmann, Kris, has no constructs for any social system generated by more than one person at a time. Within its own framework it has no concepts of social collectivities of experience shared or unshared between persons. This theory has no category of "you" . . . It has no way of expressing the meeting of an "I" with "an other", and of the impact of one person on another . . .' (28). As the counsellors and social caseworkers are so much concerned to establish some measure of health through interpersonal relationships, this deficiency in what is, in spite of protests to the contrary, still their basic creed (29), has caused some of them to see implications in Erikson that are not there or to seek consolation in role theory, but in all cases they are inevitably conducted back to their starting point, the individual and his intractable environment. They are, by the nature of their beliefs, compelled to adopt a view of maturation that is based on adaptation to the environment and they tend to forget that though the child cannot do much about his environment, the adult is not entirely incapable of bringing about change.

Notes and References

1 Davies, Bernard D. and Gibson, Alan, *The Social Education of the Adolescent*, University of London Press, London, 1967, p. 87.
2 Rogers, Carl R., *On Becoming a Person*, Constable, London, 1967, p. 262.
3 Holden, *op. cit.*, p. 49.
4 *Ibid.*, p. 145.
5 Farber, Leslie H., *The Ways of the Will*, Constable, London, 1966. 'Character assassination' does not only ascribe infantile motives to behaviour without any consideration of the effects of modification through education, socialization, or sublimation, but also labels an individual's traits in psychiatric terms, i.e. the traits are referred to a pathological condition or a neurotic condition that displays the traits in exaggerated and caricaturized form. The assassin describes behaviour that he envies in his victim as 'defence' without giving his victim the credit for having mastered the impulse by building the defence. He interprets kindness and consideration as 'reaction-formations' against sadistic impulses; gentleness is a reaction-formation against aggressive impulses; neatness, cleanliness, conscientiousness are obsessional reaction-formation against 'anality'; vivacity and animation are 'manic'; detachment and objectivity are 'schizoid' (the social caseworker's controlled emotional involvement might be thus murdered); being perceptive and observant as 'paranoid'; spontaneity and the display of emotions as 'hysterical'. This mode of interpretation is much used in 'pathobiography', that is the psycho-analytical study of historical personages based on indirect evidence that cannot be checked by direct reference to the subject himself. See Roazen, *op. cit.*, pp. 300–22, and Tuchman, Barbara, 'Can History use Freud?', *The Atlantic*, February 1967.
6 Rogers, *op. cit.*, p. 56.
7 *Ibid.*, p. 259.
8 *Ibid.*, pp. 280–1.
9 Roazen, *op. cit.*, p. 213.
10 *Ibid.*, p. 217.
11 Kris, Ernst, 'Art and Regression', *Transactions of the New York Academy of Sciences*, Vol. 12, No. 4 (1943). Menninger, Karl, *Theory of Psychoanalytic Technique*, Science Editions, New York, 1961 (Harper & Row, London, 1966).
12 Freud, *Standard Edition*, Vol. xxi, p. 49.
13 Landers, Ann, 'Are you Immature?', *Reader's Digest*, November 1970, p. 183.
14 Jersild, Arthur T., *Child Psychology*, 4th ed., Prentice-Hall, Englewood Cliffs, New Jersey, 1954, p. 19, italics in original (Staples Press, London, 1969).
15 Kagan, Jerome and Moss, Howard A., *Birth to Maturity*, Wiley, New York, 1962, p. 276 (Wiley, London): 'Boys with small muscle

mass are likely to have more difficulty perfecting the gross motor and self-defence skills encouraged and rewarded by young boys and therefore, less likely to gain acceptance by the same sex peers. Moreover, a boy with little muscle and small frame perceives that he deviates markedly from the culture's definition of a masculine physique, and he is apt to anticipate difficulty in obtaining acceptance from men and love from women.'

16 Jones, Edward E., 'Conformity as a Tactic of Ingratiation', *Science*, 1965, 149, No. 3680, pp. 144–50.

17 Erikson Erik H., *Childhood and Society*, Penguin, Harmondsworth, 1965 (revised ed.).

18 *Ibid.*, p. 238.

19 *Ibid.*, pp. 253–4.

20 'The youth clubs that various voluntary associations began to found during the nineteenth century were not instituted with the idea of simply facilitating the recreation and amusement of juveniles. The aim of the founders of the youth movement was to help to make young people into useful adult members of society and to steer them clear of immoral and anti-social influences. The para-military organization of many of the early youth clubs betrays the fact that their concern was more with the training of the young for a disciplined adulthood than with merely providing opportunities for recreation. It is really only since the Second World War that the idea of providing youth clubs to which young people can go simply to relax and to enjoy themselves has received any significant support.' Roberts, Kenneth, *Leisure*, Longman, London, 1970, p. 89. Although this comment is true, it has to be modified by the reminder that since the mid-fifties, the faith of the counsellors has begun to play a very significant part in the orientation of youth clubs. The number of youth club leaders who would claim that the main function of a youth club is to provide 'activities' is rapidly declining; those who would say that the clubs are places for relaxation and enjoyment only (with or without activities) are an even smaller minority, and a deviate minority at that. Most club leaders today subscribe to the view that the clubs are places where young people are helped towards a satisfactory and fulfilled adulthood not by the discipline of the earlier clubs but by the 'meaningful interaction' of members and leaders whereby the latent capacities of the individual are guided to realization. The meaningful interaction is greatly facilitated by the relationship with the leader who acts as a counsellor. This approach does not, of course, exclude activities or relaxation and enjoyment. Roberts favours a view that reduces the significance of the Protestant Ethic in all this, and argues, and quite rightly so, that what causes many juveniles concern is not that their educational or occupational expectations have been unfulfilled but that their leisure achievements fall short of their expectations. This may be true of members, but for the club leaders the influence of the Protestant Ethic is still potent in

its new guise of the psychotherapeutic ideology and it is this that makes them want their members to attain 'social maturity' and live a 'good' life rather than just be catering managers to a lot of under-privileged hedonists.

21 Davies and Gibson, *op. cit.*, p. 52.
22 *Ibid.*, p. 53.
23 *Ibid.*, p. 89.
24 *Ibid.*, p. 94.
25 *Ibid.*, p. 93.
26 'Definition of the situation' is a phrase used by W. I. Thomas. He argued that there are objective conditions that mould an individual's behaviour, and that these conditions partly define the situation for any given person; 'the definition of the situation' is begun by the parents, is continued by the community and is formally represented by the school, the law, the church'. But the actor coming to a decision to act is the other element in the definition of the situation. The definition consists not only in a verifiable, objective form but also in a subjective form, i.e. as it seems to exist to the actor: 'If men define situations as real they are real in their consequences'. E. H. Volkart, *Social Behaviour and Personality: the contributions of W. I. Thomas to theory and social research*, Social Science Research Council, New York, 1951. For a more recent formulation of the concept of the definition of the situation and the part played by the participants, see Goffman, Erving, *The Presentation of Self in Everyday Life*, Doubdleday, New York, 1959 (Allen Lane, The Penguin Press, 1969).
27 The distinction between two opposed styles of social life was formulated by Ferdinand Toennies in his most influential work *Gemeinschaft und Gesellschaft* (1887). Briefly, he meant by *Gemeinschaft* what is usually referred to in English as 'community' while *Gesellschaft* indicated 'association' and these societal forms of living together correspond to types of will that manifest themselves in different kinds of social relationships. 'Community' is manifested in the family, friendship group or neighbourhood in village or town, while 'association' is represented by the city and the state. The former is based on concord, tradition, custom and morals, and is characterized by intimate primary face-to-face contacts; the latter's traits are laws and conventions based on common aims, and is characterized by the great number of relatively impersonal secondary relationships. The one form represents the past of traditional societies, the other, the present and future trends leading to mass society. To some degree, Louis Wirth in his seminal article 'Urbanism as a Way of Life', *American Journal of Sociology*, Vol. 44, 1938, pp. 1–24, reinforced the pessimistic outlook implicit in Toennies by his own rather gloomy views of the consequences of urbanization. Georg Simmel, a contemporary of Toennies, held contrary views and in 'The Metropolis and Mental Life' (reprinted in Wolff, Kurt (ed.), *The Sociology of Georg Simmel*, The Free Press, Glencoe, Ill., 1950) he emphasized

the stimulation and advantages of living in a great city. This argument will be taken up in a later chapter when the nature of industrialized society is under discussion.

28 Laing, R. D., *The Politics of Experience*, Penguin, Harmondsworth, 1967, p. 45.

29 'While psychoanalytic group therapy is not unknown, psychoanalysis for the most part continues to take place in a two-person environment comprising the analyst and his patient, the essential theory of which differs little from that established by Freud himself', Rogow, Arnold A., *The Psychiatrists*, Allen & Unwin, London, 1971, p. 194.

Chapter 5

The Myth of Adjustment

'Since the goal of treatment in casework is to stabilize or to improve the functioning of the client in terms of social adaptation or adjustment, especially in the balance of inner and outer forces, the psychosocial approach in study and diagnosis is also the characteristic of treatment aims and methods. . . . One way of expressing the objective of psychosocial adjustment would be to say that the caseworker is interested in preventing social breakdown, in conserving strengths, in restoring social functions, in making life experiences more comfortable or compensating, in creating opportunities for growth and development, and in increasing the capacity for self-direction and social contribution. A person's ability to maintain himself depends on his constitutional equipment, his acculturated personality, his self-awareness, and the resources and opportunities available to him' (1).

So says Gordon Hamilton in a frank statement of what most counsellors and social caseworkers attempt to do.

She uses 'adjustment' as if it were synonymous with 'adaptation' and here again, as in the parallel case of maturity, we find a confusion between a biological concept 'adaptation' and a value judgment 'adjustment'. Adaptation is a biological term referring to the processes whereby an organism accommodates to its physical environment. 'Adjustment,' declares Mitchell, 'is a term . . . used by some social psychologists to refer to the process whereby an individual enters into a harmonious or healthy relationship with his environment, physical or social' (2). Humber and Dewey define adjustment in a different way, though the meaning is essentially similar. Beginning with a statement that man has to acquire common perceptions of himself and the world, partly because they are *essential to the explanation of social order*,

119

they continue by adding that these two processes (perception of the self and of the world within the framework provided by a common consensus) are incorporated in the greater process of adjustment, which comprises two major elements; socialization and enculturation, and the seven minor elements: accommodation, compensation, identification, projection, rationalization, repression, and sublimation. 'Each of the adjustment processes is shaped by the interaction of the biological heritage, the simple or complex environmental possibilities, and the acquired knowledge, beliefs, and attitudes that the person brings to each episode or act in terms of which an adjustment is attempted. Both the variables and attributes held in common by mankind, as well as the distinctive cultural variations, become, inevitably, involved in these adjustment processes' (3). The two chief factors that they mention—socialization and enculturation—are two aspects of the same process. Socialization is learning the essentials of living in company with one's fellow human beings and in adopting the requisite attitudes and developing the ability to perceive oneself as an object among other objects. It also includes learning that living has to be a compromise between competing impulses, motives and needs and has to be based on the ultimate commanding authority of what Freud called the 'reality principle' over the 'pleasure principle'—the latter involves doing whatever is immediately pleasurable without heeding the consequences, while the former is rational action based on an assessment of the consequences. The reality principle is essential for all human life and is the main item in an inventory of those aspects of socialization that are common to all human beings and allows it to be distinguished from enculturation which is learning the particular cultural variations upon universal human themes.

'The socialization of man is understandably more complex than that of animals because human social institutions, as expressions of man's culture building ability, take on such varied and changing forms. This means moreover, that the process of socialization is only a part of the process by means of which men adjust themselves to their fellows in working with the total body of traditions—economic, social, technological, religious, aesthetic, linguistic—to which they fall heir. . . . The aspects of learning experience which mark off man from other creatures, and by means of which, initially, and in later life, he achieves competence in his culture, may be called *enculturation*' (4).

A child has to learn to speak because it is in the nature of man to do so—this is socialization—but learning to communicate in a particular language peculiar to the group is enculturation.

The remaining seven attributes of adjustment fall into two categories that Daniel Katz refers to as 'ego-defensive' and 'value-expressive' (5). Ego-defensive functions are negative and the individual protects himself from acknowledging harsh truths about himself and his motivations, by using such mechanisms while by the same means he can also defend himself from admitting the harsh realities of the external world. These are the mechanisms by which his ego is protected from his own unacceptable impulses and also from the threatening external forces. 'They include the devices by which the individual avoids facing either the inner reality of the kind of person he is, or the outer reality of the dangers the world holds for him' (6). Freud, and those who favour an orthodox Freudian approach, view these ego-defences as deriving from internal conflicts resulting in feelings of profound insecurity; they are adaptive only in the very narrow sense of relatively reducing the internal conflicts and helping the individual to escape from complete breakdown; ultimately they are unadaptive as they impede the individual from making a social adjustment that would obtain him the maximum satisfaction available to him from the world he inhabits. The most non-adjustive defences are those of complete denial and complete avoidance that result in withdrawal and retreat into a fantasy world; the less non-adjustive are the devices of rationalization, projection and displacement. The degree of awareness by the individual of his use of these devices varies greatly, some realize their nature after their use and have some understanding of how they are protecting themselves, others appear to have no comprehension of what they are doing.

'Value-expressive' attitudes are those by which a person derives satisfaction from expressing himself in keeping with his personal values and his conception of himself. The satisfaction comes, not from the relief of internal tensions and conflicts, but from confirming the identity that the individual has constructed for himself.

He gains from expressing attitudes and opinions that reflect his cherished beliefs and his self-image. By this the self-image is sharpened and defined and becomes more like that which the individual desires. Such attitudes lead to involvement with groups (reference groups) to which the individual desires to belong, and also to identification with 'significant others'. The self-image itself originates from the basic process of socialization and enculturation. These mechanisms lead to the internalization of the values of reference groups, and on acceptance by the group, the individual becomes aware, because of the appropriate 'good' feelings, that he is approved of. Neo-Freudians of the ego-psychology movement stress the importance of value-expressive behaviour in self-development, self-expression, and self-realization, all of which are the aims of ego-psychotherapy. Such attitudes, therefore, tend to be adjustive (7).

The clue to the problem of the social caseworker's preoccupation with adjustment and maladjustment is provided in the observation by Dewey and Humber that adjustment is 'essential to the explanation of social order', in other words, adjustment can be considered as the process whereby the individual comes to see 'reality' as others 'see' it, and to acquiesce in their consensus. The adjusted person not only conforms with our notion of what the world is like but also confirms that it is just as we thought.

To return now to Hamilton: the critics of social work treat the term 'adjustment' as if it means trying to make the client accept and acquiesce in a social situation that is 'harsh, depriving and unjust'. She denies the validity of this interpretation and argues that the caseworker 'may, however, help the client to identify what is real in the external world, whether he or anyone else acquiesces in it or not' (8). She cites, as an example of what she means, an imaginary case, that of a child whose parental environment is unfavourable. The caseworker (and not all caseworkers would agree with her) first makes an approach to the problem through the relationship between parents and child, and tries to modify the parental attitudes and behaviour towards the child. If he succeeds, the parental pressures on the child will be diminished and the relieved child's own behaviour will improve, and probably nothing more need be done. But supposing the parents are unable to respond to the approach in this way, or that the child's rejection of the parental behaviour is too profound, then an alternative environment such as fostering may be offered. The child in his new environment may be able to 'make a happy "adjustment"' and the situation will now be less unfavourable to him than of his parents' home. This is, however, only likely to happen if his former situation was one in which he was struggling against the environment, so that 'shifting the factors and reducing the pressures' might enable him to 'handle the conflict' better. The success of the expedient of foster care is most unlikely if the original situation has been of such a kind as to set up 'a personality conflict' because of the child's own 'angry, retaliating and anxious feelings' and so merely altering the external elements alone will not assist him. The caseworker will then have to try psychotherapeutic treatment (counselling) in order to 'modify the child's feelings'. When the individual, child or adult, 'cannot accept himself or others, when his social behaviour and attitudes are affected, when his feelings are complicated, confused or contradictory, psychological treatment is usually indicated' (9). If there are severe symptoms, behaviour disorders or the suggestion of a 'disease process' then psychiatric treatment is probably indicated. A situation similar to this may exist in the case of an adult living in an unfavourable environment, and providing him with another job and some financial aid might resolve his problem, but not when the 'struggle' with a hostile external world has been internalized', and if this is the case, then, as with the imaginary child above, the goal of social work will be the client's 'emotional readjustment', the necessary condition for this being that 'the client himself wishes to change and that he will pursue whatever course of treatment will help him either to change his situation or to modify his attitude and behaviour patterns'. Such 'personality adjustment' may be attempted by psychotherapeutic treatment or 'environmental manipulation' or a combination of the two.

It is clear from these examples that two rather different processes are involved and that confusion results from using adaptation and adjustment synonymously and omitting to qualify the term adjustment. If 'adaptation' were to be used for the child's successful translation to a foster home, and 'social' or 'personality' adjustment to describe that process by which his view of himself and his environment is modified we should have a much better comprehension of what is taking place. Changing the environment when possible has been a way of dealing with problems for generations and it has frequently been subjected to criticism on the grounds of justice and humanity, though it is part of an adaptive form of behaviour that has characterized man throughout his recorded history and typically includes the boy who runs away to sea and the impoverished European farmer seeking his fortune in the New World. The crucial difference between these examples and the imaginary child in foster care is that the agent of the change in the foster care case is a social worker while in the traditional seeking-one's-fortune-elsewhere the agent is the person actually making the change, albeit compelled to do so by impoverishment or economic pressures. 'Personality or social adjustment' is something quite different; for how do we know that the 'client himself wishes to change?' Does the wish come from persuasion or some form of brainwashing or does it originate far back in that inner being that manifests itself in actually seeking aid? 'If they did not want to change, they would not come for counselling' is a stock answer to this question. It is permissible to assume that to seek aid could indicate in many cases a wish to change one's attitudes and behaviour, but what if the client is not a voluntary one, and many social workers' clients are not volunteers? If seeking aid indicates the wish to change, the client still may have no clear idea of the direction he wishes change to be in, and even if he has, he may find himself opting for a direction that is not the one he had hoped for; he is, after all, a client not a peer and the presumption is that he is faced with a more determined, convinced and 'integrated' personality than his own. Hamilton is aware of what might be involved in 'personality adjustment' and makes the telling comment: 'No treatment goal can be envisaged which does not involve a value judgment which is itself culturally determined' (10). Is this justified? The justification, apart from helping to make the client less unhappy, seems to be that the 'value judgment is culturally determined' and the social worker is acting as the vehicle of his and the client's common culture. Concrete assistance in the form of jobs, environmental changes, and financial and educational assistance is one thing, while treating the client so that he can come to terms with his culture is another matter altogether. Hamilton quotes Ruth Benedict in support: 'Just as those are favoured whose congenial responses are closest to that behaviour which characterizes their society, so those are disoriented whose congenial responses fall in that arc of behaviour which is not capitalized by their culture.' She argues that an individual whose 'congenial drives' are not catered for by his culture is in difficulties and when his desires are strongly disapproved in his culture then he is a deviate and might suffer considerably. A so-called 'closed culture' of the kind that Benedict is describing provides the possibility of adequate and satisfying personality adjustment because the traditions and mores act as a 'collective conscience' or super-ego. Ideologies to which people make total submission or that they internalize completely seem, she adds, 'to create a condition of tranquillity' for the individual, but in an 'open culture' such as that of Western Europe or the USA personality adjustment is more difficult in the confusion created by the interaction of many cultural influences, some of which contradict others, and the 'adaptation of external pressures to the inner life may well conduce to a more delicate equilibrium of the total personality'. It is not clear what she means by 'adaptation of the external pressures' unless she means the opposite of the whole concept of personality adjustment and that is doubtful for the rest of her argument tends to belittle 'environmental manipulation' except in relatively few cases. If the social worker is the agent of the culture, even be it an 'open' one, then Hamilton omits to take into account that culture is forever changing in historical societies; about what happens in the simpler, pre-literate societies we know almost nothing because we know little of their history, and without a knowledge of their pasts we cannot make meaningful statements about the immutability or otherwise of their cultures. It would be unwise to assume that cultural changes do not occur within them, though the *rate* of such change may be almost imperceptible.

This doctrine of adjustment does not meet with much approval from circles outside that of the psychotherapists and social workers. Both from a theoretical and a practical point of view it has little to commend it to those concerned with a study of the forces operating within the individual and society. Peter Kelvin (11), for example, suggests that social change is the product of non-conformity. Of course, this does not mean that every individual who suffers from tension, insecurity, anxiety or a 'person-ality conflict' by which he is at odds with his society, is an agent or even a vehicle of social change. More than the mere possession of a 'neurotic' disposition is required if one is to fulfil that role. Kelvin uses 'adaptation level theory' but warns against applying it directly to social behaviour because it is a theory that derives from the field of perception and not from the study of social behaviour; but he argues that it can be used as a model and not simply as an analogy. 'Adaptation (he is using this term in its biological sense) has two aspects. On the one hand it makes the organism unres-ponsive to the stimuli to which it is not adapted. . . . Adaptation is not simply to one stimulus value, say 70 degrees Fahrenheit, but to a range, and minor differences pass unnoticed.' Adaptation in this sense is akin to the acceptance of kinds of behaviour: 'Thus bearing in mind that conformity to norms in everyday life is usually unconscious and automatic, the acceptance of a norm can then be seen as a kind of adaptation. The individual adapts to certain forms of behaviour much as he adapts to the temperature of the room or of his bath, or to the noise of road-drills outside his window . . .'. The range of adaptation, that is the stimuli which *do not* evoke a response, is akin to the latitude of acceptance of kinds of behaviour.

'Theoretically every single stimulus has some effect, however marginal, on the level of adaptation at a given moment of time. Norms also change, and the deviate must be assumed to affect the group. He is not merely a focus for group pressure; at the very least he increases the apparent probability of a form of behaviour, or of an attitude, which was previously "unthink-able", even if it was thought of. The "normal" behaviour of one time will often have been deviate at another; it becomes "normal" as the group adapts to its increasing frequency. In effect, the possibility of change in level of adaptation is akin to the possibility of a shift in latitude of acceptance or of rejection. In both cases it reflects the potential for flexibility, a flexibility which is necessary for the organism to adapt to changes in physical stimuli, and for the social order to take account of new circumstances . . . conformity is essentially static and represents the way of life as it has always been lived; a dynamic group or society, however, is constantly developing, and therefore changing: change inevitably begins as non-conformity, the changes becoming the new norms as society and the individual accommodate to them. (12).

Is 'personality adjustment' as advocated by social workers an attempt to relieve individuals while at the same time, unwittingly, preventing them from exercising those influences that might materially alter the societal environment which has brought about their internal conflicts? If, as the authorities on matters medical and social would have us believe, such large numbers of persons have psychic conflicts and problems, i.e. if the need for psychotherapy is as great as its advocates claim, are they not, in their rescues operations impeding the social change that might ultimately bring about a situation in which fewer such conflicts appeared? Environmental manipulation is unlikely to block social change because it contains the germ of change within itself, but personality adjustment induces at its worst conformity and at its best a fatalistic acceptance. Richard Wollheim in his plea on behalf of socialism sums the matter up very well when he writes:

'Socialism properly understood has no easy remedy for anxiety or unhappiness or for the various disorders of the mind. There are, however, things that in a Socialist society we may reasonably hope for. We may hope that the absence of certain kinds of conflict and certain kinds of privation will aid the study of fundamental conflict and fundamental privation. We may hope that in a society of universal prosperity and literacy these findings will be widely diffused and acted upon. . . . And we may further hope that, not merely in childhood but throughout their lives, the finest effort of the society will be expended in presenting everything that culture and civilization have produced that could relate to or affect or enrich their choice.

'It should be the ultimate boast of socialism that it decreases the possibility of bad upbringing, that it increases the possibility of good education, and that, having in this way realized the conditions upon which free choice depends, it further offers a man reasonable security that as he chooses, so in fact he will be able to live' (13).

It is possible to reply 'pie in the sky' to this, but whether or not we agree with the author's politics, we have to admit that here is the voice of authentic human flexibility and development, in other words of social change, if those terms have any meaning at all. It is not surprising that the myth of social adjustment coincides neatly with those sociological theories based on concepts of stability, equilibrium, consensus and the absence of change. What is remarkable is that out of the Freudian theories such a politically loaded doctrine should have emerged. Freud's patients were, as far as we know, drawn entirely from the educated, comfortably-off middle classes for whom a *modus vivendi* had to be negotiated between themselves and their family and intimates. The social worker's clients are drawn, in great part, from those who could never afford a private psychoanalyst and who are the materially impoverished and drop-outs of our society. Their psychic problems are undoubtedly similar to those of Freud's patients, but the social framework of those problems are vastly different; there is a difference of degree in being feckless on a large income and being feckless on a small one, but the degree is so great as to constitute a difference of kind. The trouble with the myth of adjustment is that it is most applicable to patients or clients who are already in the material circumstances of the well-to-do. The psychotherapeutic approach offers caviare to those who still require the brown bread. It can be argued that the Neo-Freudian approach of the social workers is merely making good a deficiency in Freud's thought, i.e. his apparent disregard of political change as a means of meliorating the inevitable consequences of the societal constraints on man's impulses, contraints that would continue to exist in one form or another in spite of the changes in the political structure of society, but need not block the widespread application of the psychotherapeutic approach. But I suggest that this is not so; the Freudian procedures were applicable to those who were, if not satisfied, at least contented with the politico-economic-social *status quo*, the Viennese bourgeoisie of the late nineteenth and early twentieth centures. Some writers such as Roazen have gone so far as to assume that Freud's apparent lack of interest in political solutions stemmed from 'the discrepancy between the official ideology and the facts of political reality' in the Austro-Hungarian Empire (14). This might be true, though if true of the Austro-Hungarian Empire it is even more so today when the Neo-Freudians live in a world in which the 'credibility gap' between political action and political utterance is probably greater than at any previous historical period. The psychotherapeutic ideologists are following the Master's path, and perhaps for the same reasons, but those whom they are helping and advising are not a similar clientele, because for the most part, they are not a clientele living tolerably satisfied with the social world they inhabit.

Barbara Wootton's attack on the psychotherapeutic notion of adjustment is now almost a classic, and the arguments she adduced in 1959 are just as cogent now. 'Adjustment means adjustment to a particular culture or to a particular set of institutions; and that to conceive adjustment and maladjustment in medical terms is in effect to identify health with the ability to come to terms with that culture or with those institutions' (15). She then becomes enmeshed in a discussion of 'mental health' and adjustment. Although this aspect of the controversy has an interest from our point of view it is not really central. The conception of 'mental health' can only be a metaphorical one in the sense that no disease processes can be identified in the conditions described as states of mental unhealth, and the conditions to which the terms 'mentally healthy' might be applied are ones in which the person concerned shows attitudes and social behaviour in conformity with prevailing norms and has nothing to do with the medical notion of 'health', the whole abstraction must be relegated to that category of modish ideas such as phlogiston and the luminiferous ether that in time are outgrown and replaced by others more appropriate to the general climate of opinion but destined to be abandoned in their turn at some future date. The greater the degree of apparent consensus to norms, the easier it will be to designate forms of behaviour or attitudes and opinions that do not conform to them as symptomatic of 'mental unhealth'. In societies going through rapid social transitions, the consensus, in any case probably more apparent than real, is tenuous and it is difficult for those charged with keeping the moral order of their society to distinguish between what is 'healthy' and what is not. An example of what is meant is provided by that episode at the end of the seventeenth century and the beginning of the eighteenth when witchcraft

E

began to be replaced by mental disorder and possession by insanity. The gravamen of Wootton's complaint against the social workers is that they concentrate on 'social maladjustment' rather than poverty and deprivation; relevant in 1959 but less so in the 1970s when the poor have become the maladjusted: to be poor in the 1970s is, to use the terminology of the psychotherapeutic ideologists to describe a situation that most of them seem unaware of, to be maladjusted.

Adjustment to what? Does it mean only that the adjusted or adjustment indicates the possession of sufficient cunning to appear to conform or to conform through expediency? Is the operation of the reality principle but the recognition of the expediency? The operation of the reality principle is that degree of apparent or actual conformity that enables the individual to survive and is embodied in the precept of 'knowing on which side one's bread is buttered', i.e. adjustment is the ability to make use of the man-made world for one's own ends and within the limits that world imposes.

Once again it becomes necessary to examine the ways in which this term is used. There seem to be three specific ways in which social workers use it:

(a) Adjustment to a specific situation, such as a patient adjusting to the routine of a hospital or to taking a medicine regularly; here the meaning is similar to that applied above to 'adaptation'.

(b) Psychological adjustment; it is difficult to know exactly what is meant by this because if it is assumed that it means being free of major inner psychic conflicts and relatively free of minor ones, then a psychologically well-adjusted person could behave antisocially if his socialization processes had not succeeded in so developing in him a super-ego strong enough to inhibit him or cause him sufficient suffering to make him feel guilty. '. . . the relationship between good psychological adjustment *as such* and criminal behaviour *may frequently be mutually supporting rather than mutually exclusive*. The relationship is frequently seen in precisely this light by law-enforcement authorities—and by offenders themselves. The police tend to regard the clever and calculating professional with considerably more apprehension than the terrified and bungling amateur. The discriminating bank robber will have nothing to do with a get-away man upset by neurotic feelings about bank-theft' (16). Attempts at psychological adjustment undertaken by the sufferer can misfire (assuming that a psychotherapist is required for any successful adjustment to take place is a cardinal belief of the psychotherapeutic ideology) as in the example of alcoholism, a technique of adjustment that usually fails to achieve its goal, though the reluctance of many alcoholics to be 'cured' or to admit their condition should make us wary of accepting the failure as obvious. Alcoholics Anonymous, more aware of this fact than most outsiders, will not accept for membership someone who does not 'want' to be cured.

(c) As a self-evident truth that is beyond definition so no serious attempt is made to define it any more than most people define 'health'. It seems to imply a conformist, level-headed, happy private life—coming to terms with the social *status quo* and one's own situation in it.

All three variations on the theme of adjustment are brilliantly confused in a passage in an article by a social caseworker on rehabilitation counselling: 'Recognition of the conscious further-ance of a relationship between the Rehabilitation Counsellor and the handicapped individual to help him to understand both his problems and his potentialities to carry though a programme of adjustment and self-improvement so that his optimum personal and social adjustment will be concomitant with his vocational adjustment' (17).

The objection to (b) that is most frequently heard is the blanket declaration by psychotherapists and social workers that there is no such person as a 'normal' criminal, that is to say 'economic crime' or crime that pays off in pecuniary terms and can be undertaken as a rational activity does not exist. All criminals are by the very nature of their activity 'maladjusted' or they would not do it. If this view is held, and it is often supported by the claim that it applies to all convicted criminals, which is a weak argument because it avoids consideration of those that get away, then it makes nonsense of the belief held by many sociologists that certain societies encourage crime. Such societies are those whose social structure is such as to facilitate the attainment of socially sanctioned goals by socially disapproved means. In some societies of this type, it is claimed that it is easier to achieve approved goals by illicit means than by those that are socially approved (18).

It is this preoccupation with adjustment or maladjustment that distinguishes contemporary social work from the earlier narrowly psychoanalytic approach and it is the Neo-Freudian ego-psychology of Erikson and others that provides the vehicle for the transmission of the values of the adjustment thesis. The problem alleged to be facing today's psychotherapist is less one of the individual's neurosis in the form of a symptom-bearing disorder than one that takes the shape of a symptom-free neurosis, the so-called 'character neurosis' that it is suggested is distinctive of our days. Erikson says, 'the patient of today suffers most under the problem of what he should believe in and who he should be—or, indeed, might—be or become; while the patient of early psychoanalysis suffered most under inhibitions which prevented him from being what or who he thought he knew he was' (19). What better confirmation could be wished for than this statement for the contentions made above that the concepts of health and disease are irrelevant here and that the context in terms of the kind of persons involved was very different in Freud's time and from the clients of social workers today. The symptoms may have changed as the late Ernest Jones believed (20), but what is more important is that the orientation of the psychotherapeutic ideology has changed as it has spread out from the small élite group of psychoanalysts to the larger mass of social workers. To the psychoanalyst, the aims of treatment are still virtually the same as Freud's, i.e. 'We seek . . . to enrich him (the patient) from his own internal sources by putting at the disposal of his ego those energies which, owing to repression, are inaccessibly confined in his unconscious, as well as those which his ego is obliged to squander in the fruitless task of maintaining these repressions' (21). Admittedly Freud had stated earlier that he aimed 'at making the individual capable of becoming a civilized and useful member of society with the least possible sacrifice of his own activity' (22), but even this is a long way from the social workers' adjustment aims, and it is very unlikely that Freud had as an individual in mind someone similar to most of the persons who form the clientele of agency social workers. Freudian psychoanalysis was never a form of treatment aiming at the adjustment of the individual to the social *status quo*, though frequently the end result was that the individual's performance and outlook came more into tune with the prevailing social norms, but this was in the nature of a by-product rather than an attempt to bring about a successful adjustment to contemporary society; as George Devereux puts it, 'It is the duty of the therapist to free the patient of his personal neurosis, without converting it into the prevailing social neurosis' (23). Eissler even goes so far as to claim that 'the resistance a person can put up against the onslaught of strong mass sentiments is an index of the degree of personality integration' (24).

The contemporary psychotherapeutic practices of social workers owe much to Abram Kardiner, though Karen Horney's statement on the common Freudian heritage of all the Neo-Freudians is true, and especially so in Kardiner's case as he is the only one of the Neo-Freudians to have had a training analysis with Freud himself. Kardiner probably did more than any other to introduce the 'sociological' approach that gives those practices their special flavour. He argues that there is no such thing as a pure human nature, there are only specific types of human nature that are given shape in the 'basic personality' that is characteristic of any specific human society or grouping. The only features that all societies have in common is the helplessness of the infant. We must, therefore, cease concentrating on the individual's psychological processes apart from their cultural contexts and turn towards locating the societal sources of pressure on the personality in its struggle towards adaptation. The ego-structure or basic personality is the individual's adaptational faculty and is in direct contact with social institutions; the complexes or neurotic manifestations are the result not of phylogenetic factors but of the interaction between the 'primary institutions' and the individual. The internal adjustments that the individual makes are necessitated by the external reality, and express themselves as anxieties and defences psychically elaborated and often demonstrated in fantasy. The primary institutions are those that are utilitarian in helping to facilitate the purposes of adaptation in the progress of social evolution. Kardiner, who is an American born psychiatrist and thus not directly stemming from the European mainstream, subscribes to the view that there is a natural selection at work in social evolution as in organic evolution—the societies that survive are those that display 'effective patterns of adaptation'—this does not seem to be quite the same as the Social Darwinists' belief in a social evolution of institutions, but a confused theory that the 'basic personality' comprises the effective mode of adaptation. The primary institutions are those that satisfy human biological wants, and include family organization, the formation of social bonds, methods of child-care and rearing, patterns of feeding, weaning, anal training, sexual prohibitions, and the techniques of obtaining food. In this conglomeration, the role of the family, not sex, is of paramount influence. It is in the family that morality is created and the 'basic personality' is shaped to accord with the requirements of adaptation to social life, a life that has its restrictions as well as its benefits. 'The family is the locus of personality formation, and hence the most reliable avenue for the transmission of culture.' Social collapse can come rather from within than from without by the failure of its members to achieve adaptation. The 'basic personality' is somewhat akin to the 'ideal type' of Max Weber and Alfred Schütz with which sociologists have made us familiar. It is a norm constructed from the range of permitted individual differences and so the individual has some measure of autonomy because he does not accept enculturation passively but selectively, so that he takes on some of the alternative personal attributes out of the total of possibilities provided for him by his society: normality is then the set of attributes lying within the range of those encompassed by the 'basic personality'. Kardiner's theory of the secondary institutions is not important for the psychotherapeutic ideology, indeed his mixture of psychoanalytic insights and comparative anthropology is itself too complicated and confused, especially in its terminology, to have much practical influence. What is significant is his focusing of attention on the role of social institutions and the ego activities in guiding the individual's life career, and his diminishing of the importance of the unconscious. In doing so he directs attention away from the id and sexuality towards the family and personal relationships, and it is this that is at the basis of the social worker's approach. He stresses the importance of adaptation, however unclear it may be, while at the same time he accepts the value of social engineering in improving the institutional framework, within which the basic personality is formed. This is the aspect with which Erich Fromm takes issue when he argues that if the social institutions turn out damaged personalities in large numbers then there is something seriously wrong with the institutions rather than with the individuals who are damaged, and a lot more than piecemeal tinkering in the form of social engineering is required to put things right. There are no 'sick' people in a 'sick' society, says Fromm, because there can be no criteria of sickness. But Fromm's influence on social work has been negligible.

Franz Alexander's views on the need to bring about social change are not dissimilar to those of Kardiner and have influenced the psychotherapeutic ideologies to a considerable extent. If social change, i.e. reshaping institutions, jeopardized the integrity of the individual in the process, the psychotherapist would have to forgo social change. The institutions of a society are the products of slow growth and cannot be changed over-night without doing great damage to individuals, and furthermore, the main direction of social evolution cannot be pointing in the wrong direction. The radicalism of Fromm is thus opposed by the conservatism of Alexander and Kardiner (they sound a little like Burke). Kardiner echoes the view of Alexander and makes the strongest plea for opposing social change as a solution to our problems both individual and collective. He and Alexander agree that a reduction in material deprivation can go a long way towards lessening deviant and 'anti-social' behaviour, and a higher standard of living could improve the quality of life for many but, they ask, will it improve the interior life ? The problem is really one concerning the degree of inner psychic conflict, and a stronger ego structure is more important than a big bank balance in achieving this; economic security is less significant than psychic security (it is interesting to observe that such views always come from those who have the big bank balances and the economic security and parallels those economists who argue in favour of 'limited unemployment' without any danger to themselves or those militarists who advocate conscription when they are long past the age of service). If, as Merton suggests, the socially approved ends can be achieved only by socially unapproved means, if at all, by most of the population, then psychotherapists counter that it would be better to modify existing ideals so that the young can accommodate themselves to their society. Dressed up in the language of psychotherapy, they are putting forward a sociological interpretation of contemporary American society in terms of expectations that are unfulfilled or unfulfillable. Ideally, they advocate not the changing of society but the elimination of specious values or the abandonment of unrealizable expectations. Is this a theory of passive but cynical adjustment? It does not materially alter the situation if what recent critics of the 'expectations' school say is true, i.e. that what is unfulfilled are not expectations regarding occupations and social status but expectations regarding leisure. It hardly matters what the ideals are concerned with, what matters is: can they be fulfilled in some measure that is satisfying. Both Kardiner and Alexander support an evolutionist theory of adaptation to the social environment based on natural selection and the survival of the fittest, but the fitness to survive is reckoned in terms of 'mental health', so the selection of individuals to evolve to their maximum development and of societies to evolve to more advanced levels of civilization depends upon success in liberating and forming the dynamism of personality development and in our kind of society 'selection' is not proceeding 'naturally' because those factors that are susceptible to human influence are being allowed to move in directions that distort both individual and collective development. In other words, the social conditions of our society are inimical to the fullest expression of the individual's adaptive capacities: too much psychic effort is diverted into defences that protect mental balance and self-esteem; too much psychic energy goes into maintaining damaged identities instead of assisting psychic growth. Fundamentally the failure stems from the inadequate and inappropriate interpersonal relations in our society and it is this that blocks or reduces personality development. A competitive society creates psychic conflicts by the drive to compete conflicting with the need for security, love, belonging and rest and in the outcome of the struggle the latter needs are repressed (25).

On the whole, the Neo-Freudian approach with its concentration of interest on interpersonal relations, the family, and love should not be against social change and, as has been indicated, it is not totally opposed, but it favours either slow piecemeal change of the kind beloved by conservatives since the days of Aristotle, or a reduction in the super-ego power of hopelessly elevated ideals. From the practical point of view, its protagonists approve of reform along the lines that social policy has been taking in

Britain and the USA for the past thirty years, but even more, they favour a revolution from within. A revolution within the individual towards more attainable ideals and this can best take place within the setting provided by a liberal, humanistic, individualistic, democratic society such as already exists (it is assumed) in the USA and Britain—only a bit better. Salvation lies within each of us, and if we all make the same kind of effort, the world will become a better place and no revolutions are required; it is really only a variant of the traditional anti-radical view.

Historically, the Neo-Freudian doctrines come from that period in which psychoanalysis moved its abode from central Europe to America, and they can be viewed as efforts to accommodate the European-based ideas of Freud and his immediate circle to the very different ambient in the USA. They had been transferred to a society in which the American Dream still exerted a powerful influence over individual attitudes and where, in spite of the massive social problems, no solution to them in political terms had seriously been considered since 1776. Freudian beliefs and theories had been transplanted to a soil whose inhabitants had an overwhelming faith in the efficacy of the social equivalents of engineers and in the power of the accurately applied dollar to solve all problems.

The American Dream lays heavy stress on the ability of the individual, by his own conscious efforts, to achieve the goal of material success. The Neo-Freudian ego-psychology has a great deal of affinity with this Dream. The Neo-Freudian approach is basically: the Oedipus complex (a main element in Freud's schemata) is considered as only one type of interpersonal relationship and is not exclusively associated with the sexual development of the child; instinct theory is virtually abandoned; a theory of adaptation to the environment is incorporated instead of the instinct theory; the libido hypothesis is dropped together with its biological determinism and strict materialism; the parallel of phylogenetic and ontogenetic development is given up partly because of its speculative nature and partly because it serves no practical purpose; the ego is given a preeminent status in its own right, and there is a move away from psychopathology towards the study of the psychic and social development of individuals, i.e. id-psychology is replaced by ego-psychology; less attention is paid to infantile experiences and their reappearance in adult behaviour and more is paid to the societal environment and its effects, particularly in interpersonal relationships: 'It is a question, not of "actual versus past", but of developmental processes versus repetition' (26). The elements that have superseded the Freudian id and unconscious are personal relationships and development: the yearning for 'togetherness' has replaced the conflict between impulses and society.

The concern with adjustment has, since the end of the Second World War, spread to Europe, and the lead in adopting such an idea has come from West Germany. Its leadership has, however, been a confused one, partly because Neo-Freudianism has clashed with Freudian orthodoxy in persons who had but recently been converted to the latter, and so were intellectually reluctant to abandon or greatly modify their beliefs, and partly because the emphasis on conformity, even 'democratic' conformity in a 'democratic' society seemed to raise fearsome spectres of the not too distant past. Some understanding of the confused acceptance of the concept of adjustment can be gained from Alexander Mitscherlich's answer to the question, 'What is adjustment?' (*was ist eigentlich Anpassung?*) in his paper 'The Sicknesses of Society and Psychosomatic Medicine'; Professor Mitscherlich is director of the Sigmund Freud Institute of the University of Frankfurt am Main (27).

According to Mitscherlich 'adjustment' does not describe a 'one-sided submission of the individual to existing social and natural conditions' but—and here his language becomes unclear—a situation that arises from the 'passive acceptance of a style of behaviour in unison with an active expansion of the individual's character'. He defines the 'truly socially adjusted individual' as one who 'is capable of socially developing his own activities'. Furthermore, the stability and internal consistency of a social structure depends on this unison between passive acceptance and the opportunities for individual expansion. The dangers for the individual and his society lie in a set of social norms that are too flexible and too tolerant and that therefore permit 'the manifold impulses' of the members a too unrestrained expansion. An unrestricted development of individual capacities will lead to a 'false' individualism that ignores social sanctions.

Society always imposes restrictions on the individual in that it demands the renunciation of instinctive urges, but when the renunciation demanded reaches an intolerable degree of constraint, the society begins to disintegrate. Restrictions must be within tolerable limits and must be compensated for by the possibility of the development of individual capacities. 'The limit of what is tolerable cannot be determined objectively, but results from the sum of pleasure and aversion experienced.'

Totalitarian regimes demand absolute submission and attempt to inculcate it by socialization processes aimed at achieving 'in man an automatism of behaviour similar in function to the innate control by instinct in animals'. By doing so, it is assumed that all social conflicts will disappear. There is, however, an essential difference between this man-induced automatism and the environmentally adjusted animal: in the case of man the submission (or conformity) can only be enforced by fear of those holding positions of power within the society. Fear has its limits. When it goes beyond a certain intensity it is no longer a productive element in socialization, and can become panic in extreme situations. In general, when not taken to extremes, fear encourages the ego-orientated aspects of behaviour among a great number of the masses. Fear is conducive to isolation and a-sociability. The 'cultural aptitude' (a term used by Freud) of a person, i.e. all that is achieved through the intensification of external social commands into internalized commands dictated by conscience, decreases when the pressures exerted by fear grow too great and are converted into 'cultural hypocrisy' which is only a superficial adjustment unsupported by super-ego dictates. This effect displays itself in the outbreaks of barbarism that, in the long run, accompany every dictatorship and which characterize societies that do not reflect the ego-ideal of their members but are mere jungles in which the strong can take advantage of the weak.

Apart from the fear engendered in totalitarian dictatorships, there is another source of fear that afflicts our kind of society today: the fear that originates from the dissolution of accustomed forms of interhuman communication, the dissolution of traditions that are subjected to a relentless decomposition by industrialization, and the societal changes in the environment that are its consequence. These environmental changes are due to the fact that 'man's level of consciousness has been altered because he has succeeded in influencing the external reality to an unthought of degree'. Thus his accustomed 'predecisions established by a well-defined "set of roles" lose more and more of their validity, and in this state of relative abandonment there arises an ignorance of our own inner reality which causes a chronically effective though submerged anxiety'. The American sociologist, Riesman, describes, in his type of the 'other-directed man', a being who seems as if equipped with radar by means of which he constantly scans the behaviour and attitudes of his fellows so as not to lose his own conformism to their ways. Such an individual remains 'ego-weak' and wide open to suggestions that promise him a relief from anxiety. Another type produced by this kind of society is the beatnik, mods and rockers, *Gammler* and so forth who possess negative attitudes towards their societies and gain their relief from anxiety through attachment to a group with its own strongly asserted new group ideals. These groups find strength in opposition, though they usually express themselves aggressively and destructively rather than through positive and kindly action. Groups of this nature draw our attention to the fact that the social task of dealing with libidinous and aggressive instincts is still unresolved.

There is much of original Freud in Mitscherlich's views together with something of Kardiner's basic personality concept, but he does face up to the 'dual' nature of adjustment, which is more than many contemporary British and American psycho-therapeutic ideologists do; but like them he cannot offer a way out of the impasse. It is easy enough to speak of conformity on the one hand and opportunities for the development of individual capacities on the other, but so far the mean between the two extremes has escaped us. Rhetoric is not a substitute for clarity of thought, it is only an alternative. Brim sums the situation up with lucidity and brevity when he writes:

'In closing we have reached the intersection of two great interests in the study of personality and social structure: how society manages to socialize the individual so that the work of society gets done, and how individuals manage gradually to transform the social system in which they live. The deviant person who cannot be resocialized is the source of innovation and change in the behaviour and ideals of society. The fundamental problem to be solved by an enduring society is to train individuals to be responsible, and yet provide for the development of the free and creative person. A middle way must be taken between producing the undersocialized and the oversocialized person. A society must develop members who conform and fit into the existing order, as well as those who, although deviant now, are better equipped to live in the world to come' (28).

Nicely put, but what if the society itself is irresponsible and its values confused and unrealizable? What if we are advocating conformity for the many and deviance for an élite as existed in the Russia of Nicholas I, when any book selling at more than two gold roubles was free of censorship, for who could believe that a person able to afford such a sum for a book could possibly be seditious?

Social adjustment or psychological adjustment, when it is more than a mere analogy for 'adaptation', is a fiction in two senses: the first because it is an article of faith, without objective and definable criteria; secondly because if it means a 'middle way' then it has never historically been realized or is likely to be because innovators, to some degree, must always be non-conformists and by definition 'not adjusted' in some respect or other. Innovation, for better or for worse, is the main force in the historical process, whether one believes in development or progress in the evolutionist's sense or in the more limited sense implied by an 'episode of progress'. A general theory of social adjustment is a fiction or myth that brings to mind the words of Fourier: 'il semble que la nature souffle à l'oreille du genre humain qu'il est réservé à un bonheur dont il ignore les routes, et qu'une découverte merveilleuse viendra tout à coup dissiper les ténèbres de la civilisation' (29).

But in another sense, adjustment is not a myth but a consolation. Techniques and procedures that can reconcile an individual to his lot can, no doubt, be of inestimable value in making such an individual happier or more contented, and if in the process some fraction of his potential capacities, if he possess any, be actualized,

141

then all the better. If social work is for what previous generations would have called, without being mealymouthed, the 'lower orders' or what social workers refer to themselves as 'the socially or culturally deprived', the drop-outs and casualities of our society who cannot afford private psychiatric treatment or possess sufficient wealth to shield themselves from the pressures of the legal and economic systems, then social work, except as it provides material assistance and environmental manipulation, is a confidence trick, just a modern version of the 'opiate of the people', neither more nor less reprehensible than any other opiate. It is unlikely, though this is completely unsupported speculation, however, that the majority of the social workers' clients are in the category of innovators, and their deviance even if they are not just those who have failed in what Malthus called 'the perpetual struggle for room and food', is not of the kind that will, if unchecked, threaten to change the society in which they live. It can thus be argued, both from the point of view of humanity as well as of expediency, that bringing the client into harmony with his society's values will do no harm and might be of some benefit to the client as well as the society. But then, it has to be admitted that the social worker doing this is not the kind of person that the textbooks from which he learns his trade claim or the tutors that teach him say he is; he is but a mere trouble-shooter if he is professionally motivated and a secular priest if he is indoctrinated.

A very different situation exists when the social worker makes sweeping claims to extend his ministrations to all in his society. It is one thing to offer consolation to those who, with or without a revolution, are unlikely ever to be anything more than the mute, inglorious members of their society; quite a different matter to act upon the whole of society without discrimination. The first might be described as a laudable act of charity, the second is an act of political and social indoctrination. Not all social workers are concerned to 'adjust' in the wide sense or to stimulate towards 'maturity' and suchlike; many still hold views similar to that expressed in a recent paper on counselling in which the view is put that 'counselling may be appropriate to "nursing" individuals through psycho-social transitional processes whether they be commonly experienced dramatic events or personal problems experienced only by the individuals who have them' (30). The commonly experienced events are of the crisis type such as bereavements, birth, marriage, retirement, divorce, all of which tend towards breakdown on the part of individuals. With this, one can have little quarrel, but the most powerful and influential voices in the social work field are putting forward claims of a much wider and more penetrating kind.

Notes and References

1 Hamilton, *op. cit.*, pp. 237 and 239.
2 Mitchell, G. Duncan, *A Dictionary of Sociology*, Routledge and Kegan Paul, London, 1968, p. 3.
3 Dewey, Richard and Humber, W. J., *An Introduction to Social Psychology*, The Macmillan Company, New York, 1966, p. 201 (Collier-Macmillan, London, 1966). This is a textbook favouring the 'interactionist' approach and the psychotherapeutic ideology. The seven minor elements that the authors include in the process of adjustment figure largely in textbooks of psychoanalysis and psychopathology but this should not detract from their participation in 'adjustment'. If we subtract from the concept of adjustment any notion of 'good' or 'bad' then value judgments will not obscure our appreciation of these elements, though some may be morally reprehensible and others ineffective.
4 Herskovits, Melville J., *Man and His Works*, Knopf, New York, 1948, p. 39.
5 Katz, Daniel, 'The Functional Approach to the Study of Attitudes', *Public Opinion Quarterly*, 1960, 24, pp. 163–77.
6 *Ibid.*, p. 169.
7 The ineffectiveness of ego-defensive behaviour depends on the point of view taken. A consideration of the example given by Katz will make this apparent. A worker who acts out his own internal conflicts by persistently quarrelling with his colleagues and employer might relieve himself of some of his emotional tensions and thus bring about an adjustment; but his behaviour at work might impede his promotion or even lead to his dismissal so that in terms of adjustment to his work situation, the behaviour is ineffective.
8 Hamilton, *op. cit.*, p. 237.
9 *Ibid.*, p. 238.
10 *Ibid.*, p. 5.
11 Kelvin, Peter, *The Bases of Social Behaviour*, Holt, Rinehart and Winston, London, 1970.
12 *Ibid.*, pp. 104–5.
13 Wollheim, Richard, *Socialism and Culture*, Fabian Tract 331, Fabian Society, London, 1961, p. 48.

14 Roazen, *op. cit.*, p. 257.
15 Wootton, *op. cit.*, pp. 218–21, 237–8.
16 Korn, Richard R., 'The Counselling of Delinquents', in Harms and Schreiber, *op. cit.*, p. 131, original italics.
17 Usdane, William M., 'Rehabilitation Counselling', in Harms and Schreiber, *op. cit.*, p. 277.
18 The leading exponent of this sociological theory of deviant behaviour is Robert King Merton in his *Social Theory and Social Structure*, The Free Press, Glencoe, Iii, 1949 (Free Press, London, 1968).
19 Erikson, *op. cit.*, p. 239.
20 Jones, Ernest, *Free Association*, Hogarth, London, 1959, pp. 124–5.
21 Freud, Vol. xx, p. 256.
22 Freud, Vol. x, p. 146.
23 Devereux, George, 'Maladjustment and Social Neurosis', *American Sociological Review*, Vol. 4, No. 6, December 1939, p. 846.
24 Eissler, Kurt, 'Objective (Behaviouristic) Criteria of Recovery from Neuro-psychiatric Disorders', *Journal of Nervous and Mental Disease*, Vol. 106, No. 5, November 1947, p. 501.
25 Alexander, Franz, *Our Age of Unreason*, Lippincott, New York, 1942, 2nd ed., 1951, and *Psychoanalysis and Psychotherapy*, Norton, New York, 1956 (George Allen & Unwin, London, 1957); Kardiner, Abram, *The Individual and His Society*, Columbia University Press, New York, 1946 (Columbia University Press, London, 1939); *The Psychological Frontiers of Society*, Columbia University Press, New York, 1946 (Columbia University Press, London, 1945); *Sex and Morality*, Bobbs-Merrill, New York, 1954.
26 Horney, Karen, *New Ways in Psychoanalysis*, Norton, New York, 1939, p. 153.
27 Mitscherlich, Alexander, *Krankheit als Konflikt, Studien zur psychosomatischen Medizin, 1*, Suhrkamp Verlag, Frankfurt am Main, 1966.
28 Brim, Orville G., Jr., 'Socialization through the Life Cycle', in Brim, Orville G., Jr. and Wheeler, Stanton, *Socialization after Childhood: Two Essays*, Wiley, New York, 1966, p. 46 (Wiley, London, 1966). These papers were originally given at a conference organized by the (American) National Institute of Mental Health.
29 Fourier, François Charles Marie, *Oeuvres Complètes*, tome 2, Paris, 1843, p. 20.
30 From a privately circulated paper on counselling by R. E. Morley.

Chapter 6

People Matter, Not Money:
the Human Relations in Industry Ideology

In a recent survey of firms in the United Kingdom offering health schemes for their managerial staffs, 3·1 per cent of the 134 companies that replied to the questionnaire stated that they offered 'psychiatric counselling' as one of the facilities available (1). A little more than 3 per cent of a hundred large companies (about a thousand managers in each) providing their top employees with psychiatric services when needed should occasion little surprise; indeed it is a remarkable testimony to the manner in which British management has lagged behind that of the USA that the figure is so small. This kind of service to employees is a logical development of the human relations in industry approach that, in spite of the slow growth of fringe benefits of a psychotherapeutic nature, has still made considerable gains in Britain.

The human relations approach as applied to industry has had a long history, and dates back to the early 1920s in the United States. Briefly, and in the words of Georges Friedmann, it aims at 'strengthening the psychological bonds connecting the worker with the firm, at combating, neutralizing or overcoming the forces which separate him from it, at making the enterprise a collective reality in which the worker is mentally integrated (in a manner he is more or less conscious of, depending on the methods used) and, consequently, in which he will be induced to contribute his physical and technical working capacity more fully' (2). It concentrates on the relations between management and workers and is based on many assumptions, not least among which, is a managerial ideology postulating that the skills that nowadays lead up the ladder of success are 'not technical ones but skills in coordination, that is skills in dealing with relations between people' (3). Though the approach is eclectic and pragmatic, as one would expect from its business setting, it still has its origins in the same source as that of the psychotherapeutic ideology itself: 'Influenced by the discovery of the unconscious (Freud) and of non-rational motives (Pareto), the Human Relationists proposed that Man's social needs were rarely satisfied by formal structures. Man's major allegiance was to the primary groups of friends and family. It followed that most attention should be paid to informal activities and to the factors influencing the formation and character of work-groups' (4). Even when it appears in the shape of learning theory (now currently fashionable) Halmos claims: 'the practical prescripts are still based on assumptions about facts in human relationships which are not distinguishable from the assumptions about facts in the thinking of the counsellors' (5).

To Halmos, the spread of the counsellors' faith to the business sector is viewed as an extension of an unmitigated good and worthwhile attitude towards one's fellowmen in an area that for generations has been regarded as one in which exploitation and greed have predominated. Even though the motives for adopting such an attitude may be confused, unclear and even suspect, this does not, in his opinion, detract from their effect or seriously affect his main thesis that the human world is becoming a better place for it. After all, the Dale Carnegie creed of making friends and influencing people is easier to live with than a creed of overt coercion. Business's top men are becoming more concerned with doing 'good' (or even being 'good') than with the unscrupulous pursuit of the maximization of profit. If, however, doing 'good' also does not conflict with making a profit, so much the better, but even if it does so conflict, Halmos suggests that such businessmen might well do 'good' and suffer a relative loss. Halmos deliberately takes this optimistic view because he believes that the future of western society (perhaps of all human society) depends on the spread of this faith, and he is concerned lest the negative, debunking propensities of many sociologists should hinder our appreciation of this evolution. But much of his optimism stems from a particular view of the nature of contemporary industry that is also held by most of the 'human relationists'.

The hypothesis that underlies this view is that (a) big business is in the hands of managers who do not own the firms but run them on behalf of the shareholders; (b) these managers have evolved a new ethos, a 'professional' one so that their aims as well as their viewpoints are quite different from those of the great entrepreneurs, the Lords of Creation as F. L. Allen once called them; (c) they manage on behalf of their shareholders but they also exercise stewardship on behalf of their colleagues and fellow-workers and the general public, and (d) they do so not only because it is profitable (a debatable point) but because that is the way their ethos compels them to behave; (e) the new managerial ethos derives from professionalization and is linked with role playing because the new professional manager plays a 'role of concern'. There is an additional proposition that does not much concern us here because it takes us well beyond the scope of this work and it is that (f) managers have the same kind of ethos whether they be managers in the USA, the USSR or the UK and this is because they are faced with essentially similar problems and they resolve them in fundamentally similar fashion because their stewardship is basically the same the world over. Within a nation state the same applies, the problems of managing a nationalized industry are close to those involved in running a free enterprise corporation; this may be expressed in rather a different way by saying that free enterprise management is following the patterns set by the management of nationalized industry. One of the consequences of this hypothesis having been widely accepted and rarely challenged is that the great non-subject of management and all its academic ramifications has come into existence and become the theology of the business and industrial world.

Closely connected with the above propositions is the further belief that we are entering a world in which ideologies are passing away: this is the 'end of ideology' thesis that has had such a remarkable impact over the past ten years. It is argued that the common professional viewpoints of managers in the East and West, for one thing, makes ideologies anachronisms (6). The thesis is that 'capitalism' has been regenerated and redeemed, while socialism has become 'liberalized' and in the affluent societies of the West, these two modes converge and are leading us towards a new social order that will soon surpass the 'welfare state' as we know it today. Ideologies are thus irrelevant and are being replaced by scientific and technological expertise. (It all sounds a little like Comte's vision of the age of positivism in a new frock.)

The contemporary situation in the industrialized countries of the West has been analysed by Ralf Dahrendorf who finds the origins of the human relations school in the changed structure of industry, rather than in the adoption of a particular psychological movement's theories; not that his sociological analysis rules the latter out. His approach is non-reductionist in that he follows Durkheim's precept of finding a sociological explanation for a sociological fact.

Dahrendorf classifies thinkers on the contemporary issues of class and management into two groups and uses an unusual nomenclature to describe them: he calls the men of the left and of radical and revolutionary stances the conservatives, and those that one would normally describe as centre or middle-of-the-road conservatives he terms radicals. His reasons for this seem to be that the 'conservatives' are those who accept traditional views of industrial society, i.e. still believe in 'capitalism' and 'class conflict'; 'haves versus have-nots' and so forth, while his 'radicals' accept the view that the whole industrial-social scene has changed and new attitudes are required to deal with new situations. For the sake of clarity, I shall refer to Dahrendorf's 'conservatives' (who include such radical thinkers as C. Wright Mills) as the 'pessimists' and his radicals as the 'optimists', for the very good reason that the first group believe that there have been no significant changes and the talk about such changes is mere propaganda and 'conning', while the second believe that there have been great and important alterations in the whole socio-economic structure of western society. Needless to say, the optimists in some way or another subscribe to the 'end of ideology' thesis, while the pessimists do not.

The pessimists claim that ownership, and particularly institutional ownership, is still sufficiently concentrated to control many of the most powerful industrial and commercial firms. Owner-control is also reinforced by an elaborate and complicated system of interlocking directorates, so complex that very little is known about its extent and its ramifications. Major decisions on policy are still taken at the board of directors' level, as W. L. Guttsman has emphasized. Even when professionalized managers do exercise control, they do so in the interest of the owners and there is no empirical evidence of any value to support the contention that they do not. They also argue that there is very little evidence for the belief that ownership and control are now divorced; what has occurred is a reorganization of the propertied strata into a more or less unified stratum of the 'corporate rich' which includes the very rich whether they be aristocrats, plutocrats, entrepreneurs, and the chief executives (the mangerial élite); *the managerial élite and the very rich are not two distinct and clearly separated groups*, and the evidence that claims that they are is too trivial to be taken seriously.

Among the pessimists must be included Norman Birnbaum who discusses at some length the controversy over non-owning management and ownership control. He makes the following propositions: that there is something of a symbiosis between managers and shareholders (he uses the European term 'rentier'); that the rewards of management include 'privileged access to ownership through stock bonuses, share acquisition plans, and the like'. He also argues that not all managers manage equally, some manage much more than others, especially the heads of banks, and the chiefs of insurance companies and financial groups. He claims that the attitudes of managers 'would appear to be quite indistinguishable from those of entrepreneurs'. Furthermore, he denies the validity of the thesis that there is a continuum between the membership of boards of directors and middle and junior management after the manner of the Napoleonic career open to talents, a belief that is fed to each annual intake of business studies undergraduates. There is no such continuum; there are differences in the decisions made by boards of directors that put such decisions into a quite different category from those made by members of the lower echelons. In addition, those at the summit have a consciousness of power that sets them apart from their subordinates, together with financial gains that are of a different order from the rewards of the latter. It is extremely difficult to reach any definite conclusions because 'the conspicuous fact about the new form of élite organization is that it is not conspicuous'. The vague terms 'manager', 'executive', hide the range of power and influence that the holders of these titles may exercise. The managers of corporate property, the managers of political power, and the managers of the mass media are united into an informal group but they are not a conspiracy, 'not even a club, but simply a happy coincidence'. The concentration of power at the top might seem to those lower down the ladder a quite legitimate division of labour and gives them the warm feeling that they are participating in some joint enterprise: 'The diffusion of share-ownership . . . has not seriously affected the concentration of property—but it has had important social-psychological effects. Among which is that it has obscured the objective situation of dependence and relative powerlessness of those who have an assured career on the middle levels, with regular and predictable salary increases, a recognizable status giving a share in prestige, job security, and limited opportunities of hobnobbing with those really at the top' (7).

The optimists see the industrial scene very differently. In advanced industrial societies such as the USA and UK (other advanced industrial societies such as those of West Germany, France and Italy do not correspond so closely to this pattern) two-thirds of all firms are joint-stock companies and they own four-fifths of all economic enterprise property; their shares are fairly widely dispersed, at least among the wealthier strata, and therefore individual and family ownership has ceased to be the dominant pattern of economic organization. Ownership has been superseded by management. The separation of ownership from control has led to the emergence of a new group of managers whose outlook in terms of ideology, goal and values is quite different from that of their predecessors. To call such managers 'capitalists' is inappropriate (and so to refer to the enterprises that they manage as 'capitalist' is also inappropriate). These managers are bureaucrats who owe their positions to their managerial skills and abilities instead of 'owning the company' or is some way controlling a majority of the voting-stock. Their different training, backgrounds, and experience make them think and act differently from owner-managers and capitalists. This popular and fashionable thesis, which in this country coincides very neatly with some of the current myths developed since 1945: myths such as 'there is more upward mobility now than ever before', or 'the poor are getting richer and the rich poorer', or 'the gap between the rich and the not-so-rich is narrowing', or 'there are no obstacles any longer in the path of working-class children in our egalitarian society'. Such myths receive support from this 'managerial ideology'. But the bases for this belief do not rest on very secure empirical foundations. The blanket term 'joint-stock company' tells us very little about the nature of any specific company; the wide dispersal of shareholding can sometimes lead to control being in the hands of persons actually holding very few shares, but still shareholders for all that. A private joint-stock company can 'go public' and still retain control in the hands of a few shareholders who are family members and friends. We know too little about the backgrounds, training and experience of non-owner managers compared with those of owner-managers, and we know little or nothing about the possession of shares by non-owner managers in companies that they manage (8).

Dahrendorf says that the term 'capitalist' is only appropriate where the legal owner of the enterprise is at the same time the practical manager of production and the supreme commander of his workers. This argument introduces something additional to the standard controversy between the optimists and the pessimists, and makes explicit what Berle and Means implied in 1932 when they wrote that societies such as the USA and Britain were no longer 'capitalist' (9), but this seems to me to be a mere piece of hair-splitting; it is not vital that owner-control means actual day-to-day management, because what is at issue is the belief that only owner-controllers want to 'maximize profit'; professional non-owner managers have wider and more humane aims, and Dahrendorf's distinction between 'capitalist' and others begs the question.

Class may best be defined in terms of authority relationships, and authority is the major factor determining class and class conflict, are views that Dahrendorf puts forward. He does not share the optimists' belief that there is no conflict between the workers and the 'non-capitalist' – non-owner managers. Previous assumptions about class conflict have always supposed that property is the source of such conflict, but Dahrendorf contends that today the possession or otherwise of property is hardly relevant—what is important and at the root of conflict is authority. Every organized and imperatively co-ordinated association contains within itself a dominant and a subservient group. Authority relationships of this universal kind are found in every type of enterprise; churches, armies, schools, hospitals, trade unions, political parties (the contention is really only a restatement of Michels' famous thesis that all organizations necessarily assume an oligarchical character in the course of their development) (10). There are ruling groups in the state and ruling groups in industry and ruling groups should therefore, at least initially, be regarded as ruling only within the framework of separate and defined associations, and there can thus be as many co-existing, though possibly competing and conflicting, ruling groups in any society as there are organized associations in it. Each ruling group has its non-ruling supporters so that the society is broken up into competing and conflicting power and interest blocs. To speak of a 'ruling class' in the older sense of the word can nowadays be misleading. The connection between groups, ruling and otherwise, and the connection, if any, between leaders of industry and other ruling groups has yet to be empirically studied, but Dahrendorf believes that contemporary industrialized societies are 'pluralist', i.e. theoretically, ruling groups only exist within separate associations and there is no self-evident relationship between managers and capitalists and the ministers and top civil servants. If the rulers of industry were also the rulers of the state, then the first government by a socialist party would refute this. Power is shared unequally amongst the ruling groups and in spheres such as government and the control of industry the spheres of influence merge and grow confused. In a pluralist society the difference between dominant groups is emphasized, not their similarities in what J. K. Galbraith calls 'countervailing power'. The struggles are not class struggles, but conflicts between functional groups possessing concentrated power; Big business, Big Labour, Big Agriculture, and so forth. Dahrendorf asserts that class action is noticeably lacking in contemporary industrialized society (11). Here he dislodges one of the main planks in the platform of the optimists: they claim that Big Business exercises its power with a strong and growing sense of responsibility partly because it is subject to the greatest pressure and public scrutiny and also because it is now led by a professionalized managerial élite; Dahrendorf denies there is any evidence to support this (the harsh criticisms of Big Business by the Conservative Government for sabotaging its wages restraint policy in Britain in 1970 and 1971 certainly support Dahrendorf). Although Dahrendorf accepts the optimists' belief that ownership and control have become separated, he also believes that conflict is not excluded between labour and management in spite of the appearance of a new business ideology on the part of the non-owning managers.

The new ideology has arisen as a consequence of this separation of ownership from control and the emergence of a new dominant group of managers. The old bases for the legitimacy of entrepreneurial authority no longer hold. The old style capitalist's authority was legitimated by his ownership, or from being one among the owners. The new type of manager still, in private enterprise, derives his authority in part from representing the shareholders, i.e. their rights are delegated to him, but unlike the actual owner, he cannot afford to exercise his authority in direct and deliberate contravention of the wishes of workers and subordinates or even against some alleged public interest (it is unlikely that the owner-manager could flagrantly do so today either). So the non-owning manager has been forced to seek an additional and perhaps even more powerful legitimating basis, and he has found it in the idea of a kind of consensus among those who are bound to obey his commands (12). The 'human relations' school of management is a symptom of this new legitimacy. His views are not, in essence, dissimilar to those expressed by Reinhard Bendix (13) that in modern societies managerial ideologies develop that serve to justify the power of management in terms of basic cultural values. While Bendix concentrates on these ideologies as legitimating the managers' powers to society as a whole, Dahrendorf concentrates on the legitimation of managerial authority over labour, a legitimation that is powerfully reinforced by the belief that managers are now 'professionals' and as such, like all professionals, owe a responsibility to society as a whole; or to put it in the rather cruder and emotive terms of the Chairman of the Reed Paper Group: 'The Reed philosophy is that it is people that matter, not money'.

But the human relations approach, in spite of the massive literature devoted to it and the colossal investment in it, has quite clearly, save in marginal instances, failed to achieve industrial peace and contentment. Why? Because it is seen by workers as either (a) a confidence trick or (b) irrelevant (this does not mean that some of its by-products in the form of welfare amenities and welfare schemes are not appreciated). It is suspect because in order to be a reflection of a new approach, the optimists' thesis must be true. The human relations approach has to be validated by a genuine change of heart on the part of management or else it is nothing but a hypocritical gimmick designed to persuade workers and subordinates, not to mention the general public, that the bosses are not really in business just for the greatest long-term profit (or short-term in some cases) for themselves. Where the approach has apparently succeeded it is associated with shorter working-hours, better pay and better chances of advancement, so that it is impossible to know which element has affected what. The initial experiments carried out in the period 1927 to 1939 in the United States were deceptive in the long run, and since then few exponents of the approach have bothered to take account of the specific historical context of those experiments and their novelty. Even if, some critics urge, it were not to be a manifestation of hyprocrisy, it would still be largely irrelevant because for the majority of industrialized workers, work is not a 'central life interest' and so the benefits of human relations, welcome though they are, would only affect the periphery of the workers' lives.

The concept of a 'central life interest' (for convenience hereinafter referred to as CLI) is a fairly old one (14), but still a valid formulation of something that has been observed for some considerable time.

By a CLI is meant that complex of interests and associations supplied by primary relationships that gives a 'meaning' to life and also provides the major source of satisfaction. The work of Dubin and Orzack indicated that the central interests of industrialized workers were not in their work; rather, they found their preferred associations and interests outside the work situation. They also found that less than 10 per cent of workers preferred the informal relationships of the work situation to other possibilities. But workers do place higher value on the work organization than they do on other organizations in which they have membership. They concluded that workers have a well-developed sense of attachment to their work and work place without being totally committed to them. Blauner's investigations have not contradicted these findings (15). Using the concept of alienation as his measure, and the type of work as his significant variable, he contrasted craft work with machine tending and then assembly work, and finally with a continuous process industry, such as the chemical industry, where work is highly automated. Blauner found a regular progression of feelings of greater alienation, particularly in the form of powerlessness and meaninglessness, from craft work, where it was low, to motor-car assembly work, where it was highest, with a reversal of the progression in the circumstances of automated continuous production. Where alienation is lowest is where the workers feel that they have control over their jobs, are freer from supervision and are not mere instruments in a technical process. Among craft workers, printers rate their work interests high and give as their main reasons for liking their work, its variety, creativity, challenge, and educational stimulus. Motor-car workers, while they are among the highest paid 'blue-collar workers', find their work routine and boring, but give as their chief satisfaction the fact that their high wages offer an opportunity of buying a better outside-of-work-life.

When Orzack turned to investigate professional workers, he found a very different picture. In contrast to the industrial workers, nurses reported in four out of five instances that work and the work place were their CLI, almost a complete reversal of the findings relating to industrial workers.

Stephenson confirmed these findings in his study of clerical workers in Chicago. Among those who had little change of advancement, such as secretaries and typists, work was not a CLI; they were content if the pay was good and the boss pleasant; their main interests were outside and in what their wages could buy. But when he investigated supervisory personnel whose careers were still, theoretically if not always actually, open, he found that many reported work as their CLI.

The inescapable conclusion that is to be drawn from such studies is that they clearly indicate that for the mass of industrial workers, work can never be a CLI, and so a human relations approach can never be more than peripheral in importance compared with short working hours and high pay; only after those have been achieved does the human relations approach have any significance. But for professionals and those doing skilled jobs with prospects of promotion and advancement, work can be and often is a CLI, but again the human relations approach is relatively unimportant as such groups rarely engage in the more bitter forms of conflict and industrial strife with management.

David Riesman goes so far as to advocate what is virtually 'the happy alienated worker'. As work will never be a CLI to the majority of workers, and as the intellectual and moral climate of Western industrialized society is changing from the domination of the Protestant Ethic to the domination of some ethic of leisure, it would be reasonable to abandon concern with alienation and concentrate on short working hours and high wages so that people could gratify their leisure wants that are now the locus of their CLIs. Though Riesman's thesis might be most applicable to the USA, there is good reason to suppose that this change of moral climate is detectable throughout the Western world, though cultural modifications will still account for individual national variations.

If we turn to West Germany where the policy of *industrielle Mitbestimmung* or co-determination of management by workers and managers has been implemented since immediately after the Second World War, and was experimented with in the days of the Weimar Republic, we do not find any very significant differences between the attitudes of workers there and in the USA or Britain (16). The work of Heinrich Popitz and his collaborators (17) indicates that the workers, while admitting that co-determination does prevent the bosses taking dictatorial measures, still do not feel deeply involved and committed to the firm, and that the phrase is empty of any significant content. A worker is only able to do the limited job that he is paid to do and does not really know much about anything else, and no boss worthy of the title would pay much attention to the uninformed opinions of workers, seems to be a fair summary of what workers feel about co-determination according to Popitz. What is, however, of more importance in the Popitz study is that the workers still tend to view employers, bosses, the management and even the clerical and administrative staffs connected with them with intense suspicion. Even intelligent workers doubt whether white collar workers really work. The rather primitive approach to work that has characterized much working-class thinking in the past two hundred years is still strong: work is either physical or if mental then it is of such a nature that one can be seen doing it, as one can see an engineer operating an instrument panel or performing mathe-matical calculations or a surgeon intervening with his scalpel and other instruments. The rest, the kind of things that the managers, the accountants, the marketeers do is not work. Fundamentally, the workers believe that these gentlemen become rich only at the expense of the workers' own efforts, and so we are back with the first objection made above; all human relations techniques are forms of confidence trickery, they are hypocrisy. They are methods whereby the worker is conned into involving himself and believing that his knowledge of what is going on and even his participation actually make any difference to the running of the firm and its policy. He is diverted from attending to those things that really concern him and is made an ally of the bosses at the expense of allegiance to his own kind. (These findings may no longer be relevant as Popitz's work was published in 1957, long before the *Wirtschaftswunder* and the full effect of membership of the Common Market was felt.)

The human relationists ignore the fact that the sources of industrial unrest and conflict are complex and not only vary from culture to culture but are determined to a great extent by factors that are outside the relationships between employers and employ-ees in any given firm. The manner is which the historical factors have been ignored in the discussion of industrial disputes in Britain is almost unbelievable. It is of very little use to evolve refined and 'sophisticated' theories about the nature of the relationships between power blocs and groups and to deny the existence of 'class conflict' in Britain. What Dahrendorf says about conflict in Germany might well be true, but anyone who denies the continuance of class conflict and animosity in Britain, France and Belgium today is either a fool or a hypocrite. The distinction between 'us and them' might not be a symptom of class conflict to sociologists but in the language of everyday life it is, and until sociologists devise a jargon that has no relationship to the usage of everyday life, this kind of hostility will be called by those wanting to be understood by the time-honoured designa-tion that it has had until now; class conflict. Friedmann says of the human relations school: '. . . there is nothing more instructive than the orientation of English industrial psychologists who, at the end of their studies, in order to imbue subdivided and monotonous tasks with interest, turn to the *esprit de corps* which they find in the regiments, public schools, universities and athletic teams of their country. The question is supposed to be one of creating in the factory a team spirit which would transfigure all tasks. Led by their particularism and misjudgment of the social reality outside the firm, these psychologists therefore persuade themselves that this sort of interest may be inspired, so to speak, on order, by an appropriate psychological propaganda. But the worker's feeling for his work, as well as the fatigue or resistance which he displays in the face of difficult tasks cannot be localized within a job and restricted to these frontiers. They certainly set in play physiological and psychological factors, but also the relations between the worker and his work, that is, his personal problems and his ties with the various groups to which he belongs, such as family, trade union, and social class, as well as his status in the society or State in which he lives. Here there is a fabric the threads of which cannot easily be separated. Anyone who tries to affect the psychology of the worker at his work will have no success if he ignores this interdependence' (18). Beyond the technological aspect, there lies a psychological one and beyond that there exists a sociological reality that is ignored. Silverman (19) asserts that the human relationists have managed 'almost totally to ignore environmental factors' and he could have added 'historical factors also'. The bias of psychologists inclines them not to perceive historical factors but their blindness is only equalled by the disregard of history exhibited by many industrial sociologists.

In nationalized industries it would be expected that the attitudes of workers would be less hostile to the bosses (Popitz cites a preference by many German workers for nationalization rather than *Mitbestimmung*) but the available information indicates that this is not so. Some of the most bitter of recent industrial disputes have taken place in the field of the nationalized industries and public corporations, and it has become a myth, perhaps without foundation, that the traditional animosity towards bosses has been perpetuated in the British nationalized industries and public corporations. How much truth there is in this belief is hard to ascertain. The work done by Scott and his colleagues in their study of the coal industry (20) neither supports nor denies the assertion. Their findings seem to indicate that low morale in the mines is associated mainly with dissatisfaction about pay, but that when pay is considered reasonable by the workers, then 'effective productive organization and managerial behaviour would appear to be conditions for the achievement of really high morale'. Human relations rank after pay, which is what a commonsense approach would lead one to expect. Sociology is, after all, at its best a shade above common sense, at its worst, many levels below. Scott and his team admit that workers' attitudes to management do not constitute 'a simple emotional response to frustration'. It should be borne in mind that the study concerned an industry with a high proportion of Blauner's category of craft workers and his findings were replicated in that most of the craft workers in coal were 'work-oriented'.

The studies made by J. H. Goldthorpe and his colleagues into the attitudes and behaviour of affluent manual workers stress the social nature of the orientation that workers bring to their work as well as the instrumentality of work, i.e. as a means of gaining an income to satisfy wants, and in so far as these findings and investigations have any bearing at all on the psychotherapeutic approach, they tend to offer negative evidence. Even Friedmann, who has attacked 'atomized' jobs and calls for 'job enrichment' (his term is 'job enlargement'), has not changed his views on the ineffectiveness of the human relationists' endeavours (21).

The actual practice of counselling in business is not widespread, and takes place mainly in the USA. In 1929, V. V. Anderson, a psychiatrist, was employed by the New York department store of R. H. Macy and Company for the purpose of assisting in the selection and evaluation of personnel, the ultimate objective being to reduce costs and increase sales. Anderson found that some 20 per cent of the store personnel were 'problem individuals' and many of these suffered from 'personality disturbances'. Although the matter was considered from the viewpoint of efficiency and sales, Anderson was encouraged to use therapy where it would increase the effectiveness of an employee and reduce friction (22).

At approximately the same time, the Western Electric Company embarked on a series of interviews with employees to determine those aspects of the worker's (work) environment that were regarded favourably or unfavourably. The investigators, under

W. J. Dickson, discovered that the 'talking-out' aspect of these interviews not only had a beneficial effect on the individual but that the complaints made originally by an individual tended either to disappear or to be restated. Dickson and his collaborators discovered one of the basic beliefs of the counselling mystiques: the complaint as originally stated was not the *real* source of the individual's troubles. After a trial period, the company decided to inaugurate an on-going counselling programme for their ordinary workers. The company believes that the programme improves the mental health and morale of employees to their own individual benefit quite apart from any benefit it brings to the firm.

There are very few such general counselling programmes in existence even in the United States; what has developed is a modification of counselling applied to the training and selection of supervisory and executive personnel. 'Man evaluation' or the selection of candidates for responsible positions, relies to a great extent on evaluative procedures that make use of the counselling approach, and this aspect has grown in recent years as 'man evaluation' has broadened into not only selection but also the development of executives' capacities. In this context, counselling is seen as being concerned with clarifying the executives' ideas about themselves, defining their personal objectives, and diminishing tensions between individuals, and also with making such organizational changes as will reduce confusion and enable areas of responsibility to be devised that are commensurate with the capacities of individuals.

A further development of counselling in the industrial setting has been the growth in the belief that the experience of undergoing counselling is beneficial to top executives. This is an extension of the widely held view among certain groups in the USA that psychotherapy, particularly psychoanalysis, is something that we can all scarcely do without in the stresses and confusions of contemporary living. Men at the top, with a heavy load of responsibilities, benefit from the opportunity to talk freely, personally and privately with a counsellor. If the notion is true that executive ability is a reflection of an integrated personality, then top executives will derive benefit both for themselves and the company from undergoing what is held to be a 'maturing experience'. The fact that top executives may also be lonely on their summits and welcome the chance to unburden themselves is another point in favour of counselling. The advocates of such practices argue that the new professional business executives with broader objectives than those formerly current, see no need to justify them beyond their practical utility to the firm and any general social utility that does not conflict with the interests of the business. On the desirability of extending such counselling facilities to the mass of the work force, they are not so certain. Apart from the difficulties involved, because of the large numbers and the shortage of trained personnel to do the counselling, there is the opposition of organized labour that, so far at least, does not appear convinced either of the value of counselling or of its neutrality. In addition, top executives admit that though counselling could probably increase the efficiency of workers and diminish the occurrence of industrial strife, there is little empirical evidence that it does either of these things. Even the Western Electric Company's continuing programme is, apparently, undertaken more for its social value than for any ascertainable benefits to the company itself. Counselling for its social value can thus be seen as one of the fringe benefits of working for a company rich enough to afford such luxuries. To some labour leaders, however, the counselling enterprise seems more like the paternalism that is associated with some Japanese industrial concerns, or that advocated by some European Catholic industrialists who have attempted to follow the path indicated by Pope Leo XIII in his encyclical *Rerum Novarum* of 1898.

Counselling in industry has received some support from those managers who subscribe to the 'conspiracy' theory of industrial unrest. Strikes and disputes are basically the work of individual trouble-makers; these are persons who are frustrated, bitter, antagonistic and confused, they are uncooperative neurotics (they might also be 'Reds' but then Communists according to this view are also neurotics). These people fail to find the satisfactions they need and so live in a state of chronic tension and unhappiness with themselves. They find faults in their environments which relieve them from their own tendency to self-condemnation, in other words, they project onto their work situations and their employers the faults and stresses within themselves; to use a medical analogy, they are foci of infection that spread out into the industrial body.

(If this hypothesis were to be true, then why do so many of their co-workers follow their leads?). To those who believe in this explanation, counselling offers the chance of creating a 'healthier psychological climate' at work and the possibility of changing the negative attitudes of such persons and so reduce their tensions and neurotic difficulties and ultimately bring about a situation free from industrial strife. Those who feel that this is a valuable and constructive attitude towards industrial relations rely heavily on Carl Rogers' belief that the self-criticism of a counselee diminishes as counselling progresses and his criticism of others and his hostility towards others likewise declines. The neurotic whose attitudes towards himself are hypercritical and negative can disturb a whole organization because of a 'feed-back' that is generated by fellow workers who are exposed to this hostility and react defensively and aggressively.

The instruction of supervisory and executive staff in counselling techniques is also beneficial in reducing tensions and disturbances that are likely to develop among personnel and particularly between subordinates and superiors, is another claim made by those oriented towards the human relations school of thought. Not that firms train their executives and managerial staffs in counselling, but many large, and some medium-sized, concerns do teach their top personnel to use certain techniques in interviewing, reprimanding, etc. that owe much to non-directive client-centred counselling. Few firms today encourage their managerial staff to be overbearing and authoritarian towards subordinates, though the prevalence of jokes about the boss being in his desk-top thumping mood might indicate that the old-style manager is not yet an anachronism.

The fears that counselling in industry is either something to the benefit of the firm (and this does not mean that it is to the detriment of the worker), or a confidence trick, or a move in the class war are widely held, and in an attempt to allay them, Leroy N. Vernon (23) says:

'Counselling . . . is based on the belief that all human beings are capable of understanding the interests of others, even when those interests are opposed; and of tempering the pursuit of their more selfish objectives with an appreciation of mutual interdependence. A good counselling programme with employees is quite free from any hidden objectives. It does not propagandize, but has as its first purpose to listen and understand, and as its second objective to build in every person the belief that he can be understood.'

Counselling in industry, then, has no ulterior motives. This might be true but the onus is on the businessmen who use it to prove their good faith. Our opinion of their good faith depends a great deal on our belief in the professionalization of managers and all that this entails in role-playing. It has already been indicated that there are doubts about the alleged changes in the structure of management, and although new managerial ideologies have received much publicity and academic comment, there have been doubts expressed about the acceptance of such ideologies and even the suggestion that if they are not 'for the birds' then they are, at least, mere window-dressing. The 'Lords of Creation' have not disappeared from the industrial scene and the megalomaniac entrepreneur is still with us. Ruthlessness towards colleagues and exploitation of the customer, and so of the general public, are not things of the past. The social consciences of some concerns may be clear, but of many of them this is a supposition that could only be maintained if the assumption were to be made that their consciences are limited and underdeveloped. The rational nature of free enterprise militates against being too worried over matters of conscience and the public good; too often the interests of X are not those of Y. The irrationality of business (as apparent in nationalized and public industries as much as in free enterprise) likewise runs counter to considerations of social value and the common good. At the best, the situation might be as described in the organizational manual of the Koehring Company of Milwaukee, a firm manufacturing earth moving equipment:

'The primary purpose of this company is to serve the needs of three groups of people: customers, employees and stockholders. From the viewpoint of those who need shovels, cranes, pavers, etc. the primary reason for the existence of this company is to produce these products. From the viewpoint of those who work here, the primary purpose is to create jobs where people can work, produce useful goods, and receive security and the means of livelihood as well as the satisfactions of being part of a fine company. From the viewpoint of the stockholders, the primary purpose of the company is to pay a good return on their investment, and to lay the foundation for a better return in the future. Products, people and profits are the problems of business, and the success of business management can be measured in terms of how well they serve in these three areas.'

What, one might ask, is the primary purpose of the company from the viewpoint of management, assuming that its interests are not synonymous with those of the stockholders? The usual answer is that it is to integrate these diverse objectives that are not really incompatible with each other. The answer might lie in developing the kind of generalized prosperity and affluence that exists today in West Germany and that makes questions about motives virtually irrelevant, though even in that type of circumstance, the social value of much industrial activity is still open to question.

There does not seem to be any doubt that Halmos's contention that 'the personal service ideology of the counsellors is being transmitted to members of the impersonal service professions . . . and that industrial personnel trained in the experimental sciences or in the technologies are also being indoctrinated in this manner' (24) is true, but to what extent does this affect the business manager? Does he pay lip service to such ideals, use them when they suit ulterior motives? To what extent can we apply the term *professional* to such managerial personnel? I submit that in a context such as that of industry, the term 'professional', where it is not downright misleading, is inappropriate. If it is a mere claim for social status, then it is a conceit; if it means only the possession of expertise, actual or fancied, then it is a misnomer; if it implies an ideal, present in the minds of the claimants, to an obligation that transcends their loyalties to employers and shareholders, that is an obligation to individuals as such and to the public at large, then this has to be shown to exist. Direct experience of industry and business coupled with the tutoring of business studies undergraduate students in their sandwich placements in industry might lead one to conclude that quite a good portion of the literature on the education and training of businessmen, technologists, managers, etc. is composed of pious wishes and sheer ignorance. It requires a little more personal experience than that provided by the examination of curricula in schools of business management and business studies to gain some idea of what goes on in the daily conduct of business and commerce. When reading some of the material that is the result of considerable effort on the part of industrial sociologists and psychologists, it is hard for one to conclude that the personal experience of such academics is more often than not almost nil. A feeling is engendered that is similar to that which comes of reading much of the literature of political science about the actual conduct of political life; the suspicion that the authors have little practical experience of what they are writing about.

To speak on managerial roles, of the role of the professional manager and similar terms does not clarify the situation, it obscures it. The concept of the role is a useful one in certain branches of sociological theory, where it is possible to speak of roles in the same way as one speaks of ideal types, that is, appreciating that they are intellectual abstractions, but in the study of such a position as that of managerial personnel in industry, the use of the concept is marginal. The expectations and the norms are so unclear and so determined by the specific circumstances that it is not possible to make meaningful statements about them. The ideals that lie behind the expectations and norms are equally as elusive. The role concept can, within narrow limits, be applied to certain positions and result in meaningful analysis, but such positions are usually traditional, professional or associated with the machinery of the state or law. It is possible to say something about the role of the judge, policeman, nurse or clergyman in a manner that it is not possible to do when talking of the businessman, journalist, private trader, shopkeeper, etc. It is even possible to say meaningful things about the roles of popular entertainers, TV personalities and tennis stars, but nothing approaching this kind of statement can be made about the roles of managerial personalities in the world of business, industry and commerce. Dahrendorf has pointed out the limitations of role theory as an explanation of human action, and as Popitz observes, the silence with which German sociologists have greeted his views indicates their acceptance of his incontestable propositions (25); whether or not the fact that British sociologists have likewise remained silent indicates their acceptance, I cannot say.

The advent of counselling in industry clearly has some affiliations with the tendency that Riesman has designated by the term 'other-directedness' but although his analysis of contemporary social attitudes may be relevant for the United States it is not certain that it has any relevance in Britain. Both societies, it is assumed, are moving away from attitudes founded on the Protestant Ethic towards attitudes based on a creed of leisure, but this does not mean that a necessary concomitant of that creed is 'other-directedness'. 'Other-directedness' is a type of conformity that seems peculiarly American, though there are some signs of it here in the impulses that make middle-class intellectuals as well as working-class intellectuals leap onto whatever intellectual bandwagon is fashionable, that is, indicated as such to them in weeklies such as the *New Statesman*, journals such as *Encounter* or those infallible sources of the latest mode, the 'quality Sunday supplements' of the *Observer* and *Sunday Times*. That kind of intellectual conformity that reaches its lowest in BBC2's 'Late Night Line-up' and the reluctance to admit that one does not take the *Guardian;* but outside these spheres, there seems little evidence that the kind of conformity that Riesman describes as 'other directedness' has taken root here or is likely to.

Over twenty years ago Riesman and his co-authors published *The Lonely Crowd*, which, in spite of its condemnation by certain sociologists as being 'soft sociology' (26) quickly became the source of ideas that have been incorporated into our general intellectual luggage; Riesman has suffered a rare honour: his ideas have been preserved though their authorship has been forgotten. Riesman postulated three types of social character: tradition-directed, inner-directed, and other-directed. A given society seems to give rise to the kind of character that its structure needs, which is almost the same as saying that the character-type is 'functional'.

Traditional societies produce a type of individual who conforms to what is seemingly an eternal set of traditions; this is not surprising where the patterns of social structure and relationships have remained relatively unaltered for generations. But in societies undergoing rapid change, a new kind of character is produced, a character type flexible enough to adapt to changing conditions and able to find and create new patterns of behaviour, while at the same time, he possesses an interior firmness that enables him to find a way through bewildering change without breaking-down from the pressures upon him. These character types are similar in nature to other sociological abstractions, and represent an 'ideal' rather than an actuality. In transitional societies such as the United States in the nineteenth century, Britain in the time of the Industrial Revolution and its aftermath, perhaps in parts of Europe during the 'Enlightenment' such a type was produced: the inner-directed man, who learnt a mode of conformity that was created by childhood socialization in which a set of values and moral standards deriving from the parents and family were internalized and used in later life. This secure set of internalized values gave a firm moral orientation in a society that set a high premium on individualism and based its standards on an ethic of work, endeavour, and the concept of vocation. If he needed any form of response from his fellow-men, the inner-directed man needed their respect.

With changed social conditions, the twentieth century has seen the emergence of a new mode of conformity, that of other-directedness, and it is strongest among the educated urban middle-classes occupied in bureaucratic or large-scale organizations. Their societal environment demands a highly flexible, plastic, continually socializing kind of individual who is sensitive to the demands of peers and the expectations of the immediate situation and who responds with radar-like alacrity to the cues he detects in the behaviour of others (Gibson and Davies' notion of 'social maturity' has some affinity with this character type). His socialization is such that he is early made dependent on the peer group, and develops a need to be well liked and accepted. He is socialized to make adjustments in his own behaviour that will ensure his acceptance by his peers. His direction comes less from parental values internalized in childhood than from a prompt response to his peers and to the wider world to which he is oriented through the medium of his peers. Unlike the inner-directed man, who owes his moral strength and social courage to the possession within himself of personalized ethical standards, the other-directed man is never certain of his own values and opinions because they are mainly reflections of those held by his peers. He needs a great deal of response from his peers; he needs them to like him and he is unhappy if he fails to achieve their liking.

It must be emphasized that to Riesman these three types are *modes of conformity* and they do not bear value judgments about one being 'better' or 'worse' than another, but conflict and difficulties arise when two character types exist in the same society as they do today. In Western societies, the inner-directed man still exists, as is to be expected if our society is 'transitional' but he is tending to be more and more of a deviant. Thus the ruthless entrepreneur so characteristic of the last century is assumed to be odd-man-out today when we make the assumption that all businessmen, or most of them, want to be loved by employees, colleagues and customers equally. Another source of conflict exists when the myths of one age are retained into a time when they are no longer appropriate: the 'American Dream', that with effort and talent the poorest can rise to be a captain of industry, is a myth of a past age and its survival causes unhappiness and disappointment because it creates expectations that cannot be fulfilled; which is what Merton says in his discussion of anomie.

Riesman's other-directed man has become, in the opinion of many, the rather despicable symbol of contemporary Western society (though this was not Riesman's intention). He is assumed to be the typical product of the market economy with its competitiveness and acquisitiveness and he has appeared in various forms in the works of others, some of whom are indebted to Riesman while others are not. C. Wright Mills (27) describes what is essentially the same type of individual in his model of the 'competitive personality', and the same or similar person appears in the works of Erich Fromm as the 'marketeer' (28). The central theme in the work of both authors is the abuse and manipulation of personality for the sake of status and upward mobility, the loss of integrity by selling oneself, turning oneself into a marketable commodity, the abuse of friendship, so that the object of an intimate relationship is how to win friends in order to influence people; personalities, one's own as well as those of others, are all treated instrumentally as things in the pursuit of wealth and status, and more recently perhaps, in pursuit of the 'good' leisure life. The classic formulation of the type of person and his world is to be found in Whyte's *Organization Man*, the title of which has become a cliché in our society. Whyte extended the idea from the market situation into the larger world of corporate enterprise, into the bureaucratic environment of the large-scale industrial organizations (29). He describes the pliable character, almost amorphous, of the middle-management grade executive and the manner in which his wife and family have to conform to the requirements of suburban life based on constant translocation, ever onwards and upwards, from one grade to the next higher, and from one suburb to the next even more desirable one. Most of the books of Vance Packard have contributed to this depressing picture that views the public and private lives of men in Big Business as one great confidence trick that all seek to play but whose rewards are confined to the Happy Few.

This pessimistic picture is, no doubt, in many of its details exaggerated, but is it not more likely to be 'true' than the rosy-tinted vision that assumes without evidence that corporate public and private industry has major interests that do not conflict with the interests of other groups and the society as a whole? Both views are based on contradictory evidence, though the evidence for optimism is so scanty that it can scarcely be considered as such. If the view is put forward that the pessimists select their material, then the same applies to the other camp: it is usually forgotten, if it is even appreciated in the first place, that access to factories and industrial plant by sociologists and psychologists is only with the consent of the management; it is, therefore, reasonable to assume that the ideologies of management might lead to bias in the investigations, and where the situations do not support the managerial ideology, access might not be permitted (30).

The faith in the virtues of 'professionalization' also require examination. The professional manager plays a 'role of concern', he is imbued with the 'faith of the counsellors'. Let us assume that such a manager is a 'professional' in a meaningful sense of the term, does it necessarily follow that he acts accordingly? In recent years it has become fashionable to abuse doctors and lawyers for their cupidity and departure from 'old standards'. A cynical view of the pretensions of lawyers is modish; the medical associations are accused of conduct unbecoming the most militant of working-class trade unions; professional associations have been described as nothing more than middle-class trade unions. Surgeons, it is alleged, abort happily if the patient can pay; they abuse the NHS in favour of private patients who are insured by one of the voluntary insurance organizations. If these old professions with clearly defined and historical traditions are guilty of such behaviour, why should we assume that the business executive is free from evil motives, free from duplicity, cynicism and personal greed? Why should we except the social worker himself? It is no use saying that to become 'a social worker has spelt in most countries a life-long frugality and shabby respectability' (31) for this implies that wealth and material possessions are the only things that make an individual insincere. Mercenary gain may appeal to some doctors, prestige and status to some lawyers, but the choice is always an individual one. Whatever may lead to the loss of integrity among social workers it has not, until now, been wealth; it might have been and may still be prestige and status, for the evaluation of these is a much more individual and personal thing than wealth; there may be other rewards whose values are known only to specific individuals; but the point I am trying to make is that integrity is not the prerogative of a few professions and not of others, and there is no evidence to show that the processes described as 'professionalization' produce integrity and the other qualities that they are assumed to do. I am not making sweeping generalizations about 'whether *all* personal service professionals are *completely* sincere with their clients' (32) because this is not the point at issue; I am merely questioning whether or not there is any substantive evidence that can be adduced to support the notion that (a) 'professionalization' produces a certain kind of attitude, and (b) whether the behaviour of one profession is of a higher moral order than that of others. Doctors obtain money, prestige, status and, one must assume, a pleasure from doing their work well, together with a number of other satisfactions that are individually valued. Not all of them derive any satisfaction from doing the job well, some are only in it for the money, others for the prestige, others mainly because they can play god; some are, no doubt, sadists, some are saints. A similar situation applies to all professions, including that of social work and if the wealth is not there, then there is something else that gives as much or similar satisfaction to many practitioners (33).

But, and it is an important 'but' even by the vague criteria of the professionalization of such experts as accountants and engineers, the business and industrial manager is not a professional; his training, where it exists possesses none of the characteristics that distinguish a profession from an occupation, thus the claim to a professional role fails to be substantiated, and in this case, we are entitled to ask if the ascription to such men of the faith of the counsellors is anything more than a superficial adherence on their part to a fashionable creed. Ultimately, the answer does not depend on an assessment of the available evidence because there is too little to bear examination, but on a view of objectivity. Perceived objectives are multiple, who knows which view is the 'real' one? Perhaps we all fall into one of two basic categories: those whose perception comes through lenses tinted, not perhaps with rose but with optimism, and those whose vision comes through the wrong end of a telescope. If one is of the latter category, then counselling in industry and the psychotherapeutic ideology applied in industry, are part of the manipulative and persuasive techniques by which the vast irrationality of economic enterprise is facilitated, those imbecile processes that periodically re-invent the aeroplane at gigantic cost, that re-invent the motor-car annually, and that turn the Mediterranean into an inland sewer.

Notes and References

1 McCann, Roger, Parry, José and Secombe, Joan, *Company Health Care for Managers*, unpublished project report sponsored by the British Institute of Management, London, 1971, Table IIIb, p. 45. The companies offering psychiatric services were mostly those connected with an American 'parent'.

2 Freidmann, Georges, *Industrial Society—The Emergence of the Human Problems of Automation*, edited by Harold L. Sheppard, The Free Press, 1955; Collier-Macmillan paperback edition, 1964, p. 351.

3 Blau Peter M. and Scott Richard W. *Formal Organizations—A Comparative Approach* Routledge and Kegan Paul, London, 1963, p. 88.

4 Silverman, David, *The Theory of Organizations*, Heinemann, London, 1970, pp. 26–7. The author attributes an influence to Pareto that the latter is most unlikely to have exerted, and the quotation therefore gives a misleading impression.

The seminal situations that brought the human relations approach into prominence were the investigations into the problems of industrial relations carried out between 1927 and 1939 at the Hawthorne Works of the Western Electric Company in West Chicago and Cicero, Illinois; and the special circumstances existing at the Bata works at Zlin in Czechoslovakia from about 1932 to 1939.

At the Hawthorne Works, the experiments carried out indicated the relative unimportance of physical factors in morale, productivity and stability; they demonstrated the importance of psychological factors, particularly taking an interest in the workers and having supervisors who were good listeners, rather in the manner of counsellors. The Bata situation showed the significance of a charismatic and paternal 'chief' in maintaining morale and workers' identification with the firm and the job.

5 Halmos, Paul, *The Personal Service Society*, Constable, London, 1970, p. 128. Even the concept of 'empathy' has been adopted by the management consultants. See Press, Charles and Arian, Alan, *Empathy and Ideology: Aspects of Administrative Innovation*, Rand McNally and Co., Chicago, 1966, especially Chapter 5: 'Empathy' by Henry Clay Smith of the Department of Psychology, Michigan State University (Rand McNally, London, 1968).

6 Bell, Daniel, *The End of Ideology*, The Free Press, New York, 1960 (Collier-Macmillan, London, 1960). For a counter argument that destroys the basis of the end of ideology thesis see Hodges, Donald Clark, 'The End of the "End of Ideology"', *American Journal of Economics and Sociology*, Vol. 26, No. 2, April 1967, pp. 135–46. Hodges puts forward two propositions: (1) that the 'end of ideology' thesis is itself ideological, and (2) ideologies are 'waxing stronger than ever' today. The first is incontestable, and the second is supported by much empirical evidence.

7 Dahrendorf, Ralf, *Class and Class Conflict in Industrial Society*, Routledge and Kegan Paul, London, 1957, and *Conflict after Class* (a lecture delivered at the University of Essex) Longman, London, 1967; Birnbaum, Norman, *The Crisis of Industrial Society*, Oxford University Press, New York, 1969, pp. 12–14.

8 In the UK such giants as ICI and Unilever are management-controlled, while Ferranti-ICL, Pilkington's, Rank, and Woolworth are owner-controlled. Owner-management still seems to abound in joint-stock companies and the truth in an American business consultant's observation (reported somewhere by Vance Packard) that if 'you want to manage a company, the best way to achieve this is to own it' still seems to possess an element of truth. Few people would deny that West Germany is one of the most advanced industrial countries in the world, and Zapf's researches into the German industrial élite does not support the optimists' views about the backgrounds etc. of managers; see Zapf, W., *Wandlungen der deutschen Elite*, 1919–1961, Piper Verlag, München, 1965.

9 Berle, Adolf A., Jr. and Means, Gardiner C., *The Modern Corporation and Private Property*, Macmillan, New York, 1932 (Harcourt, Brace, London, 1969).

10 Michels, Robert, *Political Parties*, trans. by Eden and Cedar Paul, Dover, New York, 1959 (a republication of the first English translation of 1915).

11 He affirms this in his *Conflict after Class* that appeared before the events of 1968.

12 One of the largest pharmaceutical companies in Britain has recently adopted a training scheme for its executive personnel that owes much to the counselling approach. The firm even uses the term 'counselling' to describe the regular 'friendly' interviews that subordinates have with their superiors, though no serious attempt is made to gain 'insight' into the interviewees; the firm's top men seem to think that 'counselling' means only that the interviewer is friendly and does not make himself unpleasant and attempts to put the interviewee at ease.

13 Bendix, Reinhard, *Work and Authority in Industry*, Wiley, New York, 1956. '. . . . the propagation of the idea that the interests of the rulers and of the ruled are identical helps to confer legitimacy upon the regime', Fox, Alan, *A Sociology of Work in Industry*, Collier-Macmillan, London, 1971, p. 126.

14 Dubin, Robert and Orzack, Louis E., 'Industrial Workers' Worlds: A Study of the "Central Life Interests" of Industrial Workers', *Social Problems*, Vol. 3, No. 3, January 1956, reprinted in Smigel, Erwin O. (ed.), *Work and Leisure*, College and University Press, New Haven, 1963. Also Orzack, Louis H., 'Work as a Central Life Interest of Professionals', *Social Problems*, Vol. 7, No. 2, Fall 1959, reprinted in Smigel *op. cit.*

15 Blauner, Robert, *Alienation and Freedom: The Factory Worker and His Industry*, University of Chicago Press, Chicago, 1964 (University of Chicago Press, London, 1964).

16 *Mitbestimmung* (for which there exists no adequate English translation) is not just 'joint consultation' on the British lines. The principal difference is that German co-determination in industry gives the worker legally established direct control over the firm's activities through representation on the supervisory and management boards. See Tilford, R. B. and Preece, R. J. C., *Federal Germany—Political and Social Order*, Wolff, London, 1969, pp. 84–95; for the supervisory board (*Aufsichtsrat*) see Anderson, Beatrix and North, Maurice, *Beyond the Dictionary in German*, Cassell London, 1968 (Funk and Wagnall, New York, 1969), p. 15 under *Aktie*.

17 Popitz, Heinrich, Bahrdt, H. P., Jueres, E. A. and Kesting, A., *Das Gesellschaftsbild des Arbeiters*, Mohr (Paul Siebeck), Tübingen, 1957.

18 Friedmann, *op. cit.*, p. 382.

19 Silverman, *op. cit.*, p. 76.

20 Scott, W. H., Mumford, Enid, McGivering, I. C. and Kirkby, J. M., *Coal and Conflict: A Study of Industrial Relations at Collieries*, Liverpool University Press, Liverpool, 1963; the investigations were carried out in 1957 and 1958.
21 Goldthorpe, J. H., Lockwood, David, Bechhofer, Frank and Platt, J., *The Affluent Worker: Industrial Attitudes and Behaviour*, Cambridge University Press, Cambridge, 1968.
22 Anderson, V. V., *Psychiatry in Industry*, Harper, New York, 1929.
23 Staff Director, The Vernon Psychological Laboratory, Chicago.
24 Halmos, *op. cit.*, p. 136.
25 Popitz, Heinrich, *Der Begriff der sozialen Rolle als Element der soziologischen Theorie*, Mohr (Paul Siebeck), Tübingen, 1967, p. 41.
26 Riesman, David, Glazer, Nathan and Denny, Reul, *The Lonely Crowd*, Yale University Press, New Haven, 1950 (Yale University Press, London, 1950); and Riesman, David, *Faces in the Crowd*, Yale University Press, New Haven (and London), 1952. 'Soft sociology' does not use inappropriately the paraphernalia of the exact sciences or amass statistical material irrespective of its relevance; it is looked on with contempt by the fashionable 'hard sociologists' who attempt to apply the methods (though not the methodology) of the exact sciences to their material. 'Hard sociologists' rely heavily on statistical procedures, and today they are lost without a computer; they eschew theory; I cannot offhand recall the titles of any works attributable to them that are of any significance.
27 Mills, C. Wright, 'The Competitive Personality', *Partisan Review*, 13 (1946), p. 433.
28 Fromm, Erich, *Man for Himself*, Rinehart, New York, 1941 (Routledge, London, 1949).
29 Whyte, William H., *The Organization Man*, Simon and Schuster, New York, 1956 (Penguin, Harmondsworth).
30 Sheppard, Harold, 'The Treatment of Unionism in "Managerial Sociology"', *American Sociological Review*, 14 April 1949, pp. 310–33.
31 Halmos, *op. cit.*, p. 161.
32 *Ibid.*, p. 159.
33 'The sociology of occupations gives one a magnificent panorama of the systematic delusions which people will adhere to in defence of their roles in society. Thus ministers will stoutly maintain, in the face of all evidence, that what they preach on Sunday has a real influence on the business decisions made by their parishioners on Monday. And insurance salesmen will tell one with probably genuine sincerity that their business is akin to the ministry in its humanitarian outlook. Morticians believe sincerely that respect for the dead can only be expressed by an elaborate (and, incidentally, costly) funeral. Advertising men believe that motivational research is nothing but the building of a bridge between manufacturer and consumer—the most democratic of enterprises. Psychoanalysts believe that charging a high fee is conducive to therapeutic results. All kinds of physicians believe that

defending their right to charge what the market will bear is equivalent to defending the achievements of medicine itself. . . . And government officials believe simultaneously that the budget must be curtailed and that their staff must be expanded. . . . Occupational ideologies vary both in terms of intellectual comprehensiveness and in the degree of distortion they inflict on social reality. What they have in common is their basic function of justifying the occupational enterprise, giving the members of an occupation a particular picture of themselves and of the world in which they live': Berger, Peter L., *The Precarious Vision*, Doubleday, Garden City, New York, 1961, pp. 62–3.

Chapter 7

The Nature of Technological Society

What do we mean when we speak of 'industrialized' or 'industrial' society? What do the qualifying adjectives indicate? According to Andreski: 'We can simply define it as a society which subsists on the products of big and complicated machines'; a society whose 'sole essential feature' is 'dependence on machines' (1). Apart from its being based on machines, what else is distinctive and specific about such a society? Is industrialization the key to the problem, that is, are all the other particular features dependent on and determined by industrialization? The answer to the second seems to be an unqualified affirmative and therefore also an answer to the first. This does not imply that all commentators on industrialized society are in full agreement; although there do not seem to be significant differences about its history and its 'shape', there is much disagreement about its consequences for man. In spite of these differences, certain features, albeit under different names, are common to the many accounts supplied by sociologists, social psychologists, historians and all those others who concern themselves with the topic. I intend in this chapter to examine some of the sociological interpretations of contemporary industrialized Western societies and indicate that, in spite of their diverse sources and intellectual orientations, they lead to some consensus on the nature of the phenomenon.

That industrialization is the key factor has sometimes been obscured by the individual interests of writers, especially sociologists who have often, and justifiably, concentrated on other aspects of their societies. In considering any sociological account it is necessary to set it within its historical context, for what has interested one generation has not always interested subsequent ones. Sociology is, more than of any other factor, a product of the French Revolution and the social upheavals associated with it, but it is also a by-product of the industrial revolution—which brought

about concomitant social disturbances that coincided chrono-
logically, more or less, with the French Revolution; in short, the
Founding Fathers such as Saint-Simon and Comte, and the second
generation luminaries like Durkheim were as concerned with the
problems of order and social stability as with the fact of industrialization. Of the early sociological writers only Herbert
Spencer was more concerned with industrialization as such than
with order. Because of the predominance of the interest in order,
those aspects of modern society exemplifying this problem have
tended to conceal the overriding importance of industrialization
proper and especially the development of techniques and the
emergence of a peculiarly technical mode that has come to distinguish our society from preceding forms. A list of the facets of
contemporary societies that have been the main concern of
sociologists would include, among others, the decline of small
solidary groups and of community itself; the size and complexity
of modern societies; the growth of bureaucratization and large
organizations; urbanization; the relative lack of personal social
relationships and the growth of impersonal ones; anomie; alienation; the diminution in the influence of religion and moral teaching; the secularization of life; the growth of deviancy and of sub-
and contra-cultures. This is not to say that industrialization has
been omitted but the fact that it is central to all these other aspects
has been de-emphasized. The conditions that are described by the
list when taken together are subsumable under the blanket term
'mass society', an opprobrious name that reflects the general
disgust of intellectuals with the social environment of the twentieth century, and that contains, as Daniel Bell notes, two assumptions: firstly, that the quality of life in our kind of society is
inferior to some previous type of society taken as a standard, and
secondly, 'a presumed scientific statement concerning the disorganization of society, created by industrialization and the
demands of the masses for equality' (2). The first implies that it is
a society pleasing only to the *Lumpenproletariat* and the *Lumpen-
bourgeoisie;* the second, that it is falling apart. Mass society has
failed to provide the norms and values in which men can discover
meaning in their social and individual existences, and satisfactions
in their relations with others. The inhabitants of mass society, for
the most part, are assumed to be as Raymond Chandler described

them: 'People who look like nothing in particular and know it'.

This view of society sees individuals as lonely and isolated, living confused, unhappy lives dominated by competition, acquisition and the consumption of material goods. Their work is dehumanizing (though what exactly this means is never quite clear), their leisure is commercially organized by the entertainment industry all the way from spectator sports to sailing small boats and 'do-it-yourself' hobbies. Their intellectual nourishment is provided by the mass media and is based on the lowest common denominators in every field; their interests are founded on conspicuous consumption, sex, and nuclear family life.

One of the main omissions by the critics of mass society is their failure to take into account the possibility that this new type of society might have thrown up alternatives to the traditional values and institutions that it has destroyed or eroded. Not that this means that the new alternatives are better or worse than those they have displaced, only that they are different. The psychotherapeutic ideology is one of these alternatives: an alternative to religion and philanthropy. Georg Simmel criticised the style of life forced on their inhabitants by the great urban centres of today and said that existence among such large conglomerations of people was conducive to callousness to one's fellows and this in turn concealed a latent hostility towards others that was a product of urbanism; thus he endorsed the mass society condemnatory approach. But at the same time, he indicated that such cities made people free by providing them with privacy and anonymity as well as the intellectual stimulation that was never attainable in the smaller, tightly-knit communities of the pre-industrial age (3). No valid conclusions can be drawn from this kind of argument, though it is useful as a corrective to distortion, for the implication that there was little intellectual stimulation before the great cities came into being would lead one to some odd conclusions; nearly all the great of the pre-industrial age would have to be written off or classified as exceptions that proved the rule. Simmel is among the defenders (rather lukewarm, though) of the mass society, or at least is one of those who do not regard it with unrelieved gloom. The optimistic version of mass society describes it as a great complex or web of social groups, large and small, from which the individual gains his identity. These groups, professional, academic, political, social, sporting, and so forth are the bonds by which the individual is linked to the larger unit that is society. Membership of these groups overlaps so that the groupings mesh to form a complicated network, and it is in membership of these groups that individuals find meaning as well as satisfactory personal relationships so that great numbers of them, probably the majority, are not lonely and isolated as the critics maintain, and they are not without values and ideals either.

The opponents of mass society often pose an idealized picture of a past about which we know very little; an ideal based on alleged freedoms, the virtues of community, and the sustaining force of traditional religious and moral values; not all of them do this, and there are critics of the mass society who offer incisive assaults on the complacency of its protagonists without backward looks at an imaginary past; it is some in this category that we shall be considering later.

The harshness, intolerance, narrowness and rigidity of many past societies, especially the small tight communities of the medieval towns and eighteenth century rural areas, provide an image of conformity and cruelty that is a gift to those extolling the virtues of today. But it is easy to forget that all societies have their own versions of conformism and cruelty and if the critics of contemporary society concentrate their attacks on the negative side of modern life, it is only fair to observe that the apologists for today direct their fire on the equally negative aspects of the past; but we know very little about the evil and the good of the past; we know a great deal about those of today.

'If it is granted', writes Bell, 'that mass society is compartmentalized, superficial in human relations anonymous, transitory specialized, utilitarian, competitive, acquisitive, mobile, and status-hungry, the obverse side of the coin must be shown, too— the right to privacy, to free choice of friends and occupation, status on the basis of achievement rather than ascription, a plurality of norms and standards, rather than the exclusive and monopolistic social controls of a single dominant group' (4). Fine sentiments expressed with admirable rhetoric but do they reflect actual conditions? What of the right to privacy in the face of the powers of governmental and public agencies? What privacy does the 'data bank society' leave us? What sort of privacy does one get in a 'slab' or 'tower' block of council flats? The same kind of privacy that used to obtain in a medieval village? Perhaps, but then the danger of violence was probably less. Is there a free choice of occupations? For whom? The fortunate few, maybe. Some of the apologists talk as if political and intellectual freedoms had been won for all time and seem unaware of the precarious nature of these gains and of their steady erosion: there is a considerable difference between the 'freedom' to cast a meaningless parliamentary vote and the freedom to protest and demonstrate; a difference between freedom to exert pressure on an unresponsive administration and freedom to pursue grievances through channels until they peter out in the arid desert of bureaucracy. The 'permissive society', be it either curse or blessing, is a fragile thing but it is easy to believe that it will not succumb to a backlash when one has been conditioned to mistake indifference for tolerance: religious freedom is the result of few people caring much any more about religion; political, social and intellectual freedoms are still circumscribed and limited as they are not yet matters of indifference (5).

Another apologia for mass society comes from Edward Shils:

'As I see it, modern society is no lonely crowd, no horde of refugees fleeing from freedom. It is not *Gesellschaft*, soulless, egotistical, loveless, faithless, utterly impersonal and lacking any integrative forces other than interest or coercion. It is held together by an infinity of personal attachments, moral obligations in concrete contexts, professional and creative pride, individual ambition, primordial affinities and a civil sense which is low in many, high in some, and moderate in most persons. . . . Aside from these (external dangers such as war), it is in no danger of internal disintegration. Whatever danger it faces in this respect would be far less from those who are charged with faithlessness, and the inability to rise above their routine concerns, from the philistines and dwellers in housing estates and new towns, than from those who think that society needs a new faith to invigorate it and give it a new impulse' (6).

Enough has been included here to indicate that there are intellectually distinguished apologists for industrialized society apart from those technologists and industrialists and the academics who have jumped onto their band-wagon and who have a vested interest in minimizing its defects or denying them altogether. Men like Shils and Bell deny the validity of the concept 'mass society' in its pejorative sense, and they justifiably and reasonably attack the backward-looking conservative clericals who are always yelling for a new faith that on examination turns out to be a revamped version of one of the more authoritarian Christian creeds or who, on the basis of their own high ethical principles, want to be their brothers' keepers. But not all the critics of industrialized society come within these categories, and I now turn to some investigators who neither offer a new faith nor yearn for the past nor offer a political panacea, but merely attempt an objective analysis of what they perceive in the present scene. They are, I suppose, mostly pessimists in the sense in which this term has already been used in these pages, but only because they are not convinced that man is a member of a species that has a built-in destiny to happiness and contentment or even to survival; they do not subscribe to the opinion that the world of the future must *inevitably* be better than the present, but they all agree on one point, and that is that the present is very different from the past, and this is not the fault of the younger generation or because religion and morality have declined or because long hair on young men is sapping their virility and destroying the moral fibres of the nation, but *can* be attributed to industrialization and the elevation of a technical approach into a way of life. In spite of terminological differences, the common agreement among such thinkers can be easily discerned.

From the early years of the nineteenth century down to our own day, thinkers have attempted to elucidate what Raymond Aron has called *the historical mutation* (7), i.e. those changes in industry that commenced before 1800 but whose rate of change since has increased to such an extent that they have ushered into being a period in which the history of the whole human species has replaced that of individual peoples, the history of the world is one history because the nations have become one in the sense that they have a common cultural substructure of machines and techniques. Both Saint-Simon and Comte wrote of the *industrial society* whose main feature was the growth of machine-based industry. Comte described the essentials of this new society in terms of the contrast between industrialists, agriculturalists and financiers of the new age and the politico-theological military élites that had dominated traditional societies. The objective of the first group was the exploitation of natural resources, not the conduct of war. Wealth in the developing society (evolving would be better, as the notion of evolution was present in Comte's thought) consisted of rationally organized labour, but the wage-earner was not just a new kind of serf, but one whose situation gave promise of individual freedom and achievement leading to upward social mobility. This view of the nature of industrialized society was not, in some respects, very different from that of Marx. Comte and Marx were in agreement on work being central together with the application of science to techniques of production and related fields, and they agreed on the resulting massive increase in collective resources that followed. Comte, however, saw the future in terms of peaceful co-operation between the productive groups in society, Marx saw the future in terms of class conflict and strife leading ultimately to a revolution by the exploited workers; the end of the line, according to Marx, was the creation of an earthly paradise in the shape of the classless society, but not until after many vicissitudes. Comte considered class conflict to be a temporary phenomenon, an aberration that was symptomatic of a passing deficiency in social integration that would, sooner or later, be corrected and made good. Ideologically, and in spite of their general ignorance of him, Comte is the precursor of the human relations school in management, the sociological functionalists and the whole brotherhood of optimists. Comte and Marx were united in the paramount importance that they attributed to economic activity, and they based the whole of man's social life upon it; and although Aron argues that they ignored the autonomy of other activities, especially politics, as well as the factor of pure chance, he admits that in our century: 'Rationally organized labour is both the source and the measure of wealth' (8), an opinion with which Comte and Marx would have had no quarrel.

When we ignore the predictive elements in these two interpretations of the mutation, we see that the descriptions of what has happened and what is happening are very alike insofar as they both stress the uniqueness of the evolution of machine production and labour organized to serve it. In purely descriptive terms, it was only in their analysis of the nature of work in capitalist industrialized society that the two disagreed. Marx believed that work under capitalism was alienating while Comte believed that work under the new conditions was liberating and enlarging.

The theme of alienation has been a dominating and pervasive one during the past fifty years with the critics of mass society both in Marx's formulation of the concept and in its later variations. As Marx uses the term it defies empirical testing and it is expressed in a way that is almost mystical and thus lends itself to different interpretations (9). It has entered into everyday usage and has appeared in the 'pop' vocabulary of dissident groups and the young, thus adding to the vagueness and diffuseness of a concept already blurred by the use of the relatively uncommon word 'alienation' for a German term that could have been rendered by the more frequently heard 'estrangement'.

According to Marx, in capitalist society the worker's product is taken from him and becomes something apart from and hostile to him. What generates this is the exploitation of the worker by the capitalist which is experienced by the worker as deprivation, that is, he has a very weak market position, low income and little spending power. This exploitive capacity of the capitalist leads to the worker being deprived of the possibility of attaining his full physical and mental fulfilment through his work. Alienation is a collective experience engendered by the social structure of capitalist society; it is individually experienced as estrangement from the work situation and from society or in the words of Keynes as 'the flavour of final purposelessness'. The exact shape of this estrangement for the individual and how widespread the feeling is are perennial problems for those who use this term in their analysis of industrialized society, as is also the question of whether or not it occurs in non-capitalist industrialized societies. In Marx's meaning of the term it is more than just a feeling of powerlessness and meaninglessness.

As Marx ascribed alienation to capitalist society as one of its main and most distressing features, so Durkheim attributed anomie to it. Durkheim did not, however, suggest that anomie was peculiar to industrialized capitalist societies. It is, he argued, a feature of societies undergoing rapid and sweeping changes and it could occur in societies that were not capitalist and not industrialized in our meaning of the term; but the conditions of capitalist industrialized society were singularly conducive to anomie. Briefly, Durkheim posits that man has insatiable appetites (ambitions, wants, needs, etc.) that are kept in check and within reasonable limits by the norms and values contained within the ethical consensus that the society possesses, in other words, society imposes a set of rules that prescribe 'normal' behaviour. At times of rapid social and economic change, individuals' fortunes fluctuate, they become richer or poorer, successful or bankrupt, and the existing moral and ethical code is weakened and may even break down entirely, so that individuals are left to face their fortunes as best as they can, thrown back onto their own interior forces and without the firm guidance provided by societal norms. Ambitions generated by prosperity are limitless, they are deprived of the conventional restrictions that previously kept them within reasonable limits. Despair engendered bye conomic failure and made insupportable by the successes of others becomes an impulse to suicide. Sudden affluence as well as sudden poverty can bring about disruption which can drive the sufferer to what Durkheim called 'anomic suicide'. As with Marx's alienation, anomie is something that arises from the social structure; it denotes the inadequacy of traditional norms confronted with socio-economic change and the 'uselessness' of these customary ways and values can be described as leading to a state of 'normlessness', but it is a characteristic of a society and its structure, not something that is explainable in psychological terms as a personality trait of certain individuals and their inability to adjust to their social situations. It is a 'social fact' as also is alienation.

That anomie is a characteristic of a society has, like alienation, become lost in the confusion occasioned by the take-over of these terms by social psychologists and students of deviant behaviour. To talk of 'alienated individuals' and 'anomic personalities' robs both concepts of their essential sociological attributes. *Anomic* can only be applied to societies and societal situations; *alienated* can be applied to individuals but this tends to obscure the fact that it is society itself that is the alienating agent.

Recently, partly as a result of technological developments, the unfolding nature of industrialized society has been re-examined and much that was historically relevant has had to be abandoned as explanatory material for the contemporary situation. It is no longer the machine as such that is the predominant and unifying feature of modern industrialized society but *technique*. Jacques Ellul goes so far as to say that as technique is dominant not only in the West but also in the East and as technique is the same everywhere, all ideological, philosophical, and political differences are relatively trivial and superficial compared with the underlying uniformity of technique—but this is not quite the same argument as the 'End of Ideology' (10). By technique is meant, in the words of R. K. Merton, 'any complex of standardized means for attaining a pre-determined result'. Spontaneous and unreflective behaviour is changed to deliberate and rationalized behaviour by technique. The faith in and fascination of technique, i.e. its ideology, endows the man who believes in it with a personal commitment to the search for 'the one best way' of attaining any goal. A society composed of technical men is committed to just this search. This is the element of truth that lies behind the 'End of Ideology' and the belief in the common professional problems of managers the world over in spite of political differences. Under the layers of political and philosophical differences, the technical expertise is the same: brainwashing is the same in the People's Republic as in the United Kingdom. The man-made world is the same electrified, refrigerated, computerized and televised place no matter where you are (except for those 'backward areas' where the techniques have not yet been adopted, but for them it is only a matter of time). The culture of techniques is based on seeking without pause improved means to ends that are only scrutinized in the most sketchy fashion or whose implications are ignored or not even appreciated. In such a culture, means become ends: the means justify the end, and 'know-how' is the most prized and honoured attribute of men. One of the most impressive aspects of technique is that it brings into existence the reality that it postulates; this constitutes its greatest triumph: it is concrete, objective, and it works.

Technique must not be confused with machines; it includes machines but is more. Without the machine, the techniques of today would not exist, but although the machine is the origin and is central to modern techniques, the techniques have proliferated into every sphere of human action and have taken over all of men's activities, not only those of production, but even of sex, as the numerous popular manuals on coitus indicate. It is true that the machine is 'pure' technique and is the model (*Urtyp*) of all the other techniques and the latter 'recognize' this by transforming everything to which they are applied into a machine or a simulacrum of one. The men who use the most complex of modern machines, the spacecraft, have to become machine-like in their reactions; and in their control of emotions they have to simulate the unfeelingness of the machine.

The machine has created an environment that is 'un-natural' in the sense that it is mostly a man-made construction. There are areas of cities in which, unless one looks skywards, one can see nothing that is not a product of man for as far as the eye can reach. The machine and its own techniques were the first to have had an impact on man's environment and the results are to be seen in our conurbations, those vast conglomerations of 'built-up' areas with their varieties of slum, their absence of open spaces, light and air; with their man-made surfaces under foot, and their polluted air above and the noise that is everywhere as obtrusive are the only natural creations found in such places; and our fellow humans, who exert an even more dreadful pressure by their sheer numbers than all the other monstrosities together.

Technique is not something new. All societies have possessed techniques but not all societies have been possessed by them. A distinction must be made between the 'technical operation' and the 'technical phenomenon' (11). The 'technical operation' refers to any action performed according to a certain method for the purpose of achieving a specific aim. It is the method that gives the procedure its distinctive nature and the operation can be as 'primitive' as making a flint arrowhead or as modern as programming a flight to the moon. There is a continuity in technical procedures that transcends the vagaries of history, and the only thing that distinguishes the earlier forms from the later manifestations is the greater refinement that comes from the application of science to them. What is the demarcation between technical operations and spontaneous, unreflecting actions? The search for greater efficiency. Technical operations start out from simple, spontaneous forms of activity and need not be more complicated than the latter, but they achieve the desired end more efficiently and as the result of conscious choice. Technique creates means, but the technical operation is still performed by the worker who does the work, the primitive hunter and skilled craftsman are both technical operators and their attitudes to what they do are virtually identical.

But the technical phenomenon is very different. In the first place, it is a product of the scientific approach to the world around us, of what Weber called the 'disenchantment of the world'. It is characterized by consciousness and judgment, it transforms what was 'previously tentative, unconscious, and spontaneous' into 'clear, voluntary, and reasoned concepts' (12). As an example we may compare the making of a wooden wheel by a traditional craftsman and the production of an intercontinental missile. The craftsman's procedures could today be mathematically and quantitatively validated, though no such calculations occurred consciously in his activities. The contemporary missile is, however, constructed solely on the basis of calculation, traditional skills play no part whatsoever in the process. In place of the craftsmen, there are technicians who perform portions of the planned procedure. This example shows the importance of the intervention of rational judgment in technical operations.

In some way that is still unknown to us, man becomes aware of the possibility of novel and different ways of creating or doing things. The pragmatic approach distinctive of the traditional manner of doing things is replaced by new operational schemes that are the results of conscious reasoning and reflection, and new tools follow from them in response to more extensive and free-ranging experimentation. In the history of such a transformation, many new techniques are tested and the results are rationally evaluated in the context of the aim of the means: efficiency. A kind of 'natural selection' takes place and the multiple means are finally reduced to one: the most efficient. Reason determines which of the means shall 'survive'. Consciousness demonstrates to all concerned the advantages of the best means and what it can achieve. The appearance of the technical phenomenon drives out traditional techniques based on chance and pragmatism, they only survive in the fine arts, for even in the production of in-expensive ceramics and household ornaments, the technical phenomenon has assumed proprietorship. In the words of Ellul, 'This phenomenon is the quest for the one best means in every field', and it is the 'aggregate of these means that produces technical civilization', i.e. the contemporary phase of industrial civilization. In this type of civilization, the preoccupation is with the search for the most efficient method in every field, as much in 'human relations' as in rocketry. It is not the best relative means that is sought, but the best absolute means based on numerical calculation. Furthermore, it is the specialist (designer), not the worker, who decides what is the best, because he can demonstrate the superiority of one means over the others, not that he always succeeds without a struggle; the history of technique is full of examples of the best technique being at first rejected, but sooner or later, less prejudiced interested parties are convinced by the experts (13). Ellul calls technique 'the science of means' and its origins are to be found in the transformation of technical operations into technical phenomena. In our society, no human activity escapes this approach, though not all are equally affected, and in some the best means has not yet been discovered. The technical imperative shows itself in five main areas of our society (leaving aside the area of sport in which some of its more bizarre manifestations occur such as techniques of turning in swimming races and in high jumping contests): mechanical techniques, i.e. those that apply to machine production (these, of course, have the longest history); intellectual techniques represented by 'library science', indices, storage and retrieval of information systems, data banks; economic techniques ranging from the organization of labour to economic planning (in the sphere of production, they overlap with the mechanical), needless to add that in this particular field of application the 'best means' has not yet been found; organizational techniques, not only as they apply to industrial and business undertakings but also as applied to public and social administration, the law, police, armed forces, and bureaucracy itself plus a range of techniques from 'organizational analysis' to 'office management'; finally, but, by no means of least significance, are the human techniques: those in which the human being figures as the object of the technique. They include medicine, genetics, education, propaganda, advertising, brain-washing, vocational counselling, publicity, 'comparison literature', and the whole gamut of psychotherapeutic counselling and related techniques.

The techniques are very different from one another and there is little similarity between them as techniques but they all have the same goal: doing whatever they are doing most efficiently and by systematic procedures based on the application of rational and scientific (and where possible mathematical) principles. The technical imperative has become a faith, a worship of techniques, and Ellul derives this from what he calls 'our ancestral worship of the mysterious and marvellous character' of our own handiwork, but I suggest that the worship stems from a more mundane fact: in the short run, technique works.

The historical relationship between technique and Christianity is complicated and ambiguous. The argument that it was always favourable towards technique and its development because it suppressed slavery is untenable. In the first place, it assumes that slavery was not conducive to the development of technique and this has yet to be shown, and in the second place the historical evidence for the suppression of slavery by Christianity is doubtful, and anyway the serfdom that was distinctive of the period of Christian feudalism was not likely to have been more conducive to the development of technique than was slavery. Another contention, that Christianity secularized the natural world and thus made it available to man is probably true but at the time did little to assist in technical evolution. The argument goes that in pagan times, men were loath to interfere with natural phenomena because they feared the anger of the gods or spirits that either controlled natural forces or actually were such forces, and Christianity destroyed such beliefs. Under Christianity, the deities were ousted, and it became possible for man to utilize and exploit natural resources, but although nature became exploitable, man did not do so, and for a very good reason. Early Christianity rejected all earthly things and where it did not hold them sinful, it held them in contempt. Christianity discouraged economic activity and industrial innovation, and condemned luxury and turned men's minds away from such vanities. Even when, in the early medieval period, these doctrines diminished in intensity, Christianity was still opposed to technical development because of the adverse moral judgment that priests and theologians continued to pass on all human activities not directly related to the glory of God and the propagation of the Faith. The unity of Christendom encompassed every human activity and none could escape the question 'is it righteous ?' and chrematistic activities seldom escaped reprobation. But in the late middle ages, there was a return to earlier and more primitive forms of Christianity that broke down many of the barriers to the exploitation of nature that had been prevented by the unique conditions of medieval Christianity and that by then no longer existed. The reformation was conducive to the utilization of natural resources and the development of technique in a way that the Church Fathers were not. This coupled with the growth of humanism and the centralized absolutist state produced those circumstances in which Weber discerned the beginnings of our present rationalized, bureaucratic society.

Some of the early stages in the evolution of what we can conveniently call the technical culture were quite contrary to later developments; the exigencies of the early period of growth were different from the requirements of later stages and the inability to appreciate that the same developmental processes can have different social manifestations at different stages has caused not a little confusion. For example, in the period from 1700 to about 1900 (in the West), a process of social atomization occurred whereby the individual was 'freed' from traditional ties and enabled to participate in the historical mutation (or industrial revolution, if this term is preferred). Under the slogan of the defence of the rights of the individual, an attack was made on the traditional privileges of groups such as aristocracies, guilds, and orders. Legislation brought changes to the family structure, and the laws governing divorce, inheritance, and paternal authority were modified so that the individual was strengthened and the group weakened. In this way, the individual became more malleable and easier to use as an instrument in the new machine techniques. The break up of social groups facilitated the mobility and reconcentration of the population required by industrialization and its techniques. New academic institutions and orientations not only challenged traditional learning but devoted themselves to those studies applicable to the development of technique. A whole new environment of shocking squalor appeared in the shape of overcrowded cities, unhealthy dwellings and sordid workplaces, and in addition, a new social stratum appeared as a by-product of industrialization: the proletariat. The individual was 'atomized' and rendered pliable without family, environment or group membership that could resist economic pressure. Only one authority was left for the individual in such a society: the state. The state protected the arts and sciences when they served the new techniques (and in a desultory way even when they did not) while itself undergoing changes brought about by the bourgeoisie, the industrial innovators and the pecuniary beneficiaries of the new culture; the modern state is as much a creation of industrialization as are the technological academies and universities. The weakening of traditional authority, the crumbling of traditional moral and religious codes, gave the innovators a freedom to exploit individuals that was underwritten and justified ideologically by the doctrine that nothing ought to be permitted to stand in the way of progress. The 'underdeveloped' parts of the world such as Africa and the Middle East are undergoing today a process essentially similar in its social manifestations to that which Europe and the United States underwent in the eighteenth and nineteenth centuries. By the outbreak of war in 1914, the masses had been won over to the side of technique and society had been fully captured; self-interest (the ideal of comfort, for instance) had been made apparent to everyone and none gainsaid it save for a few intellectuals who made ineffectual protests, mainly on behalf of organized Christianity or some vague sentimental idealism. In Britain and the USA the part played by the state in this progress had been minimal, but not so in Europe, where the state was often the agent of industrial development. From the very beginnings of industrialization profit was the prime and ostensible motive while empiricism was the dominant mode of thought assisting it. Techniques were developed and experiment encouraged because it paid to do so, and states gained in international prestige by virtue of their industry, that could supply the arms to equip the great conscript armies that were the workers in disguise. Ellul asserts that the Americans began by mechanizing complex operations that finally produced the assembly line, while Europeans tended to mechanize simple operations such as spinning, the reason for this was that the Americans were in the position of being able to dispose of an exceptionally pliable working force already created for them by the migrations from Europe, whereas Europeans had to mould such a force for themselves and naturally utilized it in the simplest and most convenient way possible.

Ellul uses arguments that are similar to those used by Max Weber in respect of the origins of Western-type capitalism. He affirms that five factors came together in the West and that they had never before coincided in time and place. The five conditions were: (1) a very long period of technical maturation without the impediment of religious or state checks; (2) population growth; (3) a suitable economic milieu; (4) a society that was open to the propagation of techniques; and (5) a clear technical intention that combined the other four into the pursuit of the technical objective: the single best means. The unique historical phenomenon was the simultaneous existence of the five factors.

Primitive techniques have no substantive existence, they are merely intermediary between man and his environment; contemporary techniques are our environment. The technical culture is one that is founded on the belief that production and consumption coincide with the whole of human life. Comfort and well-being cannot be envisaged save as part of the technical order of things, the prototype of modern man is the ship-wrecked Robinson Crusoe who managed to reach the shore of his desert island with most of the contents of a seventeenth century supermarket. It is a presupposition of our day that the 'quality of life' was inferior before technical development. It very probably was, but we cannot demonstrate or prove it (the assumption made is that because our ancestors did not have our material blessings, their lives *must have been inferior*). That the rural slums of the pre-industrial age were as bad as any of the industrial slums of the nineteenth century is probably true, but *they did not have to be* (that they were, is a tribute to man's nature) while the industrial slums of the early growth of technique *had to be* otherwise the cheap labour would not have been forthcoming; the shanty-town slums of South African economic development *have to be* because of the very nature of this kind of industrialization (the question is, 'is any other kind possible?' Judging by what has occurred in Communist states, the answer is 'no').

In primitive techniques, the deficiencies of the tools are compensated for by the skill of the user; in our society, the deficiencies in the worker are compensated for by the techniques; mass production techniques insure that any high-grade moron can operate the mechanisms (14).

Ellul provides a threefold characterization of the technical phenomenon of today; the three characteristics are: (1) rationality exemplified in systematization, division of labour, creation of standards, production norms, etc.; it involves two distinct 'phases': (a) the use of 'discourse' in every operation, that is, an area to which the criteria governing the operation applies (this excludes spontaneity and personal creativity), and (b) the reduction of method to its logical dimension only, i.e. all facts, figures, phenomena, means and instruments are reduced to the schemata of logic. (2) It destroys, eliminates or subordinates the 'natural' world and does not allow that world to restore itself (for example, make good the depletion of natural resources) or even 'to enter into a symbiotic relation with it'. (3) Automatism of technical choice: when everything has been mathematically calculated, logically scrutinized and is recognizably the most efficient means, then the technical movement becomes self-directing, in other words all choice save the technical one is eliminated. (The weakness in Ellul's argument here is that he ignores the fact that the most efficient can, at least for a considerable time, pass unnoticed.) Thus everything that is not technique is gradually being eliminated and replaced by technically oriented substitutes; as examples one may take the proliferation of technical, vocational and 'practical' degrees in the newer universities and similar institutions. It is enlightening to see how the old technical colleges and institutes have been elevated into 'colleges of advanced technology' and then into 'technological universities' and 'polytechnics' and have graduated from diplomas and certificates in engineering to degrees in engineering and thence onto degrees in 'business studies', 'management', 'applied social sciences', in fact to the study of any kind of technique from social work to 'computer science' so that their catalogue of courses is a set of rubrics for the new theology of technique.

There are additionally four other attributes of the technical phenomenon that Ellul lists: self-augmentation, monism, universalism, and the autonomy of techniques.

Technical advance is assisted by the joint efforts of thousands of technicians but additionally, when a new technical form appears, it makes possible and conditions a number of others. The progression is determined by the preceding technical situation alone. A new kind of spontaneous action occurs: the evolution of technique becomes causal; it is the technical necessity (the technical 'reality') that determines that all that technique can produce is produced and accepted by the consumer. This is self-augmentation: neither producer nor consumer determines production, it is technique as an entity in itself that is the determining factor.

Monism or *unicité* is a term Ellul uses that describes the fact that the technical phenomenon presents everywhere the same characteristics. Technique does not observe the distinction between moral and immoral use of it, instead it creates an independent technical morality: a number of uses can be made of a machine, but only one is the technical use, and this technical use is always the best way of doing something. If a machine or procedure lacks this one use, then it is not technique. Technique then is a means with a set of 'rules of the game'; it is a method or procedure that is unique and not open to arbitrary choice; no advantage is gained when the machine or organization is not used as it 'ought to be'.

The linking together of techniques and the fact that technique involves the same effects everywhere constitute the universalism of the technical phenomenon. It is a mighty force in breaking up the social structure of 'backward' countries, and it creates a bond between technicians of every race and nationality, a kind of fraternity of technocrats. Once a given technique has been learned, language differences decline in importance—verbal communication between technicians, where it is necessary, can be reduced to limited and stylized forms thus both facilitating and restricting understanding.

The rules governing a technique are not those of justice or morality (or injustice and immorality either) but only 'laws' in a peculiarly narrow sense. External necessities no longer determine technique, as they once did; the internal necessities of technique itself are determinative. The technical phenomenon includes the imperative of the nature of technique. It is meaningless to speak of techniques as 'neutral'. Wherever technique encounters a living substance today, be it bacterial or animal, the latter is ultimately subordinated to the 'needs' of the former though men fool themselves and each other by claiming, in face of all contrary evidence, that external pressures and influences determine techniques. Giedion's study of the mechanization of bread production (15) shows that at first the attempts failed; then the nature of bread was changed in order to *adapt* it to mechanical manipulation and the process was successful; thus the mechanization of its manufacture depended finally on the transformation of human taste; man adapted to the machine. Whenever technique collides with a natural obstacle, it tends to get round it either by replacing the living organism with a machine or by modifying the organism so that it no longer offers a specifically organic reaction. Technique has developed so far that man is in the course of being eliminated save as the 'thing' that starts the mechanism or the procedure, or the supervisor who inspects to see that the technique is functioning correctly. Where the human individual cannot yet be dispensed with, technique demands his adjustment and the suppression of distinctively human feelings and reactions. The case of the test pilot is an example, but one that is bettered by that of the astronaut. The individual has to be trained to become unconscious of self in order to operate the technique, and experiences on the Apollo missions have demonstrated the effectiveness of this training.

These attributes and characteristics of the technical phenomenon show quite plainly that there is no common denominator between the techniques of today and those of yesterday; they are not only quantitatively different, they are qualitatively different as well.

In the early stages of its present development, technique was assisted by the breaking up of traditional group structures, but now we witness a demand for the reconstitution of the fragments. We hear pleas for 'community', the stimulation of community spirit, for new communal associations, and governments put out reports emphasizing the need for community and the dire consequences of not having it, and a new breed of social workers appears on the scene: 'community workers' and a new branch of study, 'community work', come into being to clutter the already outlandish catalogue of new higher education courses (16). In part, these demands attract the attention of the 'backward lookers', whose vision of the present is always obscured by an idealized version of the past, but in the main the demand for community appeals to those who deprecate mass society and it is seen by them as a strategy whereby some of the deleterious effects can be countered and also as a device for saving our moribund democracy. But are these attempts to resuscitate community (of the old type) really effective forms of opposition to techniques and the supremacy of technical modes? Is it the swing back of a pendulum or does the pendulum never swing back? Ellul has no hesitation in replying with a categoric 'no'. 'If we examine these new sociological forms in detail, we find them all organized as functions of techniques . . . modern collectivities and groups have no existence beyond techniques—they are representative of the major tendency of our time' (17). Contemporary man is no longer situated in relation to other men but in relation to technique, modern advanced societies are centred on technical necessities and imperatives and *on human adherence to them*. For human beings could (though they are most unlikely to), break away: thus communities and communal feeling would be desirable things in those nihilistic working-class areas of the great cities or in the new urban dormitories, in fact, they would be a 'good thing' in any area of actual or potential strife or clash between groups. If one examines the numerous community projects and schemes, they are usually to be found wherever the 'lower orders' (to revert to the language as well as the attitudes of the past) are likely to get out of control. Preaching 'community' is, like the human relations approach, the advocacy of a 'lubricant' that will facilitate the techniques of state and industry, which in the UK are, at the moment, concentrated on a joint endeavour for greater productivity. In the early days of industrialization, a highly mobile work force was required, preferably disunited and with each member competing with the others, now advanced technical society requires a stable, united work force and mobility is relatively unimportant, so it would be convenient if what had been smashed up could be put together again; but so far the attempts have failed. The really deprived, the second-class citizens of our society, see it only as another confidence trick; the politically educated elements see the futility of it; while the affluent worker, the 'know nothing', privatized individual does not want to know because he is not interested; the middle and upper classes do not require 'community' because they have never lost their own groups and associations. As for the technically trained, the real élite of our day, they have the gospel of productivity to satisfy them, it has taken the place of the gospel of work of the Protestant Ethic and is just as meaningless. The belief in the gospel of work was an act of faith (God approved of hard and *rewarded* work) and the belief in ever increasing productivity is a breed of the same order, only the object now is not God's approval but victory. It is a product of the Second World War situation; for the United States it is simple, they have never ceased to be at war since 1941 so the perpetuation of a war situation at home has not been difficult. In the UK we have been at war with ourselves since 1945 and so it has been relatively easy to call for greater and greater productivity in all fields: engineers to produce more cars, teachers to graduate more students; the situation is one of permanent war, always producing for victory, but over whom? The inexorable imperative of technique, reinforced by the Second World War, leads us to find justifications for obedience, and politics have become the rationalizations for the autonomy of technique, a fact too dreadful for most of us to accept or even perceive. The writers of science fiction, those latter-day prophets of doom, are some of the few individuals who have faced up to the contemporary situation and it is interesting to see how the themes of perpetual war with aliens, the existence of a single technical culture for the whole of the earth, and the total technicization of the human race are repeated in the vast literature, almost all of which is pessimistic, that has appeared in the past twenty years.

In spite of the foresight of the science fiction authors, we do not know the consequences of the ultimate triumph of technique. That it leads to 'mass society' in the worst sense of the term seems clear, but what this kind of society implies for individuals is not apparent. Karen Horney believed that our civilization was still based on a secularized Christianity, with brotherly relations as its highest value, but our world in action represents the opposite: the basic rule of our world is to compete; competition in every sphere: economic, political, class and status, and also in the social, even in friendship and sexual relations; in this situation 'community' has disappeared.

The realization that the demands made on man by this technical society, the modifications of the human environment, and the alteration of social structures, in short, that man is in disaccord with the world that he has created and must be restored to harmony with it, has led to the most potentially powerful techniques of all: the *maieutic* or human techniques as Ellul calls them, and they are the techniques of psychotherapy (18).

Direct action on the power of techniques is impossible, the clock cannot be put back. Only a catastrophe (a nuclear war for example) could materially change them. So the only course that is left open to us in our present situation, is to act upon ourselves, i.e. to prepare ourselves for our new role. The essential question for our age is 'what is man's role in this world he has brought into existence, but that now proceeds by its own momentum?' A question that cannot be answered and that the human techniques are not concerned with because their task is a narrower one. They are, according to Ellul, concerned with three particular avenues that offer relief to man: relief through liberation, relief through humanizing the techniques, and relief in restoring the unity of man.

(1) The 'liberation of man': the argument is that technique gives man greater opportunities for freedom than ever before; easier work and better working-conditions plus more leisure; additionally, freedom from famine and the other material constraints of the natural order of things. Then by the human techniques of psychoanalysis and related depth psychotherapies, man will be freed from his inner constraints and thus become better adapted to his present life and able to master the difficulties posed for him by the contemporary world. In this view, the mechanical and material techniques collaborate with the maieutic techniques to liberate man both externally and internally.

(2) Liberty through a humanization of the technical processes or the creation of a technical humanism. The world of techniques must be changed so that its abstract and mechanical aspects are minimized and man becomes a participant in a complicated operation that includes himself. The interests of man and the demands of technique must be made to correspond and the 'facts of human nature' must be taken into account in order to keep man from being crushed and becoming an obstacle to the development of technique; the means for achieving this is some form of 'human relations' approach, i.e. a variety of psychotherapy.

(3) The unity of man is the source of liberty and there are human techniques that can restore the unity of man. Technique can counter technique and salvation lies in the combined efforts of psychology and sociology to find a way out of the difficulties. By psychology and sociology are meant those manipulative and persuasive techniques that these two disciplines have evolved, so this avenue of escape is really only a combination of (1) and (2).

One of the human techniques that have been called into being to redress the imbalance between man and technique is that found in education. The new approach in educational methods is designed to broaden the outlook of the child, to develop his social personality and increase his happiness and maintain his equilibrium. Opposition to society expressed in a lack of social adjustment produces serious personality difficulties that lead to the loss of psychic balance. This implies that social adaptation or adjustment is one of the most important elements in contemporary education, thus it is not the child 'in and for himself who is being educated but the child in and for society. And the society moreover, is not an ideal one, with full justice and truth, but society as it is' (19). This society (both in its Eastern as well as its Western manifestations) is becoming increasingly totalitarian, and adaptation to it becomes progressively harder to achieve, or put another way, conformity becomes ever more onerous. The techniques are ever more extensively required in attempts to mould or work on individuals in order to make them content in a milieu that would otherwise make them discontented (20). The pedagogical techniques educate children to become what society expects of them and their social consciences are formed so that they strive for the same ends to which the techniques are directed. The process of adjustment is never ending and is the core element in all the maieutic techniques. Ellul argues that the Napoleonic conception of education, as expressed in the Lycées and Grandes Écoles, that it should provide administrators for the state and managers for industry in conformity with a totalitarian view of the nation, has become world-wide, and if so it is ironic if we accept Aron's opinion that Napoleon was, in most respects but surely not in this one, an anachronism. Education no longer has a humanistic goal or any value in itself, it is purely instrumental in its aim of training technicians and assistants to them. As *Le Monde* declared in

1952, 'there are too many half-baked intellectuals and not enough technicians' (21). Higher education is following the same path; it is rapidly moving away from being an exciting and unpredictable foray into human enlightenment and becoming an exercise in conformity and an apprenticeship to the gimmickology of a technical world.

The human relations approach is an equally necessary technique to adapting the worker, especially the assistants to the technicians, to the techniques of work that require the complete integration of the worker. Counsellors in industry provide the techniques required. They act as safety-valves and trouble-shooters for the grievances and complaints of employees. The worker may express his feeling and dissatisfactions to the counsellor with the full confidence that nothing he says will be reported to management in individual terms. But, as Ellul remarks, the counsellors never counsel anything: 'Their activities have nothing whatever to do with a positive cure of the soul, a mission which would suppose at least the possibility of profound changes, new orientations, and an awakening consciousness on the worker's part' (22). To let people talk relieves them, forestalls rebellion, and talking to a professional counsellor, i.e. a psychological technician, is less dangerous than talking among themselves.

In order to avoid the conflicts engendered by living in a technicized society, the individual must be adapted or adjusted and forced to find his relations with his fellows and in his group satisfying; full adaptation can only be achieved by total integration into the group. These human techniques are not remedies, they are means that facilitate, at their best, the mechanical processes and increase production and subordinate human feelings to the calculation of the technicians while at their less successful level, they are palliatives. They make men more comfortable in submitting to the imperatives of the machine and production. They cannot lead to the recovery of a sense of worth, personality and authenticity: 'they are a delusion that dessicates the individual's desire for anything better' (23), and as an example of this vocational counselling (or guidance) could scarcely be bettered.

Vocational counselling applies a modified form of psychotherapy and derives its principles from the same sources. It claims to discover an individual's vocational aptitude and to guide him into the occupation that he is naturally adapted to and in which he will do best and be most contented. The value of aptitude testing is unquestionable and is not the point at issue. The criticism levelled against vocational counselling is that it seems to discover those aptitudes that the economic policy or economic techniques of the moment require. This is no capitalist plot or communist conspiracy, all it means is that human potentialities are vast and flexible and vocational counselling modifies these potentialities in accordance with the demands prevailing at the moment. If the vocational counsellor did not presuade his clients to adjust in this way, the logical outcome would be that the economy would be founded on these aptitudes and large numbers would starve to death. The impracticality of such a system demonstrates that in vocational counselling, the primacy of the individual is a pretence, but the pretence is necessary as a part of the process of adjustment. In this respect vocational counselling is no different from any other of the maieutic procedures.

The last of the human techniques, but certainly not the least, is that of entertainment. The aim of entertainment is to distract. Propaganda is never wholly convincing, so entertainment fills up the gaps. Entertainment is nowadays mostly the display of techniques and in the cinema and on television these techniques are utilized to give life meaning. The techniques of the mass media are, above all else, skilled ways of giving life meaning by avoiding the fact of death. Life has a meaning only when death has a meaning might not be quite what Ellul intends to say, but it is the basic fact of social and individual life and it is what Berger means when he says that 'every human society is a bulwark against death'. This is probably what Ellul intends when he writes: 'Technical civilization has made a great error in not suppressing death, the only human reality still intact' (24).

The entertainment industry provides us with a world of fantasy in which the spectator 'goes to bed with the leading lady, kills the villain, and masters life's absurdities. In short, he becomes a hero. Life suddenly has meaning' (25). In the fantasy world of television and cinema what ought to change has already been altered. Everything, even the portrayal of technique, is larger than life; death is reduced to impotence by the technique of too frequent representation in news and documentaries as well as in drama and thus it ceases to shock or have any impact, it is an incident in a faraway land or a puppet-like convulsion of the body in some Western fairy tale. Heaps of massacred bodies are as common a sight to contemporary viewers as were images of the crucifixion to medieval believers. But equally important as the neutralizing of death are the mass media portrayals that emphasize those aspects of the relationships between people that are discouraged in the technicized society: non-competitive friendship, integrity and loyalty, and above all, compassion. The family or 'kitchen-sink' type of television serial stresses affection, warmth, and the essential 'goodness' of life, while a most remarkable feature of many of the most popular commercial television series in the UK is that they have 'compassionate heroes' as exemplified in Sergeant Mann of *Red Cap*, Frank Marker of *Public Eye*, and that supreme example, the most humane and compassionate of all, *Callan*, who inhabits a world of mindless bestiality. Television is not only emotional blotting-paper in the sense that it absorbs individual tensions and frustrations, but also because it soaks up social tensions.

A most significant element in the great technical achievement of modern mass entertainment is sport. Commercialized spectator sport is historically a product of industrialization and urbanization. It is a tolerated reaction against industrial life at the same time as it is a set of techniques, one might almost say pure techniques, because they are totally ends in themselves. The organization and complexities of spectator sports are a non-industrial version of the industrial society but one that is a fairy tale, for in its performances the best man wins, and justice is seen to be done. It provides the heroes that the world of work has never been able to supply: it also ensures the constant dependence on technique even when the worker is not working: commercialized sport is the technicization of leisure.

The domination and encirclement of man by technique is not a plot, plan or conspiracy by any individual or group, it is not something organized by 'them'. It is for Ellul an impersonal phenomenon that proceeds by itself once it is set in motion and it inevitably leads to the reconstitution of man. Schelsky, although not in agreement with all that Ellul says, agrees with him on this point and refers to technology as being 'self-originating'. The reconstitution of man into a 'hitherto unknown being' is achieved by the convergence of a plurality of independent and inter-dependent techniques. Each technician asserts in good faith that his particular techniques leave man intact, but the convergence of techniques, that is a stage in the evolution of the technical society, is a spontaneously created situation that does not leave man intact. The steady dissociation of man that has been proceeding step by step with the convergence of techniques has not escaped the notice of all observers of contemporary society and their appreciation of the situation has found expression in a nameless but widespread belief in the West. Shorter working-hours, well-paid happy 'alienated' workers who will find their own real personalities and their expression of them in their leisure: 'dead time' will become 'live time' and full automation is the means whereby this will be achieved. Leisure will provide the escape, the opportunity for the flight into oneself. If work is neutralized, then the only possibility of self-expression and self-fulfilment is in non-work, i.e. in the private sphere of life. The setting, the momentum or drive, the means are all provided by technique, and the leisure and private sphere of life is rapidly becoming techni-cized so the ineffable happens: sooner or later man himself becomes a 'technique' in a vast mechanized, computerized, automated and 'air-conditioned nightmare'. But like Alice in the Red King's dream, he will not even know that he is a character in a dream.

Schelsky (26) somewhat earlier than Ellul, described technology as an independent force. His use of this term should not make us less aware of the similarity between his outlook and that of Ellul; the latter uses 'technique' because he wishes to emphasize the individual nature of the separate procedures that converge to create a technical society, while Schelsky uses 'technology' to indicate the abstraction that lies behind the procedures and manifests itself in them (27). The means become ends, which is the reversal of the situation that existed in the earlier stages of techni-cal development. With very little warning, scientific research and technology extrude new techniques into our society and we have to find an application for them; that is, we have to find or devise a human purpose for something that has not been consciously planned. According to Schelsky, technical development produces unforeseen methods and unplanned objectives for them. Technical growth or development, evolution if this term is preferred, is the realization of the potentialities implicit in techniques, it is a form of immanence. The convergence of techniques is accompanied by the convergence of technology, economy, and administration into a single integrated whole in which political and social decisions are taken on the bases of technical expertise. The ability to make alternative political and social decisions is gradually being withdrawn from politicians and public to be exercised by administrators whose advice is mandatory. Events since the Second World War indicate that the administrators (in the sense of pukka civil servants) are themselves being taken over by and merged with technicians, so that politicians and administrators are becoming the spokesmen for technical experts whose imperatives vouchsafe no alternatives. A clue to the future was provided as early as 1914 when European governments accepted the irreversibility of mobilization, the logic of the military experts permitted no alternative to war once the technique of total mobilization had been set in operation. The power of the politician is slowly becoming a fiction as he is diminished by the technical expert. This is not a version of the vulgar criticism of scientists that holds them to blame for everything, since science and technology are not synonymous; science and technology did not become interdependent until the late nineteenth century; science made only indirect contributions to technical development in the early part of the industrial revolution. Modern science, however, produces a certain kind of knowledge that, with or without the intention of scientists, can be utilized technically. The assumption that in the late twentieth century science is mostly impelled by technology, that science itself has become technicized, is quite tenable—in fact any other view would not stand up to close examination. Governments in the West are less concerned with the realization of goals (social or otherwise) than with the resolution of technical problems and these, by their nature, are not suitable for discussion by an ignorant lay public. Science, research, technology, the utilization of industrial resources, and the use of raw materials have converged into one multifaceted complex of techniques, and this complex has become institutionalized. In the opinions of Ellul, Gehlen and Schelsky, to choose but three of the many analysts of contemporary Western society, politics has been reduced by the influence of technique to a mere choice by the electorate of the leaders of rival groups of administrators and technicians, the differences between the groups being minimal and historically based; the need for this electoral choice is only a residue of the politico-economic institutional structure of an age that is passing. The most industrially advanced societies, affirms Gehlen, are exhibiting characteristics associated with organisms that mainly react to external stimuli, that is to say, such societies do not demonstrate that they are influenced by norms and guided by values.

On the level of individual and personal action, the influence of internalized values (conscience, super-ego, socialization) has given way to adaptive behaviour. What operates as external stimuli for the society are the technical exigencies and they are treated as objectivities, and what the individual has to adjust to are the demands made on him by the specific technical areas within which he works and the society that surround both them and him. This has coincided with the 'de-politicization' of the masses whose demands now only represent privatized needs: more money, more leisure, but not a radical change in all or any significant part of the social order.

Techniques are modes of what Jürgen Habermas regards as *active adaptation,* i.e. human control over the external environment; they distinguish, he claims, the collective self-preservation of social animals from the preservation of the species characteristic of other animals. Whether or not it applies to bees and ants is quite irrelevant here, but what is significant is that it is characteristic of the manner in which human collectivities act in the historical process. But, argues Habermas, as far as individual human beings are concerned, the adaptation that they are called upon to make is *passive:* culturally we adapt the external environment to our needs, individually we have to adapt to the cultural demands that are predominantly and increasingly technical. Already there are indications pointing to this being achieved by human engineering; we are witnessing the rivalry between two as yet incomplete techniques, that of psychotherapy on the one hand and chemical and surgical means on the other. The eclecticism that is beginning to manifest itself in the work and writings of some psychotherapists might well be an indication of the converging of the two techniques in the endeavour to find the one best way. Other indications pointing in the same direction are reflected intellectually in the decline of anthropomorphism and the popularity of theriomorphic thinking that reduces man by conceiving him in animal terms; anthropomorphically we think of animals by attributing human characteristics to them, theriomorphically we think of man in terms of traits derived from animals. The successful popularizations of ethology are representative of such ways of thinking, but equally significant are those views of the human being that consider him some form of computer and conceive of the human brain as nothing more than a collection of electronic gadgets and deny the phenomenon of mind. All this would be amusing and entertaining were it not for the sinister implications: believe man is a machine and it is easy to treat him as one—man is apparently, then, only a robot who thinks he is a man.

Arnold Gehlen (28) links man's biological structure with his social institutions and the development of technology in his theory of institutions. In outline, his argument is as follows: man has a special and distinctive position in the animal world, both organically and environmentally he differs from even the highest forms of animal life. Man is born too soon, that is, certain essential stages in the organic development of the higher animals that take place during the foetal phase do not occur in the human until after birth and during the first year of infancy. This means that the development of the human being involves a very early, one might say, premature, interaction with an environment that is external to his organism. At birth, the human organism is 'unfinished' in a way that animal organisms never are. One of the consequences of this incomplete state is that the human being is left with an unspecialized instinctual apparatus. The non-human animal enters the world at birth with highly specialized drives (instincts) and oriented towards an environment that is specific to its species. The animal lives his whole life more or less instinctively in a specialized and *closed* world (29). Man, however, possesses at birth only unspecialized drives not directed towards a specific environment. He is characterized by being 'instinct-poor' or instinctually deprived, and has no species-specific environment. His world, unlike that of the animal's, is an 'open' one, that of the animal is 'closed'. These peculiar characteristics of man provide him with biological instability: his undirected drives have no biologically given modes of release, therefore whatever stability he is to possess must be supplied by non-biological means. This is done by social institutions.

The human being must make up for what he lacks biologically, by specializing and stabilizing his activities through constructs that he produces; he must build his own world, i.e. his culture. The social structure or institutions that make up his social world must be firm, but because they are man-made and not biologically provided they are inherently never as stable as those of the animal world. The man-constructed social institutions are in danger of erosion by internal or external forces and they have to be constructed and re-constructed by human effort; they are 'predestined' to change and thus precarious.

In spite of these built-in defects, social institutions are the main elements in cultural stability; they endow human action (in Weber's sense of 'action') with intelligibility, coherence and continuity, and provide a relatively stable (that is in the short run) background for all human activities. The areas of life that are institutionalized (work, religion, family life, etc.) are the background *for what appears to the individual to be spontaneous, unreflective activities,* that is, actions performed within the institutionalized sectors seem to the individual to partake of the nature of instinctive acts, they are innately 'natural' because the social institutions are taken for granted, they are, to the individual, the only conceivable social world and thus self-evidently 'natural' and 'right'. Against such an apparently enduring background, deliberate, conscious, reflective and purposeful actions can be performed. The background is man's substitute for instincts and without such a background, social life, that is, human life, would be impossible. Needless to add that the socialization of individuals must be adequate otherwise the self-evident nature of this social world would not become apparent; the construction of beliefs about the world we live in is the basis of socialization and this allows man to construct a world and then treat it as if it existed apart from himself.

But any given social institution is only one of many possible alternatives (the obviousness of this can be appreciated if one considers the great variety in the forms of the institution of marriage that exist and have existed in ancient and modern, primitive and developed societies) but in an integrated society, its social institutions do not appear as merely chosen alternatives, but as the only conceivable ones. It is through the institutions of a society that the 'open' world of man becomes a 'closed' one, or perhaps one should say, a relatively closed one. The open world of man is chaos, the humanly constructed social world is both an order and a defence against chaos. This 'closed' and seemingly stable world is precarious because it contains an element of openness for man is capable of changing the institutions that he has created or denying their 'rightness' and inevitability. The man-created world of social institutions is shared through the medium of language, which in its turn assists in maintaining its continuity as well as its stability.

In the so-called simpler societies of preliterate peoples and also in traditional societies, the institutions are at their most stable and provide a 'closed' ambient for most of life's activities. In modern societies like our own and in transitional periods such as the eighteenth and nineteenth centuries in Europe there is a trend towards de-institutionalization. The inherent instability becomes manifest as technical change occurs. Man's ability to think and reason as expressed in reflective rationality undermines the taken-for-granted cultural constructs. The inevitable accompaniment to change brought about by external facts, be they foreign invasion or population pressure or new techniques in agriculture and industry, is the weakening and dissolution of erstwhile seemingly immutable social institutions. Technology and technical growth cannot exist without reflective rationality and the combination and interaction of these weakens (sometimes totally destroys) the taken-for-granted world of established institutions and renders man once more exposed to biological precariousness. As the old institutional stability disappears, man is compelled to construct new settings for his life, and he does this in two ways: firstly, by trying to find principles of order within himself, this Gehlen calls 'subjectivism' and it takes place at the individual level; secondly, at the social level, man devises ideologies, philosophies, explanations and interpretations that undergo very rapid change. By these two means, man seeks support for his own personal effort to come

to terms with his world, bits of which are still taken-for-granted
though some, work for example, are not so much taken-for-
granted as seen as meaningless inevitabilities. Whatever the
success may be that man has in these efforts, the results are always
precarious, or are so to date, and the support they give him is
tenuous. The private sphere of life, that is the non-work side of
life, is the area of these efforts because one of the results of the
processes of de-institutionalization and subjectivization that have
occurred during and since the development of technique into a
way of life has been the dichotomization, the splitting, of man's
life into two spheres or sectors: the public sphere of work within
an organizational and bureaucratic framework, and the private
sphere of life that is outside. It is the nature of modern economic
structures that for most of mankind in an industrialized society
the public sphere is unsatisfying, even frustrating, even identity
damaging, only a happy few have work of such significance to
themselves and others that they can derive satisfaction and
identity from it. For the majority, the only identity confirming area
is the private sphere and that is where subjectivism provides some
opportunities for reducing the chaos that is within and without.

Closely associated with Gehlen's formulation of the consequences of industrialization is Berger's use of the concept of
alienation (30). He assumes that man's social works, i.e. those that
in some manner or other involve and concern other people, are
part of a 'reality' other than himself. They 'escape' him, but in
addition, a part of man 'escapes' himself and it is that part of himself that is the result and product of socialization, the part that is
really the product of other men's efforts. As a consequence of
socialization, man internalizes part of a social world that is not
himself. The possibility then arises that in certain circumstances
the social world might become strange to him, and the socialized
part of himself might likewise become strange to him. Indeed,
this 'estrangement' is implicit in the sociality of man, and when
the individual becomes aware of it, there are two ways for him to
proceed: the individual can recall, i.e. tell himself what he has
known for some time, that the world and the self are products of
one's own activity, but if this reappropriation is not possible for
some reason, then the second alternative is to reify and treat the
social world and the social self that confront the individual as

'external things' that are analogous to the objective world. This second alternative is what Berger describes as 'alienating'. When alienated, the individual does not understand that the social world was and is 'co-produced' by him. The essential nature of the social world (a human product) and the natural world (a non-human phenomenon) are not distinguished by the alienated individual, so alienation can be defined as a process of reification whereby the living substances of the man-made social world are converted into the meaningless non-human things of the natural world. This roughly coincides with what Gehlen means by 'institutionalization' because when this is successfully achieved, the world taken-for-granted that they constitute has about it something of the essentials of a non-human phenomenon. In alienation as in institutionalization, human products become de-humanized.

Berger's concept is linked to that of Marx's because according to him, activity, especially work, loses its 'meaning' as the product is only 'apprehended' in terms of the product itself. This is in Berger's theorizing not something that can be 'blamed' on capitalism because alienation like institutionalization is not an aberration, not something that happens only when something has gone wrong with the social order. Alienation is not anomie; alienation makes the world of man, i.e. the institutionalized world, that is inherently precarious as Gehlen argues, stronger and more stable since it takes on an aspect of immutability, it is 'given' and 'permanent' because it is constructed of things external to man and so it seems everlasting. Berger argues that alienation is 'normal' insofar as simpler, primitive peoples seem to live in an entirely alienated social world as do also the peoples of archaic and traditional societies; the child also sees the world around him as alienated. It is only relatively late in human history and late in the life of an individual that the apprehension of the social world as being man-made appears. The technical approach as described by Ellul is alienating just as the world created by capitalism is alienating and Gehlen's public sphere is so also. The pain of alienation comes from the prevalence of what Marx called 'false consciousness' and Sartre 'bad faith', that is to act as if the man-made world cannot be altered, defied and modified. The truly alienated individual is one who acts as if the role he plays cannot be modified, as if his behaviour is always determined by forces acting on him from the outside, as if the rules of the game were the same as natural laws.

A technical culture, both at its inception and during its growth, requires that some, an élite, must always be partly, if not wholly, de-alienated, otherwise the reflective rationality that is required to bring about change cannot come into being. De-alienation is thus precarious because of the need that man has to construct new institutions to replace the lost ones, otherwise chaos reappears. It does not affect the argument that such new constructs are short-lived, they serve their purpose albeit inadequately until replaced by fresh ones. The public sphere in our kind of society is still alienated and therefore 'de-humanizing', and this provides us with a paradox if our society is seen in this light. Adjustment in accordance with the psychotherapeutic ideology is adjustment to alienation, adaptation to a world that is still historically primitive and infantile, that is the new taken-for-granted world of the technologists and technocrats. Adaptation to 'reality' is recognition that one cannot change this world and has to accept it as a given immutability though historically one knows that it has changed and is a man-made thing. Adjustment or adaptation means that the individual returns to viewing his circumstances through the eyes of infancy and consoles himself with play.

The kind of sociological theory that is inspired by the examples of model-building in theoretical economics is alienating and must therefore be instrumental in reinforcing the status quo, because all such model and system building gives to man-made creations the status of the objective externality of the natural world.

The feature most characteristic of contemporary industrialized society is heresy. Men question the taken-for-grantedness of the technicized world; it is composed of shattered institutions, residues of others, reconstructed ones and those that are in the uneasy process of being constituted; it is a partly closed world with great open gaps in it through which man can peep at chaos, and like sunspots, the opennesses expand and contract as attempts to fill the holes succeed for a time and then fail.

Is this present stage of industrial society one from which the previously endemic class struggle has disappeared? Is it still a class society even though a masked one as Holz declares it to be? (31)

It is not only Dahrendorf who asserts that the Marxist theory of class struggle is no longer relevant. Habermas, writing in 1968 (32) said that the regulation of private enterprise by the state had suspended the class struggle by guaranteeing rewards to the wage-earners and thus avoiding open conflict, but the disappearance of class conflict was only apparent; the conflict between capitalists (even in the guise of the alleged professionalized managers) and the wage-earners is still latent, and should remain so provided that the 'system' ensured that the rewards continued forthcoming. Then how to account for the continuation of social strife in parts of industrialized society? Not by the bogeymen beloved of managerial ideologists and psychotherapists, that is, not by the actions of psychological misfits and rabble-rousers. Social strife today in the form of open conflicts about social matters is, according to the opinion of Claus Offe (33) confined to peripheral groups. Offe puts forward the hypothesis that social conflict is likely to become overt the less the frustration of the interests of the protesting group has dangerous consequences for the system. In other words, conflict breaks out at the edges of society where the state and the powers-that-be feel that there is no great need to placate or worry about those who feel wronged. Indications are that when open conflict does occur it is at the point where state intervention is least. But they are not class conflicts in the Marxist sense but sub-cultural protests and sometimes contra-cultural protests. They are reactions to attenuated governmental regulation, indifference, neglect or discrimination; the groups doing the protesting are minorities such as unemployed, coloured people, and similar underprivileged, pauperized or disfranchized groups. The violence of their protests together with the violence of the reaction to them should not lead us to imagine that a revolutionary situation exists but rather a condition of rebellion in some social groups. For a revolutionary situation to come into being, an alliance between the dissidents and one of the major privileged groups in society would be required. Violence and numbers may create rebellion, they do not necessarily bring about revolution. For a short time in 1968 when French students allied temporarily with French workers, a revolutionary situation appeared probable, but then it became clear that workers and students were only in appearance in coalition.

As Hannah Arendt has emphasized, the protests by coloured people in the USA and in Britain are not based on revolution but on a demand for a larger and fairer slice of the national cake, all the violence notwithstanding. But what of the rebellion of students? In spite of a rhetorical froth of revolutionary notions, their protests seem based on legitimate criticisms of university organization and a demand, fully in keeping with the ideals of a technical society, that their courses should be more relevant to earning a living in such a society. The gloss that is thrown over the nature of the demands by protest on things unassociated with them such as war, social injustices, and the lack of idealism, in industry and the Establishment, does not conceal the true nature of most student protest in the West: too high expectations of the educational process and the fact that the middle-class ideology of achievement has, in part at least, been displaced from the market to the school and university thus creating discontent at an earlier age. If it is true that young working-class people in Britain are less concerned than their American counterparts with occupational status and more concerned with leisure, then this would account for the relatively mild outbreaks of student discontent in the UK compared with those in America, and provision in polytechnics and colleges of technology of courses of study adapted to the requirements of the technical society would also contribute to a lessening of this kind of violent protest in the UK (34).

It has been assumed that drug-taking, hippydom, yippydom, the ecstasies of pop music, the antics of the young in what is called 'the permissive society' represent some kind of protest against the technicized industrial society, its banality and its absence of spiritual content. It is hard to come to any reasonable conclusion in regard to these manifestations. Whether they represent the eternal demand for meaning in life or whether they are merely the result of boredom and a backlash to the rigours of sexual socialization imposed by parents is not clear. It seems an odd sort of search for meaning that takes the shape of the puerilities and four-letter words of the so-called underground press. It seems that in an advanced industrial society, the dissatisfactions of the young do not take the form of the traditional protests couched in political terms perhaps because the adults in such a society have shown how empty the political mumbo-jumbo is. If as the analysts of technicized living maintain, politics has ceased to be the sphere of politicians and is becoming the concern of experts, then conventional political remedies are not likely to be of much appeal to the dissident. They, one would expect, are more likely to resort to older forms of pressure such as violence in lieu of any new forms offering themselves. The generation gap, that may or may not exist, and if it does, is not likely to affect every group in society, might account for what to the older generation appears as the triviality of youthful demonstrations. In most cases, the behaviour of the young seems designed to affront, intimidate and aggress rather than to achieve any thought-out aims.

The demand for 'community' seems to have made some people blind to the fact that community, in both its good and bad aspects, is being amply demonstrated in the behaviour of certain youth groups. Anthropologists have drawn attention to the tribal nature of some of the activities of Japanese student groups; the long lines of dancing, singing students at a demonstration are reminiscent of tribal dancing, and the uniforms, banners and helmets with insignia of such Japanese students look strangely similar to tribal regalia. In the West, especially in England, teenagers and young people indicate their 'belongingness' as well as their 'togetherness' by wearing similar clothes ranging from beads and medallions, floppy hats and ragged jeans to the sinister outfits of Hell's Angels and Skinheads. To the psychotherapist these manifestations represent the need for belonging experienced by teenagers, and they console us with the argument that the Teddy Boys of a past generation have all turned into respectable fathers and citizens (the empirical evidence for which where it exists is highly doubtful) and so will the Hell's Angels and Aggros of today (they could well afford to do so as they commit enough damage in their late teens and early twenties to last them for the rest of their lives). Is then the major part of discontent in our kind of society not a product of the search for meaning but merely the result of inadequate socialization and faulty conditioning? Have the processes of adjustment, of facing the 'reality principle' failed and all that is needed is some effective psychotherapy to put them back on the right path? This, at any rate, is the view of the run-of-the-mill psychotherapeutic ideologist.

So far we have considered only the obviously grim aspects of

THE NATURE OF TECHNOLOGICAL SOCIETY

contemporary society, but what of its other side, its leisure side? Some sociologists are of the opinion, expressed in a variety of ways, that one of the most important features subsidiary to its industrialization is its leisure or non-work side. Some have even gone so far as to speak of a 'society of leisure' and assume the autonomy of leisure in our lives. They are convinced that leisure and its associated institutions and the values connected with it are the major interests of the mass of people and to which the entire 'system' is subordinated; leisure has become the central life interest of industry. This reasoning is partly based on the quantity of leisure that people have at their disposal today, and because of this, leisure becomes the dominant component in their lives, but this argument declines in significance when another view is considered: modern Western man is most conscious of himself in his leisure activities. It is not a matter of mere quantity or amount of time disposable but a question of identity. Work (the public sphere) is not for most of us, the locus of identity formation and maintenance. Leisure is the sphere in which an individual's identity is confirmed even if it is not constructed there, although many are now asserting that identities are actually creations of leisure pursuits. Leisure pursuits include more than hobbies and skills at pastimes or the achievement of success in a field of action that is not that of one's work. Leisure or non-work must also include the areas of sex and family but these are so important that at this stage it is better to distinguish them from conventional leisure pursuits and to discuss them later and separately.

Of the many roles that an individual plays, some are merely performed, that is, there is outward conformity with the role requirements but little involvement and little or no conviction; there is distance from the role that may manifest itself in humour or deprecation in some cases though more often only in indifference; the performer goes 'through the motions'. Other roles are, however, played 'with feeling'. These are the roles that the individual feels exhibit qualities and attributes with which he wants to be associated. Many of these roles are leisure roles and as they are choices made by the individual, it can be assumed that the personality he displays in their performance is, to him at least, the 'real' personality. The injunction to people about to retire that they should have a hobby is a recognition of this fact because losing the role of active worker or breadwinner and gaining no other can, as is known from common observation, be a disaster leading to premature death.

This identification with leisure roles is found again and again in examples such as the supermarket assistant manager who, in his spare time, is the producer for the local amateur dramatic society, or the typist who is an amateur ballroom dancing champion. What is as cogent is that these leisure-based conceptions of the self are sometimes transferred to other role situations even those of work, and the working personality is stamped with the impress of the leisure time 'I'. Work roles tend to be played in a minor key, and this is perhaps one contributory factor in the failure of the human relations approach in industry.

Leisure activities are not those that necessarily incur a minimal amount of effort; the effort, physical and mental, that go into some leisure pursuits far exceeds that which is occasioned by the work the individual does. Dumazedier (35), among others, states that leisure is the main factor in determining a person's self-consciousness or perception of identity, and is the basis for attitudes affecting his behaviour in all other areas of life. This might, in many cases, be an exaggeration, but there does seem to be considerable agreement that work has become relatively meaningless and that people arrange their lives around their leisure activities and needs. Needless to say, these observations are based on studies made in the affluent nations of the West. Leisure has ceased in those societies to be the prerogative of the rich, while the view that the 'lower classes' are better off without it has all but disappeared. The Protestant Ethic still lives on in some of these countries, particularly in the USA and UK, and it manifests itself in the justifications that some still feel obliged for their consciences' sakes to give for their leisure and non-work acts: what they do is good for their health, or for their character, or exhibits a technical skill that is a self-evident good and might stand them in good stead in the event of some catastrophe.

Advertising gives a massive impetus to leisure activities and to the general orientation towards leisure. Leaving aside the motifs of home and housework displayed in many food and detergent advertisements, the predominant motifs are sex and leisure, the two being equated. Themes of leisure, always of the conspicuous consumption variety, are represented in a fairly large proportion of American and British television programmes, and many of the most popular series have a background of leisure and consumption. Tom Burns has asked if the rituals of leisure have been created to make life worth living or to give it meaning? He argues that in the early phases of industrial society so little free time was permitted that everyday life was swamped by the demands of industry, but in the technical age, social life outside of work has re-emerged: 'It has been created afresh, in forms which are themselves the creatures of industrialism, which derive from it, and which contribute to its development, growth and further ascendancy' (36). He quotes the studies of the Italian sociologist, Pizzorno, that leisure is now a source of moral values that is replacing the values of production and work associated with the bourgeoisie and that the latter were enabled to foist onto the workers. It has taken time for the obvious inappropriateness of such values for the working-class to become apparent; such an ethical system has never reflected the true situation of the industrial proletariat. With the passage of time and the transformations that have resulted in the technical society, a new set of values, leisure values, has arisen as a countersystem to those of the middle-classes. Pizzorno suggests that just as the bourgeois virtues developed as an alternative to the values of the aristocracies, so leisure values have evolved as an alternative to those of the middle classes. Leisure values are the ethics of the affluent worker and of the new technical workers and is reflected in their privatized do-it-yourself lives. Another Italian, Alberoni, argues that the emulation of the middle-classes by the working-class has given way to emulation of a new reference group: the élite of the entertainment industry and the mass media, the pop stars and 'personalities' of radio, television, the cinema, stage and commercialized sport, plus the models, fashion designers and all the other creations of publicity and the image-makers. These are wealthy and live ostentatiously as part of the jet set and millionaires' world; but they are, as Burns calls them, a powerless élite as distinct from the still ruling economic and political élites, although some persons are members of both the powerful and the powerless élite. 'The powerless élite is there to suggest ways of behaviour and to influence popular values without making decisions about them. Although few and privileged, this élite does not constitute a social class or group, and, as such, does not arouse envy or class resentment' (37). Pizzorno and Alberoni describe the adoption of an imitation, as far as possible within their limited means, of the style of life and activities of this leisure élite by others as a means of escape from the pressures of work and the local community and that provides an entrance into a wider world in which one can, to some extent, participate. Every year thousands do so in the form of inexpensive package holidays to Spanish resorts and the Canaries and Mediterranean islands where members of this élite are also to be found, sometimes even in the same or neighbouring hotels, though they stay for three months instead of twelve days. Burns indicates that this style of life based on the leisure and 'fun' people is not just an addition to social and economic life, it is everyday life itself. It helps to account for the failure of human relations in industry and the other schemes related to that approach because 'who cares?' and it assists us to understand why there is the apparent absence of class conflict and why there has been no effective challenge to the power of capital and management. It also explains why the psychotherapeutic ideology has been so successful in obtaining recognition for itself: like leisure pursuits, the psychotherapies turn the individual in upon himself so that he seeks salvation within.

Do leisure activities provide a measure of excitement that would otherwise be missing from our society? The technical society is popularly considered to be singularly unexciting, but this could well be just another of those beliefs that abound with very little evidence to support them. Natural disasters, bad harvests, decimating epidemics are comparatively rare today in the West; the need for great physical effort and manual skills is at a minimum, so much so that a few individuals feel it necessary to sail round the world alone or backwards or counterclockwise in order to make good the deficiency (at a good financial profit too). Crime in some of the affluent societies has reached new high levels in the great cities and is accompanied by violence that leaves the excesses of the eighteenth century out of the running; it is true that the victim is the main one to suffer, though in some of these societies the criminal is likely to be shot down without the benefit of a trial. There has been a considerable degree of public violence in demonstrations and the reactions to them by the forces of the state in large areas of the advanced industrial world, but some of the insecurities of life have been reduced and the welfare schemes of many states relieve living of some of the most distressing burdens though nowhere have they been totally eliminated. All together, and bearing in mind how little we know of the flavour of life in the past, it might not be unreasonable to suppose that social life has become less 'exciting' than in the past. We control our emotions in our private and social life to a degree that was unknown in the past; we seldom participate in the great excitement of national disasters and equally as rarely in great public rejoicings; we have internalized our emotional controls to such an extent that they are now beyond our control. We no longer have any public outlets for emotion and excitement save in the form of organized leisure and entertainment. Leisure gives us today what religion, social myths, and communal ceremonies once gave us.

There are still a few survivals, in attenuated form, of such communal celebrations: *Fasching* in some of the Rhineland districts of Germany, and the drum-beating ceremony at Calandra in Spain. In the old university town of Marburg on the Lahn, the inhabitants of a street called Ketzerbach (built by covering over a stream sometime in the seventeenth century) annually celebrate the building of their street with a beer drinking and singing jamboree that takes place in the open air and lasts for hours. But these examples are mere residues.

The missing ceremonies and celebrations and other forms of emotional release are supplied today by (1) commercialized spectator sports, especially football, boxing, wrestling, rugby football, tennis, and to a lesser degree by athletics, cricket, and by motor car, motor bicycle, and cycle racing: (2) by gambling, often associated with a spectator sport such as horse-racing; (3) dancing, and listening communally to 'pop' at festivals; (4) dramatic entertainment on television, in the theatre, cinema, and on radio; participating in musical events such as promenade concerts in which a great deal of emotion is released from a very large audience also comes in this category. There are variations in these outlets depending on the country: baseball and bull-fighting might take the place of rugger and cricket.

The controls come off temporarily in the mass reactions at

football matches, and in certain forms of dancing which permit unrestrained sexual feeling to display itself, and at 'pop festivals' where sexual emotions and a general wild enthusiasm escape from control.

But what is really important is that these forms of leisure (in the sense that for most of the participants they are non-work) are substitutes for the lost rituals of the past. The great rituals of the past were distinguished by a special order of time; they took place and while they took place, 'ordinary time' or 'working time' was temporarily in abeyance, such rituals were actually 'time out' and ordinary life stopped until their time had been completed. *Fasching* is a good example of this in towns like Cologne and Mainz, not only does everyday life retire for a few days, but most of its conventions too, and for the brief period of the celebrations, strangers talk and bosses and workers meet intimately and all kinds of odd things happen until suddenly it ends and then things return to 'normal' as if the interregnum had never taken place. In a similar way, the football match takes 'time out' and for the duration of the game the rest of the world ceases to exist.

In another way, the ritual of games, sports and entertainments provide what ritual has always done: stability and continuity and the reassurance that all is right with the world; ritual confirms that things do not really change. The rules of the game are the reflections of social pressures, the assurance that the womb of society, of our fellows, is all around us, but within these limits success is possible for one side, reflecting the freedom that society offers to us. A singularly good example of this ritual element is wrestling. Here the good meet the bad. The baddy breaks the rules, the referee is virtually ineffective, and if the goody wins, faith in the stability and justice of life is reaffirmed; if the baddy wins then it is always because he is dirtier or heavier than the goody and in a strange way this is reassuring because his victory could only come through immorality and the penalty for such wickedness is the jeering and booing of the spectators. The ritual nature of wrestling is exemplified in the fact that the bouts usually go the full length and when two baddies meet, the crowd always chooses one as being for the time, at least, an honorary goody. The bouts do not run their full time 'just to please the crowd' in the simple sense of this phrase, but to ensure that the ritual is adequately performed. There is also a Till Eulenspiegel element in spectator sports such as wrestling, and some baddies who are also jokers receive the applause of the spectators but this is reassurance of a different kind, the reassurance that one can make a long nose at authority and, if you are clever enough, get away with it.

What our contemporary leisure activities do, and I mean the organized, ritualized events and also such games as bridge, billiards, golf, as well as the stereotyped entertainment of the Western and the thriller together with the sexual frenzy of 'pop', is to give us a meaning and a reaffirmation of the worthwhile nature of living. An over-excited football crowd that smashes shops, cuts up railway coaches and attacks passers-by might well be demonstrating its 'togetherness', its identification with a group, that is, its group solidarity, as well as its sheer devilry and destructive urges but at the same time it is expressing that it has taken part in a great confirmatory ritual. It is probably true that the quality of life in industrialized society is so poor that the only person that the masses have to identify with is a football star, a Pelé, but this does not detract from the assertion that he is the principal performer in a ritual that affirms all that we hope for from society: a continuity, a meaning, and an eternal rightness.

Apart from the technical phenomenon, how does our society differ from those of the past ? In the first place, it can be assumed that work (meaning what one did in one's non-leisure time) had a significance in so far as it was clearly and unequivocally the means whereby vital wants for oneself and family were satisfied. In order to give work a meaning it is not necessary to postulate anything more than this; any other kind of satisfaction, aesthetic or otherwise, is extra and unimportant in this context. Secondly, time that was freed from work, and this excluded time spent on household chores, rearing children, communal duties and suchlike, was in great part organized around religious and communal ceremonies, festivals and celebrations which affirmed the permanent meaningfulness of life and were connected with the social institutions that Gehlen describes. Thirdly, there was a sacred order expressed in the religion or some ideology of the group that encompassed every aspect of individual and group life and gave meaning to all its manifestations. It is not in question whether such a state of affairs was a good or bad thing, it is, as far as we can know anything of the past, what existed. Life in such circumstances might have been satisfying and of high quality, it might, by our standards, have been awful, but it was a unitary thing. In medieval Christendom there were no public and private spheres, no dichotomy between one sector of life and another, no set of ethical norms that were relevant in one context and irrelevant in another. Right was right in all circumstances, wrong immoral everywhere. This does not imply that people were always moral and righteous, but only that they were quite certain about it when they were not. Nothing was superior to the sacred; nothing had existence apart from its affiliation to the sacred.

In advanced industrial societies work has, for most people, no intrinsic significance. At best, it is a means of 'earning a living', just one among many alternatives. It seems to have an obscure relationship with satisfying vital wants but this is so indirect as to be easily lost sight of. Screwing up nuts in a factory to buy goods in a supermarket with money obtained for the nut-screwing by collective bargaining and at a rate that seems in no way connected with the worth or value of what is being done is a very different thing from tilling a field on a medieval manor. The paper consuming nature of bureaucratized clerical work is even more remote from satisfying vital needs. But there is a tendency to lose sight of the fact that for many people routine work, 'monotonous' work is far from unsatisfying; doing the same thing day after day can be a reassuring ritual that all is well in addition to being pleasurable for other reasons. What is essentially different about most modern forms of work is that its connection with vital needs is so tenuous and obscure, and alternative forms are relatively easy to turn to, and ultimately welfare schemes make the whole business unrealistic.

But the meaninglessness of most peoples' work is not the most important difference between our world and that of yesterday; what is really significant is the absence of a sacred order in which individuals find justification and satisfaction. The absence of such a sacred order means that prestige must come from somewhere else, and it can only come from two sources: power and the ability to command material resources in the form of consumption. It was fashionable some years back to argue that Thorstein Veblen's notion of conspicuous consumption as characterizing the leisure classes or upper classes was a thing of the past (the assumption was based mainly on changes in American car consumption, the richer you were, the less conspicuous your car was but it was forgotten that large inconspicuous cars or small foreign inconspicuous cars as well as discreet Ivy League suits cost a lot of money and everybody knew it) but there seems no reason to think so. The very notion of the powerless élite is based on gross conspicuous consumption, and power, except in a few aberrant cases, accompanied by expensive dwellings, cars, gadgets, leisure pursuits and sexual relations. Failure to achieve a modicum of power and a consumption pattern higher than that of the average leads to dissatisfaction with the working life and a disregard for the working self and to a turning away for self-fulfilment in the private area of life.

The absence of an encompassing religion, philosophy, ideology, or sacred order (the terms are here interchangeable) means that the individual is forever at the edge of the night-side of life (38) and in danger of slipping over and into it. The night-side, the dark side, is the chaos that stands outside of a society, the meaningless, howling wilderness that is kept at a safe distance by a sacred order that gives meaning to human behaviour, the external universe, and the vicissitudes of living and the ultimate phenomenon of dying. Without a sacred order, the rituals cannot be efficacious.

This brings us to the third major difference between ourselves and past societies, our rituals in the form of games, sports, leisure activities, etc. are poor substitutes for the real thing: they give only temporary relief, and the best they can do is prevent us from slipping over the edge—for the time being.

Work is for most meaningless; it is not the source of prestige and self-respect and fulfilment for most of us. We have ritual activities that are inadequate and sustain only briefly. We have a thousand sacred orders, all equally invalid and suspect instead of a single encompassing and supporting one. We are determined by techniques that are means but have become ends in themselves and exert their influence and direction by a kind of innate momentum. Individual and social life is not unitary but fragmented, on the one side there is work, the economic sector, the public sphere of living, while on the other side are the fragments of the private sphere: friends, leisure, sex, family, beliefs, pleasures, in short everything that is not work. For a few, the lucky ones, this dichtomization does not occur. In their case, their work and other interests are bound together in an identity that is created by the occupation and this identity can be carried over into every segment of life. It is not necessary that the work be of a very special nature, though it is reasonable to suppose that the lucky ones are mostly among those who wield power and command prestige, but a few are found among the postmen and craftsmen, bureaucrats and junior executives. What enables an identity to be found at work seems in great part an individual matter that is the result of as yet unknown processes in the individual's socialization, education and development; suffice it here to observe that such processes do not usually succeed in achieving this felicitous result and that what seems to occur is a continuum with the work-confirming identity at one end through infinite graduations of identity weakness and damage down to the other extreme at which work supplies no identity at all.

Only the psychotherapeutic ideology, in lieu of anything better, can provide some support in such a situation as this. It provides an answer and an explanation and the possibility of salvation to those who have found this society too much for them and who have been adrift for too long; it provides a rationale for those who are tolerably able to manage, and a justification for those wielding power.

The twin principles of the psychotherapeutic creed are apposite to the industrialized society: (1) adjustment that means adjustment to the meaninglessness of the external social constraints and phenomena and that is expressed by the 'reality principle', i.e. acceptance of things as they are; (2) finding an identity within oneself with the aid of the salvationist who knows the way into the hidden mysteries of the self. The psychotherapeutic ideology is to the advanced industrialized society what discipline is to an army. The irony lies in the nature of the creed, it is not really an ideology at all, but a technique (39).

Notes and References

1 Andreski, S. L. in Halmos, Paul (ed.), *The Development of Industrial Societies*, *The Sociological Review* Monograph No. 8, University of Keele, 1964, p. 14.

2 Bell, *op. cit.*, pp. 26–7.
3 Simmel, Georg, 'The Metropolis and Mental Life' (1908) in *The Sociology of Georg Simmel*, edited and translated by Kurt Wolff, The Free Press, Glencoe, Illinois, 1950 (Collier-Macmillan, London, 1964). It is interesting to note that Durkheim and Simmel were Jews. Some of Durkheim's interest in order might have been the consequence of his Jewishness and the fact that he came from Alsace, the most anti-Semitic part of France. He also lived through the violence and excesses associated with the various scandals that swept France and often led to outrages against Jews: the Daniel Wilson affair, the Panama Scandal, the Dreyfus Case, and the anti-clerical disturbances as well as some bitter strikes. Simmel, because he was a Jew, had his academic career blocked for years, and the popularity of his lectures only led to sneers from some of his gentile colleagues. He found the lively atmosphere of Berlin with its cosmopolitanism and its relative freedom congenial, and this might have coloured his views on life in big cities.
4 Bell, *op. cit.*, p. 29.
5 See Warner, Malcolm and Stone, Michael, *The Data Bank Society*, Allen & Unwin, London, 1970, and Packard, Vance, *The Naked Society*, McKay, New York, 1964 (Penguin, Harmondsworth, 1970).
6 Shils, Edward A., 'Primordial, Personal, Sacred and Civil Ties', *British Journal of Sociology*, 8 (1957) pp. 130–45; p. 131 and 'The Theory of Mass Society' *Diogenes*, Fall 1962, No. 39.
7 Aron, Raymond, *The Dawn of Universal History*, Weidenfeld and Nicolson, London, 1961, p. 15.
8 *Ibid.*, p. 68.
9 The concept of alienation implies that one is alienated from something. Attempts to ascertain what the thing one is alienated from have been made but without much success; see Clark, J. P., 'Measuring Alienation within a Social System', *American Sociological Review*, XXIV, 6, 1959. For attempts to 'operationalize' the concept, see Dean, D., 'Alienation: Its Meaning and Measurement', *American Sociological Review*, XXVI, 5, 1961. The most readable account of Marx's concept of alienation is to be found in Fromm, Erich, *Marx's Concept of Man*, F. Ungar, New York, 1961. An excellent discussion of the concept of alienation is to be found in Etzioni, Amitai, 'Basic Human Needs, Alienation and Inauthenticity', *American Sociological Review*, 33, December 1968, pp. 870–85.
10 Ellul, Jacques, *The Technological Society*, Jonathan Cape, London, 1965; originally published in France in 1954.
11 This distinction is made by Ellul, and I use his terminology.
12 Ellul, *op. cit.*, p. 20.
13 An example of the 'best way' being ignored and derided at first is provided by the history of the breech-loading naval gun. By 1870 the muzzle-loading gun, although still in favour with the British Army had been outstripped by the development of breech-loading naval

H   225 guns already adopted by some foreign navies, but the British Navy was completely dominated by its army colleagues and refused to admit the greater effectiveness of breech-loaders at sea. In 1872 a 'duel' to demonstrate the superiority of the muzzle-loaders was arranged between two monitors at Portland but the navy's best gunner only succeeded in missing his target at 200 yards. The Naval chiefs were still unconvinced and it was not until 1882 that the first heavy breech-loaders were mounted in a British warship. Ensor, R. C. K., *England 1870–1914*, Oxford University Press, London, 1936, p. 122.

14 Brennan, Mal, *The Making of a Moron*, Sheed, New York, 1953, pp. 13–18.

15 Giedion, Siegfried, *Mechanization Takes Command*, Oxford University Press, New York, 1948.

16 If only one knew what was meant by 'community', but the definitions are too numerous to quote. If we assume, as we must, that 'the community' is a fiction or hypothetical construction, we are in danger of gross reification if we forget this. In recent years, social workers have been prone to see 'community' in the coming together of the inhabitants of an area to protest, fight or lobby for some specific cause or other, they then proudly point to the emergence of 'community' or 'community feeling' or 'spirit', but I submit that this is a misconception of the idea of 'community' and what they are describing is what Herbert Blumer ('Collective Behaviour' in Park, R. E. (ed.), *An Outline of the Principles of Sociology*, Barnes and Noble, New York, 1939, pp. 221–80) calls 'publics'. 'Public' is a term applicable to groups or aggregates who engage in controversy about issues; to assume that out of this develops or arises those special qualities described by diverse authors as 'community' is merely begging the question. For a critique of attempts to promote 'community' by participation in local controversies see Zimpel, Gisela, *Der beschäftigte Mensch—Beiträge zur sozialen und politischen Partizipation*, Juventa Verlag, München, 1970, in which she asks, 'Is political participation only occupational therapy ?'.

17 Ellul, *op. cit.*, p. 320.

18 Maieutic is a term used by Ellul, and means a method of teaching that brings into consciousness what is already present in the mind but hidden in its recesses.

19 *Ibid.*, p. 348.

20 The jargon of psychotherapy for this is 'working with' people, and it is the same phrase that potters use when they talk about 'working with' clay.

21 Quoted by Ellul, *op. cit.*, p. 348.

22 *Ibid.*, p. 353.

23 *Ibid.*, p. 356; Goodman, Paul, *Growing Up Absurd*, Random House, New York, 1960 (Sphere, London, 1970).

24 *Ibid.*, p. 376.

25 *Ibid.*, p. 377.

THE NATURE OF TECHNOLOGICAL SOCIETY

26 Schelsky, Helmut, *Die sozialen Folgen der Automatisierung*, Diederichs, Köln und Düsseldorf, 1957.

27 Generally the French and German usage of 'technology' refer to the *study of techniques and technical means*, while the English usage confuses 'technics', i.e. actual techniques and their application with 'technology'.

28 Gehlen, Arnold, *Die Seele im technischen Zeitalter*, Rowohlt, Hamburg, 1957; 'Ein Bild vom Menschen' in *Anthropologische Forschung*, Rowohlt, Hamburg, 1961, pp. 44–54; Jonas, Friedrich, *Die Institutionenlehre Arnold Gehlens*, Mohr (Paul Siebeck), Tübingen, 1966; Lepenies, Wolf, 'Handlung und Reflexion, Aspekte der Anthropolgie Arnold Gehlens', *Soziale Welt*, 18 (1967), pp. 41–66; Zeltner, Hermann, 'Dilemma der Freiheit zur Philsophie Arnold Gehlens', *Soziale Welt*, 18 (1967), p. 67; Berger, Peter L., and Kellner, Hansfried, 'Arnold Gehlen and the Theory of Institutions', *Social Research*, Vol. 32, No. 1, Spring 1965, pp. 110–15.

29 See Uexküll, Jacob von, und Kriszat, Georg, *Streifzüge durch die Umwelten von Tieren und Menschen*, Rowohlt, Hamburg, 1956, especially the Foreword by Adolf Portmann.

30 Berger, Peter L., *The Sacred Canopy*, Doubleday, New York, 1967, pp. 85–7.

31 Holz, Hans Heinz, 'Die verschleierte Klassengesellschaft' in Kruger, Horst (ed.), *Was ist Heute Links?* List Verlag, München, 1963.

32 Habermas, Jürgen, *Technik und Wissenschaft als 'Ideologie'*, Suhrkamp Verlag, Frankfurt am Main, 1968.

33 Offe, Claus, 'Politische Herrschaft und Klassenstrukturen' in Kress, Gisela, und Senghaas, Dieter (eds), *Politikwissenschaft*, Europäische Verlags Anstalt, Frankfurt am Main, 1969.

34 It has been suggested that differences between American and British youth in respect of occupational and leisure expectations stem from the differences in social mobility in the two cultures: in the UK it is 'sponsored' social mobility while in the USA it is 'contest' mobility. See Turner, R. H., 'Sponsored and Contest Mobility and the School System', *American Sociological Review*, 25, 6 December 1960, pp. 855–67.

35 Dumazedier, J., *Towards a Society of Leisure*, Collier-Macmillan, London, 1967.

36 Burns, Tom, 'A Meaning in Everyday Life', *New Society*, 25 May 1967, pp. 260–2; p. 261.

37 *Ibid.*, p. 261.

38 The term is borrowed from Peter L. Berger.

39 Halmos, Paul, 'Sociology and the Personal Service Professions', *American Behavioural Scientist*, March/April 1971, Vol. 14, No. 4, pp. 583–97, especially p. 584 on techniques in social work.

Chapter 8

Fulfilment Through Sex

If personal identity cannot be created at work and, as we have already noted, this is a rare achievement, then it must be discovered elsewhere and the most likely areas in which this can be done are those of leisure and non-work. Most of us are not creative artists, do not possess much musical talent and only in relatively few cases have the kind of skill that enables us to excel in sports. Some may find their 'real' selves in gardening or even in washing and polishing the car on Sunday mornings; others might find them in the mileages achieved in the shortest possible time during their annual fortnight's holiday; the intense pleasure that some people seem to obtain from driving from one place to another in the fewest number of hours should not be too harshly denigrated though it is hard to believe that such feats create a satisfactory identity. For most people there are, however, two areas that offer this possibility: sex and the family. These are not necessarily separate; conjugal sex can provide an identity and this is the kind of sex advocated by the psychotherapeutic ideologists, but identities can also be created by extra-marital sex and this is another form of identity creation that the psychotherapeutic ideology has helped, unintentionally, to produce because of its influence in destroying or weakening those moral and sexual taboos that previously had restricted this kind of activity to those who did not care about social censure or were powerful enough to flout it.

It does not require much perspicacity to see that our society is sex-obsessed. A trite observation that contains within it the assumption that other societies are not and were not. About past societies, even our own historical past, it is not possible to say; as for other contemporary societies, they form what is virtually one culture if we omit the Communist Bloc. What we have witnessed growing in intensity since the end of the First World War is the

228

sexualization of everything. This is the unique feature of our culture, not that we are 'sexier' than in the past or more inclined to 'fun' but that a pinch or two of sex is required dressing with almost every aspect of our lives—sexual objectification is paramount in the mass media. It cannot be attributed to any one factor. It is as silly to find its origin in some Freudian revolution as in some vast advertising conspiracy; a number of disparate elements have come together and contributed to the great myth of sexual relations, but the single most influential one is the secularization that has accompanied the growth of technique. The 'disenchantment' of our terrestrial existence some generations back, and now the 'disenchantment' of space, coupled with the evidence of man's omnipotence, have displaced and rendered untenable religious views of human life and its nature. Nothing, however, has replaced them and the lack has compelled us to turn inwards to those areas of intimacy created by sexual relationships within and without the family. A meaning to everyday life, or a rejection of senselessness in everyday life, can now come about for most people only through sex and familism. 'Proper' sexual relations are as self-evidently worthwhile and desirable as the family, and how else can a meaning be given to living and the social order be saved from falling apart?

The part that the psychotherapists have played and the impetus given to the sexualization of life by the psychotherapeutic ideology must be conceded as one of their major achievements. It stems quite simply from the Freudian contention that neuroses have a markedly sexual content and that disturbances of sexuality originate in the family: the family is the setting for neuroses, all of which have a sexual component that is determinative. Subsequent developments in psychotherapy have changed the emphasis a little and these changes have found expression in the work and attitudes of practitioners, but on the whole the earlier clinical findings have remained an accepted canon. The problems with which the social caseworker deals: delinquency, fecklessness, 'dropping-out', marital conflict, inadequacy and 'maladjustment' are all traceable to the dual sources of family disorganization and conflict and sexuality expressed in infancy, and in relations at both early and later stages with parents and siblings. The counsellor-social caseworker bases his techniques on a set of beliefs that have as their main axioms: (1) sex is a component and determinant of all human behaviour; (2) sex is the determining factor in all neuroses; (3) the family is the location in which infantile sexuality manifests itself and in which the Oedipus complex and the Electra complex (term denoting the oedipal feelings of females) originate; the family and child-rearing are thus of paramount importance for the personality of the individual; (4) because of (3) the family is the major source of good and evil in life: it is the locus of the making or marring of an individual. The significance of the sexual component has, in part, been concealed under a mass of verbiage about its nature, about genitality, sexuality, libido and so forth by which the definition of the sexual element swings from what is essentially a life-enhancing drive at one extreme to what the man-in-the-street usually means by sex at the other. These interminable pages of turgid hair-splitting and logic-chopping have only previously been equalled by the discussions of medieval theologians, and are as absorbing to the clerics of psychotherapy as they are boring to the laity. As the esoteric nature of the original formulations of psychoanalysis have been simplified, even to a certain extent bowdlerized, in order to meet the needs of popularization for the benefit of rank and file social workers and the general public, so the sexual factors have tended to be toned-down and the familial elements played-up; a process in which the post-Freudian concentration on ego-psychology and 'character disorders' has played a big part. The works of Erikson, who has become the gospeller of these later developments in the psychotherapeutic ideology, concentrate markedly on the family and child-rearing but in spite of this, the basic orientation has not changed. The new avant garde psychiatrists such as Cooper and Laing lay a similar emphasis on the family and so continue the currently fashionable trend. But sexuality is still a key concept and is fundamental to the 'devaluation' that is at the heart of counselling insight, and it is also vital in the transmission of the values of the ideology to those undergoing induction into the ranks of the ideologists. In observing training seminars for intending youth counsellors and teacher-counsellors, I have noticed that the older members of both groups often put up quite strong resistance to accepting the notions of infantile sexuality (that tiny infants have strong sexual drives and manifest them long before true genital sexuality has developed) and oedipal feelings (incestuous feelings), while the younger either accept them without question or display indifference; though it is significant that there are a few of the younger ones who show resistance as well, and they are more frequent among the teachers than among the youth workers.

The controversies over what Freud meant by sexual can be by-passed if we accept the opinion of G. Seaborn Jones (himself pro-Freud):

'It is widely assumed that Freud's extension of the concept "sexual" was arbitrary and perverse, whereas it was due to the scientific discovery that the core of neuroses (as opposed to its superficies) can best be modified by the therapist who treats the symptoms "in the same way as things normally called sexual". But this is merely the technological aspect. It is necessary to add that for the purpose of *understanding the origin* of neurotic symptoms, as well as for therapeutic purposes, the analyst needs to treat them in the same way as things normally called sexual' (1).

Among the Neo-Freudians, Sullivan does not mention infantile sexuality, and assumes that sexuality makes its appearance in the early period of adolescence, while Fromm claims that the Oedipus complex is not so much concerned with sexuality as with authority and the reactions to it, and though it is a fundamental element in interpersonal relations, its incestuous aspect is secondary (2). Karen Horney doubted the universality Freud assigned to the Oedipus complex and the significance that Freud gave to the sexual element in it: she argued that the dependency of infancy might take on a sexual tinge, but that sexuality is the usual accompaniment to an attempt to relieve anxiety, so the sexuality manifested in the Oedipus complex is really an example of the neurotic need for affection, and later signs of the oedipal conflict indicate disturbed interpersonal relations rather than sexual difficulties (3). These views represent a change of emphasis towards the family and interpersonal relationships that is so strongly marked in today's psychotherapeutic ideology and that Marcuse criticizes as part of the reversal of Freudian theory that is turning psychoanalysis into a programme protective of the cultural constraints that characterize our type of society (4). Abram

Kardiner denies the importance of the sexual relationship in the parent-child configuration but stresses the importance in general of sexual gratification for which he claims there is no substitute, and argues strongly in favour of a reconstruction of our sexual mores as they no longer serve the needs of social survival. He stresses the need for status and success and that this need includes sexual success as well as economic and other forms that bring prestige. Sexual inadequacy or disability means losing the status race in this particularly important sphere because failure in sexual relations in Western society can be a blow to pride and self-respect that can bring on anxieties that can break up the individual's link with his fellows; thus sexual relations can become competitive and exploitative as well as being a means of self-enhancement (5). Alexander, like Sullivan, tends to minimize the significance of sexuality in favour of drives towards stability and security, one achieving the necessities basic for survival by adaptation, and another towards creativity and novelty (6). The directions of contemporary psychotherapy are fairly indicated in the writings of these Neo-Freudians: more emphasis is laid on family and relationships between persons, and on the struggle for status, security, and identity in the public as well as in the private sphere. Guntrip gives expression to these views:

'We are thus not tied down to Freud's conclusions that a relaxation of cultural and moral standards is the only escape from neurosis for the majority. The position is rather that cultural and moral standards, which, however, need to be subjected to rational and enlightened criticism and development, are, at their best, an expression of the way in which reasonably mature individuals behave, the way in which in fact Freud himself behaved in private life. . . . It is because neurosis is already there that reasonable moral standards cannot be lived up to. Relaxation of moral standards could be called for as a concession to the ubiquitous low level of mental health in all communities, but is not called for as a concession to the innate instincts of reasonably mature and healthy-minded persons. The notion that civilization rests on the renunciation of instincts is a misleading ideology that there is now urgent need to discard' (7).

This statement of faith is almost pre-Freudian and indicates quite clearly how far from Freud the ideologists have gone and it also indicates the new conformity that they have assumed in their role of defenders of the existing social order. To deny the Freudian claim that civilization rests on the renunciation of instinctual drives is to destroy the sociological theory implicit in Freud's work.

But the vulgarizations of Freud that led to his being condemned as a 'pan-sexualist' are still paramount among the laity, especially the notion of the dangers connected with 'frustration of the sexual impulses' about which Frankl has this to say:

'The shibboleth of sexual frustration is occasionally called forth for purposes of sexual propaganda. In this sense it is a misconception and vulgar misinterpretation of psychoanalysis. The implication is that the ungratified sex instinct itself—rather than the repression of that instinct—must necessarily lead to neurosis. The harmfulness of sexual abstinence has been preached to youth. Such doctrines have done a good deal of injury by nourishing neurotic sexual anxiety. The slogan has been sexual intercourse at any cost, even among young people . . .' (8).

This, he argues, has been conducive to a premature entry into sexuality which impedes the transformation at a later stage of mere sexuality into eroticism. Eroticism, for Frankl, is midway between sexuality that is focused on the purely physical (sexuality) and ignores the individuality and the personality of the sexually desired person, and love that transcends the physical elements. Eroticism is a stage at which the purely physical still exerts a powerful influence but there does exist some inkling of the nature of the person who is the object of the desire; 'the merely sexual attitude is directed towards the partner's physical being and does not wish to go beyond this. The erotic attitude, the attitude of infatuation, is directed towards the psychic being; but it too does not penetrate to the core of the other person . . .' (9).

Erikson, whose book *Childhood and Society* has become the bible of the psychotherapeutic creed, plays down the role of sexuality and deprecates the exaggerations of psychoanalysis: 'While psychoanalysis has on occasion gone too far in its emphasis on genitality as a universal cure for society and has thus provided a new addiction and a new commodity for many who wished to so interpret its teaching, it has not always indicated all the goals that genitality actually should and must imply.' The goals (discussed below) are such as to win the approval of women's magazines the Western world over, but even the most uncritical reader could ask why the *should* and *must* appear in the sentence (10).

What is so ironic is that the liberating doctrines of early psycho-analysis, the new ideas that were held to be keys to release man from self-punishment and guilt without rational foundations has now turned into a new tyranny. On the one side we have all those who are desperately concerned about their sexual adequacy, and on the other side we have those parents, especially mothers, equally anxious about the quality of their affection for their children and their child-rearing methods. If there are no children to a marriage, then the couple are faced with the probability of snide remarks about the husband's virility, or they are accused of being 'immature' in not taking on the responsibilities of a family and in avoiding the demands as well as foregoing the satisfactions connected with it. Gone are the days when a childless marriage was merely an indication that in this respect God had withheld his blessing. Personnel managers probe the love life of applicants for executive appointments, and if they do not, then the applicant makes efforts to ensure that the interviewer knows that he (or she) has one. In interviewing intending students for social work courses, it is interesting to note how defensive the boy or girl becomes if the conversation turns on relations with the opposite sex and the candidate has no girl-friend (or boy-friend, as the case may be). Similarly defensive reactions are to be observed if the candidate does not show keenness to leave home, or denies serious differences with parents. The tenets of the psychotherapeutic faith have brought into existence a new conformity equally as anxiety-creating and inhibiting as the old ever was. This defen-siveness on the part of the young who do not come up to psy-chotherapeutic ideals is not confined to would-be social work students (who are often wise to what they are expected to say to impress interviewers) but is apparent, though to a lesser degree, in candidates for other types of course.

One of the effects of the relaxation of repressive sexual conventions has been to put a considerable, and new, burden on men; they have to face a fourfold set of demands that have been assiduously supported by the mass media, contemporary novels, popularizations of psychoanalysis, and even by psychoanalytic and psychotherapeutic works that achieve the same consequences though they were not intended as popularizations; to these must be added the general attitudinal climate generated by the psychotherapeutic ideology. It is, no doubt, the journalism and the vulgarizations that are directly to blame, but the psychoanalytic-psychotherapeutic movement itself cannot be exonerated from responsibility.

Men have to satisfy themselves and their partners sexually; this is a *moral obligation* that equals in its force the Christian doctrine that sexual intercourse is wicked unless it has as its aim the production of babies in holy matrimony. Sex that does not gratify the partner is an evil and immoral act is a cardinal belief of the new socially acceptable morality (sexual behaviour that is deviant and satisfying is not widely approved). The compulsion that is attached to this new stance is just as conducive to intolerance and anxiety as any of the earlier and now outmoded sexual codes.

As a corollary of the above proposition, men have to cultivate their skills at making love; they enter into competition in which their self-respect is at stake. They must not fall below a norm of sexual competence that is often a product of fantasy; Morton M. Hunt quotes the case of a man whose wife complained of his sexual inadequacy because he could not delay ejaculation for more than an hour during coitus. On consulting a physician, he was surprised to learn that his wife's expectation was grossly exaggerated and she had nothing to complain of on this score (11). Beliefs about the nature of the sexual potentials of men and women have not been rendered more rational and better founded on evidence by the psychotherapeutic ideology; folk beliefs about the nature of the sexual drives in the two sexes abound, not only among the laity but among the psychotherapists too. The crude biological fact that a woman is *physically* capable of sexual intercourse at any time, while a male *must* receive adequate stimulation to achieve erection is generally ignored even when it is known. The need to be a good performer, which includes being a 'sophisticated' one, probably accounts for the immense success of comparison literature, especially the more boring statistical variety such as the Kinsey Reports.

Thirdly, the men have to cope with sexually 'liberated' women, that is women who make demands based on the ideas that are in fashion at the moment, and who also believe the prevailing myths about their own sexuality. The educated, middle-class woman is probably aware of the latest psychotherapeutic views on her sexuality, and is also a partisan in the controversies over kinds of orgasm; she has read her Masters and Johnson as well as the latest psychiatric work in readable form (or a journalistic account of those that are unreadable). The working-class and lower middle-class woman derives her notions from the women's magazines and those for teenage girls as well as from the popular press. Magazines catering for teenagers, such as *Petticoat* and *Mirabelle*, contain a very large quantity of popular psychotherapeutic ideas, while the glossies such as *Nova* are full of them. Apart from magazines specifically directed at women, there are the newspapers, particularly the 'quality' Sundays and their colour supplements that set out to enlighten men as well as women about sex just as enthusiastically as they do about cooking, antiques, and wallpapers.

Finally there is the 'sexual goldfish bowl' (12) in which men have to live today, undergoing a continuous assessment and evaluation of their performances by friends, colleagues and acquaintances; the opposite of the Victorian obscurity is the contemporary searchlight that is directed onto every aspect of sexual relations. In addition to what occurs in personal circles, there is the spotlight of the entertainment industry focused on sex, from the box-office hits of Hollywood, always greeted as 'adult' and as reaching new heights of artistry and creativity to dirty little jokes of public house and club smutty comedians about impotence and how many times a week, day or hour 'one has it off' (13). There is a constant reminder of the possibility of sexual inadequacy to haunt the male, plus a barrage of sex-loaded material to ensure that he never escapes and that his anxiety is kept up to a high point.

The psychotherapeutic ideology is one of the factors in the sex-obsession that characterizes our society in spite of the changing emphasis of recent years; it is the 'Marxism' of psychology. As Marx postulated that the economic was fundamental to all other aspects of social life, so the psychoanalytic-therapeutic faith assumes the supremacy of sex; it is the basis upon which the entire edifice of human behaviour is erected. It also provides an outlet for those energies dammed up in the automated, computerized industrial processes of today and the unsatisfying roles played by people in them. The psychotherapeutic ideology provides a justification and a legitimation for our interest in and absorption with sexual matters, they are, after all, the basic ingredients of personal life failing all else. It also provides us with an incentive: by plunging into these inner depths we are doing a good thing, we are laying the foundations for a happy personal existence, ensuring a happy family, and ultimately making social life better by stripping it of the repressive, harmful, neurosis-creating sexual taboos of an earlier age. There is here clearly an affinity between the needs of industrialized society for a contented, stable, quiescent and acquiescent 'work force' (the industrialists and economists love military metaphors) and psychotherapeutic ideals that turn us inwards to find fulfilment in sex for the deficiencies that otherwise cannot be made good. There is, however, an apparent paradox here, parts of the sexual revolution have escaped from the psychotherapeutic cage: the first is sexuality for its own sake, i.e. Frankl's mere sexuality and to some extent his eroticism also, and that movement that is usually called women's liberation.

Freud might or might not have been a pan-sexualist, but he was certainly no libertarian or advocate of promiscuity. Kardiner and Fromm are agreed that Freud had no intention of undermining the overt sexual mores of Europe, and never recommended sexual profligacy as either a preventive or curative measure for neurosis. Fromm accuses Freud of having lamented sexual repression but, being a conservative, he had not advocated any drastic changes in the society that encouraged such a repressive sexual code. What Freud indicated was that the prevailing sexual code of his day and culture demanded sacrifices by individuals that were not worthwhile in terms of human suffering, and that were not based on honesty or wisdom but mainly on hypocrisy. He never advocated anything more than an internal coming-to-terms with the demands of society without feeling overwhelming guilt at having transgressed: emancipation from current sexual standards was an individual psychic matter that did not affect, or was designed to affect, the external social situation: 'I should go so far as to say that revolutionary children are not desirable from any point of view', he said in his *New Introductory Lectures* (14). Nothing in Freud's work should encourage 'permissiveness', 'sleeping-around' or any of the other present-day manifestations of the sexual revolution, but ever since the popularizations of psychoanalysis began to appear it has been easy to lay the blame for neurotic symptoms (or whatever term is the fashionable equivalent) on sexual repression in childhood and to advocate the abandonment of sexual taboos (old style) in favour of a general tolerance of what was previously forbidden. The tolerance itself is partly engendered by the publicity given to what was formerly unspeakable and partly because 'to understand is to forgive' or at least condone. In addition a kind of voyeurism has appeared in the social sciences and in journalistic works having a connection with them that takes the form of intensive 'case studies' of other peoples' sexual behaviour and is disseminated in best-sellers, magazine articles and television documentaries (15). The commercialization of sex through the mass media, pop songs and dances, advertising, and even sociology, has powerfully assisted the development of sex as a 'currency' in competition between men and women and in the growth of stereotypes. Sex for men, perhaps for women too, is symbolized in the model, 'dolly', previously the chorus girl and now the pin-up whose individuality is lost in the demand for the right 'vital' statistics and the appropriate facial expression. This is part of the current depersonalization of sex that accompanies its commercialization and is exemplified in the 'sex-as-fun syndome', i.e. it is a simple, natural function that should be exercised without guilt because it has no personal (with adequate contraceptives) consequences any more than it has social or moral consequences that could possibly legitimately inhibit this glorious frolic. The sexual stimuli that come from the mass media, popularizations and advertising are a constant reminder that sex is fun, sex is the great liberator and the most important thing in life. It sells cigars, cider, peanuts and motor-cars, even the B.O. advertisements make it quite clear that soap is important in getting the right girl, and teeth are only to be cleaned because that gives the girls the 'ring of confidence' that enables them to get the right men. Even the monks that manufacture Chartreuse liqueur have to fight their distributors to keep sex out of the advertisements for 'Green Fire'. The pin-ups in the evening newspapers are a constant reminder that this is what living is really all about, and if it does not mean that to you, then you are not 'normal'.

Quite outside all this is the women's liberation movement, because on this issue of the sexuality of women, the Freudians, the Neo-Freudians, the fuddy-duddies and the authoritarians are all agreed: women are inferior, their function is mothering, and their sexuality is very, very odd indeed.

But how far has the sexual revolution really gone ? Probably not very far if we may judge from the amount of work that psychotherapists still seem to have. (Here a word of caution: we have no accurate figures upon which to base a comparison of past and present, and we know very little about the way in which an occupation can create a demand for its services.) Either the rejection of Victorian sexual taboos has been greatly over-estimated or the new freedoms produce as many 'neurotic' conditions as the old repressions ever did. There is another alternative explanation: the old Protestant Ethic that has transformed leisure into work might have transformed sex into work too, and as Freud noted, man does not like working and avoids it if he can.

The greatest single factor, aside from secularization, in the evolution of the dogma of fulfilment of self through sex is probably technicized society itself. It demands a very high psychic investment from its members, unless they wish to vegetate, but against this contingency the technicized society has developed potent weapons. For the middle and lower classes to vegetate is difficult because the cultural imperatives of prestige, wealth, acquisition and consumption, and competition militate against doing so. To a lesser degree, but still significantly, the working classes are also driven away from vegetating by the commands to consume issuing from the mass media, advertising, and the state. The investment does not always show a profit, in most cases a profit is either lacking or negligible, only the lucky few, that is relatively few compared with the vast numbers employed, obtain a good return. The circumstances that render the investment negative are many and various and it is only possible to indicate a few that may be more important, because commoner, than others: skills that become obsolescent; social and economic conditions that are outside the control of the individual and usually beyond the control of the industry in which he works and the government under which he lives; the arbitrary actions of employers and superiors; and finally, the limited nature of the individual's own capacities and abilities. All these and many others make the possibility of achieving success and satisfaction in one's job doubtful, precarious and, above all, capricious.

As the processes of automation and computerization proceed, so the number of skills that become obsolete increases. The possibility of being able to develop new skills depends on factors mostly outside the control of the individual concerned: his native ability may not be sufficient; there may be no opportunities offered; he may be too old to adapt to new requirements; he may not have the necessary education; he may be psychologically unable to make the changes required. The earthly paradise that the optimists predicted would be the outcome of the modernization of techniques, that work would be reduced to a few hours a week, that surplus labour would be taken up in the tertiary sector, that everybody would have several jobs and several skills (oddly Marxist ideas for capitalist technologists to put forward), that leisure would provide the satisfaction, and so forth, has shown no sign of coming about.

The ups and downs of economic activity, the complicated antics of the economic system, exert an overpowering influence on the individual and are apparently as unpredictable and uncontrollable as ever before. The shattering consequences of the boom and bust of the first forty years of the present century are certainly reduced by the war economy that exists to some extent in every country of the West, but the 'pockets' of unemployment, the 'development areas', inflation, and the other economic sicknesses that we are seemingly still unable to deal with probably have a cumulative and long-term effect that is not far short of that of the more dramatic disasters of the past. Security of employment and some stability in real wages are still goals to be achieved. When economic pressures close a shipyard or taxation robs the worker of all incentive to taxable work, these phenomena are the result of external human forces over which the individual has no control, and unlike natural forces such as drought, earthquake, floods and pestilence, *they need have no end*. Natural forces create disasters that destroy, but if the individual survives, he knows that ultimately the forces of nature change direction or temporarily exhaust themselves and disaster, like time, must have a stop. But with the man-made horrors there is no such historical assurance. The individual is helpless before the mindlessness of natural events, but they work themselves out; the mindlessness of men obeys no such laws.

The contemporary bureaucratized large scale organization that is the representative employer of most people in the West is often discussed as if its running was an example of efficiency and smooth functioning. Anybody not blinded by self-interest or suffering from intellectual myopia can easily see for himself that this is not so. It is not necessary to subscribe to any sociological theories of the 'metaphysical pathos' of bureacracy or to plunge into the viscous verbosity of those who write endlessly on 'organization theory' (16) to appreciate that arbitrary and personal decisions are taken by those in power to promote, reward and advance individuals. The small scale employer is probably no less arbitrary, and in both instances the manifest injustice of many rewards is such as to deprive a great number of employees of any real satisfaction in their jobs or much self-respect from pursuing them.

The limited nature of the capacities of the individual have, it can be safely argued, always existed, so what is so strange about the present situation? The answer is that modern industrialization does not permit the cultivation and utilization of many of the capacities that are present in large numbers of people. The economic system of the past relied heavily on skills that were fairly widely diffused throughout the population and there is no need to harp on them here. We are all well enough aware that in the past the skills of craftsman, hunter, fisherman and farmer were common enough and permitted the individual to come to terms with his environment directly through the medium of his skill. Today such skills that are common are unwanted; for most jobs little or no skill is required and for many of the others the skill that is needed is relatively scarcely distributed among the population. A relationship with the environment through one's skill is even rarer. A merchant navy first officer recently told me that to be an officer on a very large cargo vessel today hardly demanded any of the seaman's traditional skills; almost everything including loading and navigation was done by computer, and the first officer's job was more like that of a welfare worker than anything else.

In the occupational situation that exists now, consciously or otherwise, men find it wiser to seek fulfilment from sources other than their work, and where else is there better than in the private sphere or what the Germans call the *Intimasphäre* of the family and sex?

Outside this private sphere it is scarcely possible for an individual, unless fortunately placed, to be independent because the nature of industrialized society makes him interdependent to a degree that is quite unlike anything found outside 'primitive', pre-literate societies. We have the same kind of sink or swim together dependence on each other that has not existed save among the simpler peoples. The individual can only come to terms with his environment today through social organization, since his environment is now mainly man-made. Technique calls for organization otherwise it cannot function, and the environment it constructs for itself brings into being organizations of a social and economic nature so that men can 'function' like bits of mechanism within them. Technique has brought us a long way from the loose interdependence characteristic of traditional societies of craftsmen and peasants.

The well-adjusted individual will, according to psychotherapy, accept his position in this network of interlocking and alienating organizations within which he will work effectively and without being consciously unhappy; being also 'mature', he will be married, stay married, and enjoy sexual intercourse in marriage. This is the current psychotherapeutic ideal, and under the influence of the less clinically minded leaders of the psychotherapeutic ideology it is not surprising that there have been changes made in earlier Freudian formulations. Concerned, even preoccupied, with what they conceive to be the social task of psychotherapy, the post-Freudian ego-psychologists have modified Freud's original conceptions that did little to display concern for the wider social 'problems' that worry our contemporaries. Freud's work was primarily clinical. His ideal was the 'genital character', an individual who has been fully and successfully analysed, whose Oedipus complex has been resolved and who has passed through the mystical transmuting process of 'working through' the ambivalence of his pre-genital stages and has achieved the post-ambivalent genital level of psychosexual development. He will be free from all infantile dependence: he will treat his sexual partner's satisfaction as being equal to his own, thus showing neither sadism (preferring his own satisfaction) nor masochism (putting greater value on hers than on his own; ideally, the satisfactions should be equal); he may or may not be married; he will have frequent intercourse but will not change partners too often; he will not be anxious or feel guilty about doing any of these things though he will have a proper respect for the outward forms of conformity, i.e. he will be discrete not blatant, and at all times aware of the 'reality' around him; needless to say, he will be heterosexual. Altogether the 'genital character' seems rather like someone out of a Schnitzler novel or a discreet and circumspect English gentleman of the 1890s. There is a kind of élitist disdain in this concept of being able to cope with society's moralizing and condemnatory tendencies while enjoying oneself moderately while the partner enjoys herself, moderately, too.

But for those who see themselves as the saviours of society as well as of their fellows individually, restorers of the sacred conjugal hearth, worshippers of the idea of community, and who express themselves in language that comes close to the slop of digests and women's magazines, such a character has to be modified—it would not do for everybody to go around like a tolerant and cultivated Viennese gentleman of the end of the last century—so our 'mature adjusted' character has a wife, enjoys intercourse with her and makes sure she enjoys it as much as he does, raises a family satisfactorily (i.e. in accordance with the precepts of Dr Spock) and only gets a divorce if his wife is 'immature', and as soon as decently possible, after, he marries again but this time to a suitably 'mature' partner. Not very different from the conventional Victorian ideal save that divorce replaces a timely death.

It is properly within this context of adjustment and maturity that the psychotherapeutic ideology envisages the individual as achieving fulfilment, sexual as well as in other respects. Promiscuity, 'sleeping around', the wilder aspects of sex are certainly no part of this ideology as expressed by the caseworkers and counsellors though by their carefully nurtured tolerance, when it is real as well as apparent, they are, by their non-judgmental attitude, bound to 'accept' people who do all these things. Their attitude is conducive to a certain permissiveness. They come up against people who subscribe to the doctrine popularized by the vulgarizations of Freud, that frequent heterosexual intercourse is a worthwhile end in itself and an essential element in human well-being and the source of identity. Even when it is conceded that the vulgarizations grossly exaggerate the permissive nature of Freud's ideas, it still has to be admitted that psychoanalysis created, partly at least, an atmosphere in which sexuality could be discussed without undue restraint and with less hypocrisy than before and to which people could give verbal expression to the pleasure they derived from sexual relations (provided they were of a respectable kind). The subsequent progress of these ideas so as to form the bases for the psychotherapeutic ideology has resulted in the creation of a fresh climate of opinion expressive of a new conformity and a new code of conventions that can hardly be said to be an improvement on the older variety without a lot of intellectual gymnastics. The devaluation that is implicit in 'insight' and 'interpretation' has led to an easy way of destroying the reputations and credibility of those of whom one disapproves: 'character assassination' is not confined to literary critics and biographers. Furthermore, 'deviance' from the norms of 'adjustment' and 'maturity', described as 'maladjustment' and 'immaturity' or 'infantility' are subject to censure that is all the harder to bear because firstly it cannot be refuted (this is well put in the commonly heard saying that against a psychiatrist 'you can't win'), and secondly it strikes at the very roots of the individual's self-respect. Bachelors and spinsters, i.e. the celibate, are 'abnormal', they may even be perverted; the unhappily married are 'immature', those who apparently have a successful 'sex life' (the term is odd enough, indicating a life beside the others) are admired, though with the reservation that it may not really be true. The connection of sex and 'mental health' is such as to create a tyranny quite as oppressive as that of Victorian morality but even more difficult to circumvent. In the past individuals suffered from the social stigma of being profligate, promiscuous and immoral, today they suffer from feelings of inadequacy and discomfort if they do not indulge sufficiently in the pleasures of sex and even more if they do not greatly value or enjoy those pleasures. An element of the Protestant Ethic persists in Anglo-Saxon culture that tends to convert 'can' into 'ought' and 'might' into 'should', to transform leisure into a kind of work; we have to work at our pleasures and justify them. To a certain extent this tendency applies to sex, we have a 'compulsion' to sexuality that smacks of the Puritan though it is anathema to him. We have to work hard at our sex life because it indicates maturity, adjustment, being complete, having an identity, being a full and contributing member of the community; sex is justified in terms of mental health, as a path to personal salvation and the discovery of the 'real me'; it can even be legitimated as a leisure time activity, a sport for which one can be trained and exercised and then re-justified on the grounds that it is a sport (17).

The ideal of genitality that the psychotherapeutic ideology puts forward is that formulated by Erikson: 'In order to be of lasting social significance, the Utopia of genitality should include: mutuality of orgasm with a loved partner of the opposite sex with whom one is able and willing to share a mutual trust and with whom one is able and willing to regulate the cycles of work, procreation, recreation so as to secure to the offspring, too, all the stages of a satisfactory development' (18). Sentiments with which *Reader's Digest* and *Woman's Own* would agree, even with the words in which they are expressed. The ideal would also have found favour with most medieval churchmen and our Victorian grandparents, only Schnitzler's character might have smiled, a little ironically but with tolerance.

More fundamental than anything else in the legacy of psychoanalysis is the belief that the innermost nature of man is unknown to himself, that some knowledge of this hidden self is necessary to psychic (and physical) well-being, and this can only be gained through introspection. But solitary introspection cannot achieve this knowledge, the assistance of a trained analyst is required to detect the subterfuges and rationalizations that the individual puts forward to guard his secret self. The analyst, by virtue of his own knowledge and training, is qualified to assist in this procedure and to correct the distortions that are the inevitable accompaniment to attempts at self-knowledge. The analyst plays the part of reason in

245

a struggle with the forces of impulse that the analysand himself represents. The search for knowledge of the inner self, the 'real self' is a joint venture between the two parties but the analyst is in an authoritarian position because he is the one who knows how to navigate. The 'real me' has a sexual history, a sexual present and, if he is lucky, a sexual future. For the man-in-the-street who has no analyst available, the search must be conducted alone or with the help of friends and acquaintances as well as by books and articles and usually for such a person, the sexual substructure is the only part of the theory that he has heard about or knows anything about; it is the only portion that the 'vile simplifiers' have really transmitted to the general public through novels, journalism and the mass media and it has been done on a grand scale; the rest has only received perfunctory treatment. Without intending to do so, because we know Freud was no revolutionary and few of his disciples were, the psychoanalysts have produced a revolution and a counter-revolution. They have played a big part in the 'sexual revolution' by opening up to public discussion what was previously unmentionable, and in doing so they constructed a new mysticism of self-knowledge and identity. They set out to secularize the world but not to sexualize it. That they have done so is more the responsibility of peripheral groups whose members stand in different relationships to psychotherapy, either as participants, consumers, or those who merely understand it. These people serve as 'filters' for the psychotherapeutic ideology in the sense that it 'passes through' them and reaches wider publics in versions that are simplifications and exaggerations. Such groups receive the first transmission of values and then continue to transmit the values in cruder and more accessible forms. The main groups are the social workers and counsellors, medical practitioners of general medicine, personnel officers, vocational advisors, welfare workers, social scientists of all kinds, administrators, all those who regularly or intermittently take upon themselves or have assigned to them, the task of searching out mental illness, maladjustment or any of the other symptoms of individual or social problems such as delinquency or drug addiction. To these must be added the special group of researchers into sexual behaviour, whose ideological biases are rarely examined, and as rarely overtly expressed (19). The degree to which these groups have accepted responsibility for their actions and judgments and the extent to which they are utilized is indicated by the part they play now in the formulation of public social policy. Further out from the centre of professional psychotherapists are the laymen, some of whom are as or almost as 'competent' as the professionals in their comprehension of the concepts of the ideology; further still are all those whose understanding is a confused mixture of various popularizations and a facility in using the powerful vocabulary of the ideology. But the counter-revolution has come about through the 'socialization' of psychoanalysis, by its transformation from a clinical practice into a social philosophy. This has diminished the individual and elevated the group and turned it into a vehicle of conservatism with an apolitical orientation. The original values of psycho-analysis have become combined with those of the post-Freudians so that what is now percolating throughout and converging on our culture is a combination of the values of psychoanalysis proper with the new psychodynamic values and, as Halmos rightly concludes, these values are reaching and influencing the lawyers, civil servants, administrators, businessmen and engineers though not yet to the point at which they can create the popular tyranny envisaged by Philip Rieff:

'Think of a whole society dominated by psychotherapeutic ideals. Considered not from the individual's but from a socio-logical point of view, psychoanalysis is an expression of a popular tyranny such as not even de Tocqueville adequately imagined. Ideally, the democratic tyranny which is the typical social form of our era will not have a hierarchy of confessors and confessants. Rather . . . everyone must be a confessant, everyone must aspire to be a confessor. This is the meaning of the psychoanalytic re-education that Freud speaks of. In the emer-gent democracy of the sick, everyone can to some extent play doctor to others, and none is allowed the temerity to claim that he can definitively cure or be cured. The hospital is succeeding the church and the parliament as the archetypal institution of Western culture' (20).

A grotesque future only relieved, in the the comic sense, by the prospect of new developments presaged by some American experiments in running mental hospitals by patients' committees:

parliament has entered the mental hospital, and the cynic might well comment that it is the right place for it.

It is the transmission of that portion of the psychotherapeutic ideology that contains the new ideas on sexuality that has had the greatest success, that has penetrated the farthest. Those who know little or nothing of the changing opinions of psychotherapists and who are ignorant of the contemporary focus on the family, child-rearing and marital happiness are still well aware of the sexual values. They have obtained from them a permit to speak about what could not previously be spoken of and encouraged to demand a dose of sex in entertainment and journalism that was not possible before. Nigel Kneale, the author of the play *The Year of the Sex Olympics*, has expressed the view that it is not sex that is being permitted today, because it has never seriously been hindered (he has forgotten Calvin's Geneva). The Victorians, he reminds us, had big families and mistresses (and Mr Gladstone patrolled the streets at night saving fallen women, and that was pretty permissive of a prime minister, but that was in the days before expressed motives could decently be doubted). What is being permitted today is the representation, on screen, stage and in print, of sexual acts and sexual deviations (ignoring the question of how deviant is deviancy when a lot of people do it). Permissiveness is a form of voyeurism in which Peeping Tom stages grand spectacles that, thanks to the coincidence of new developments in communication techniques, can be transmitted to every home throughout the world by the entertainment industry. What makes the present situation qualitatively different from other historical 'frank' phases, he adds, is that it also coincides with an inability on the part of the spectator to distinguish fact from fiction. Industrialized man in technicized society finds it difficult to understand the situation in which he lives, the reality of his society is too tenuous and obscured for him to do anything more than make desperate efforts to affirm himself along the lines that the voices that interpret the world to him indicate. The sexual revolution with its representationally 'permissive society' is only our version of bread and circuses, and nobody knows if the circus is the 'real' world or not.

Notes and References

1 Jones, G. Seaborn, *Treatment or Torture: The Philosophy, Techniques, and Future of Psychodynamics*, Tavistock, London, 1968, p. 159; italics in the original. The reader may feel inclined to criticize the use of the adjective 'scientific' in the quoted passage; if he does, he will find himself in good company. See Ricoeur, Paul, *Freud and Philosophy: An Essay in Interpretation*, translated by Denis Savage, Yale University Press, New Haven and London, 1970, p. 410n.

2 Strupp, Hans H., 'Infantile Sexuality in the Theories of Freud and Sullivan', *Complex*, VII (1952), pp. 51–62; Fromm, Erich, *The Forgotten Language*, Gollancz, London, 1952, pp. 196, 201–2, 204–5.

3 Horney, Karen, *The Neurotic Personality of Our Time*, Norton, New York, 1937, p. 157 (Routledge, London, 1937).

4 Marcuse, Herbert, *Eros and Civilization*, Sphere Books, London, 1969, pp. 212–14.

5 Kardiner, Abram, *Sex and Morality*, Bobbs-Merill, New York, 1954, pp. 20, 61, 159; *The Individual and His Society*, Columbia University Press, New York, 1946 (London, 1939), p. 340; *The Psychological Frontiers of Society*, Columbia University Press, New York, 1946 (London, 1945), p. 412.

6 Alexander, Franz, *Psychosomatic Medicine*, Norton, New York, 1950, pp. 12, 36–8.

7 Guntrip, Harry, *Personality Structure and Human Interaction*, Hogarth, London, 1961, p. 177.

8 Frankl, *op. cit.*, p. 170.

9 *Ibid.*, p. 134.

10 Erikson, *op. cit.*, p. 257.

11 Hunt, Morton M., *The New York Times Magazine*, 1 January 1967, p. 16.

12 Sapirstein, Milton R., *Emotional Security*, Crown, New York, 1948, p. 188.

13 Such 'adult' films as *Midnight Cowboy*, *The Graduate*, *The Diary of a Mad Housewife*. For a popular example of the 'how often' type of smutty humour one could not do better than refer to the Independent Television programme *On the Buses*.

14 Freud, Sigmund, *New Introductory Lectures on Psycho-Analysis*, Norton, New York, 1933, pp. 205–6 (Hogarth, London, 1962).

15 For example, McDermott, Sandra, *Studies in Female Sexuality*, Odyssey Press, London, 1970, and the kind of material found in *Forum* magazine or *Sexology*.

16 The concept of 'metaphysical pathos' comes from Arthur O. Lovejoy, and apparently means the sentiments that are associated with or engendered by a theory, i.e. the 'feelings' that a particular theory is associated with. In the case of bureaucracy they are, according to Gouldner, feelings of pessimism; see Gouldner, Alvin W., 'Metaphysical Pathos and the Theory of Bureaucracy', *American Political*

Science Review, 49 (1955), pp. 496–507. It would be invidious to cite any particular example of 'organization theory' as almost the entire genre could be quoted; if the reader turns to any of the 'authoritative' textbooks, he will appreciate my point. Some writers, such as Michel Crozier, are not in this category.

17 The best-selling German author Oswalt Kolle is the originator of the notion of sexual intercourse as a high performance sport, for which training is required; see Holzer, Horn, 'Sexualität und Herrschaft— Anmerkungen zum Problem der repressiven Entsublimierung', *Soziale Welt*, 20/1969, Heft 3, p. 304.

18 Erikson, *op. cit.*, p. 257. Only the line arrangement has been altered from the original, and a colon added.

19 For a discussion of the covert ideological bias of writers and researchers on the sexual behaviour of humans, see Sagarin, Edward, 'Taking Stock of Studies of Sex', *The Annals of The American Academy of Political and Social Science*, Vol. 376, March 1968, p. 4.

20 Rieff, Philip, *Freud: The Mind of the Moralist*, Gollancz, London, 1960, p. 355.

Chapter 9

The Cult of Familism
and Familistic Determinism

'Psychotherapists will conduct mixed groups of professional and non-professional members to study and evaluate suitable techniques for Counselling Parents . . . Applicants should write to Parent Counselling . . .' was the burden of a recent advertisement in *New Society* (1), and seems to go some way towards confirming Rieff's prophecy of a society based on psychotherapeutic ideals. The categories of persons believed to require counselling are being extended from those stigmatized by some official or quasi-official judgment as maladjusted, immature, or infantile to include ordinary parents. There should be little to cause surprise in this since parents are already the readership for a vast psychotherapeutic literature on child-rearing and the family, so the direct counselling of parents, any parents, is a logical extension stemming from the transmission of the values of the psychotherapeutic ideology. Familism, as Luckmann terms it, is one of the essential parts of the faith of the counsellors. Familism is one of the forms of 'self-realization' that the individual still has open to him 'without directly and sharply butting against the realities of the social structure, without immediately falling under the absolute performance control of an institution' (2). There is no good reason to question the importance that Luckmann gives to familism (i.e. the elevation of the family as a system of affective relationships to a supreme position in life or 'the self-conscious recognition,' in the words of Nelson Foote, 'of family living as a distinctive and desired activity', expressed in early marriage, a short childless period after marriage followed by child-centred family life, and sometimes associated with a higher than average economic status and participation in what middle-class Americans mean by 'community' and 'togetherness') but that it is 'open' in his sense seems improbable. The family is becoming increasingly subjected to control and supervision by numerous agencies of the state, all or most of which are wholly or partly under the influence of those whose faith is that of the counsellors; all that is now possible is the realization of self within the limits imposed by these external pressures and controls.

The family, like the legendary community, seems, as an abstraction in discussion, capable of exciting a high degree of enthusiasm among its supporters and a lot of hostility from its detractors. In the recent past, the family was often the target of abuse, seen as the Victorian epitome of stuffiness, hyprocrisy, and an influence that distorted and debased the individual's character; the kind of family life portrayed in Richard Aldington's *Death of a Hero* was not exactly attractive to the young. But in this kind of literary context, it must be remembered that the family was seen as a repressive institution mainly through the eyes of youth, not from the point of view of the young married couple and small children. The profamilists still do not have it all their own way; there is a considerable attack from the quarters of certain social anthropologists that the family as we know it is out-moded, and even stronger attack from the dissident young that it should be replaced by some form of communal life. It is not surprising that the young should say this kind of thing as the defence of the family and its value as a source of self-fulfilment is undertaken by those who also support the status quo; it is not surprising that Bruno Bettelheim, an archpriest of the psychotherapeutic faith, found the children of kibbutzim so unsatisfactory (3).

In the past the family has been an economic unit, an educational institution, a microcosmic community. Now, reduced in extension, essentially emphemeral, it is no longer any of these things. Today, if we can believe the sociologists, its main function is supportive, it provides the emotional support to mother, children and father; it is, in short, a tiny haven of meaningfulness. In addition it is still the source of primary socialization. It is a good thing in itself and no surprise that the counsellors should find it so, but it is also valuable to the industrial complex; because of its present characteristics, it is a kind of ready-made trouble-shooter, all the more valuable for being a personal creation of the married pair and their children. It can, like television, sop up the tensions created by industrialized society, provided that it is not 'off-tune' itself.

In the past, the family has been more than an economic unit, an educational force, a locus of affective support. It has been a source of pride in the shape of a name indicating continuity between generations; a property holding institution, and in its extended form, especially in Europe, a most complex network of interlocking relationships of diverse kinds. But the psychotherapeutic ideal of the family is not of this kind (nor that of the ghastly Viennese families from which most of Freud's patients came) but rather, the contemporary urban nuclear family of husband, wife and unmarried children. It is significant that when the psychotherapist talks about the family, he always does so in terms of a married couple with small children, sometimes adolescent ones, but always in a context of relative youth, i.e. youngish parents and young children. The notion of a family as something that continues throughout generations plays no part in the psychotherapeutic vision.

Concentration on the family by psychotherapeutic ideologists has a twofold source. First, the psychodynamic view that (a) socialization forms personality, i.e. the abandonment of the Freudian biopsychological thesis for a straight-forward return to the *tabula rasa* theory (child born without discernible psychological traits that are later written on the unmarked slate tablet of his personality by environmental influences); (b) the family is the originating location of personality (character) disorders and neuroses (probably of psychoses too). To these is added: second, the Freudian view of women. In this matter Freudians and Neo-Freudians are in agreement and the biological-instinctual view of Freud on the nature of women has not been abandoned in the main. Ego-psychologists, as much as Freudians, find women passive, innate mothers and inherent homemakers; ordained by their very natures to be the priestesses of familism and to find their own self-realization in bearing children and making a home: woman as nest-builder is the very foundation of the doctrine of familism.

The Pauline beliefs, that dominated Christian opinion on women for such a long time, held her to be morally inferior to man and evidence of this was supplied by the part she played in the Fall. The Freudian belief is a variant of this in a 'scientific' disguise. The little boy has a penis that can be cut off, thus he has a fear of castration. This fear assists in developing his 'reality' based conscience that acts as a self-controlling device in later life. The girl is born without a penis, therefore she believes that she has already suffered castration. Thus the girl does not develop the kind of self-controlling super-ego that the boy does and she grows up deficient in matters of principle, morality and justice. Erikson supports the view that boys fear castration, but thinks that girls fear being 'emptied and left' (4). This condemnatory view leaves women as basically morally inferior because of the biological fact that they are born without a penis and their breasts develop so much later that they cannot be a satisfactory substitute. As James Thurber once observed: 'Woman's place is in the wrong'.

It is a strange irony that at a time of secularization, this essentially Pauline opinion of women should have displaced the idealization of women that was fashionable in the nineteenth century (alleged to be a Christian period). The idealization of woman (undoubtedly only an upper and middle class belief as is the Freudian and psychotherapeutic) assumed that her innate nature was pure, and as wife and mother she embodied moral excellence; she was, above all else, mother, wife, and homemaker. The two views come together in the psychotherapeutic ideology: woman has certain innate, biological characteristics that determine her psychology and make her passive, and so on, and at the same time make her mother, wife and homemaker; thus the ideology has the best of both worlds. Erich Fromm becomes lyrical when describing maternal love: 'Mother's love is bliss, is peace, it need not be acquired, it need not be deserved. It is for this altruistic, unselfish character that motherly love has been considered the highest kind of love, and the most sacred of all emotional bonds' (5).

The biological facts that have helped to create the biopsychological theory of the nature of women cannot justify the myth that has evolved. That women can bear children might endow them with an innate psychological tendency towards motherhood and maternal responses, but it cannot be directly observed and there is no way in which the 'tendency' could be isolated from the entangling and masking network of cultural factors. So far no experiment of any kind, including one using concomitant variaations, has been devised. We can no more be dogmatic about the drives to motherhood than we can about the drives to fatherhood. If Margaret Mead can claim that the social role of father is neither biologically nor psychologically determined but only sociologically (i.e. that it is a social invention to provide protection for the mother and child), there is little direct evidence to show that the *social* role of mother is other than a cultural construct. The controversy really revolves around the problem of whether women possess rigid, determining instinctual patterns of behaviour or no inherent predetermining instinctual mechanisms that automatically operate to satisfy the diffused drives for food, comfort, and sex. (Needless to add that if women have such instinctual equipment, then presumably men have something similar; they are not all that superior.) All the available material that would satisfy scientific criteria (and 'years of intensive clinical experience' and intuitive understanding derived from case-studies must be excluded) indicates that woman's presumed maternal instincts are culturally learned. The human mother shows little affinity with the animal mother (unlike the chimpanzee mother who is alleged to be able to give the kiss of life instinctively); she has to learn about caring for children, how to be kind and loving, perhaps even to learn to want children. Whether she needs to or not, her culture teaches her all of this, it is a part of the socialization process and sometimes it fails or is inadequate and then we have the apparently quite common phenomenon of the uncaring, unloving mother or the woman who does not want children; do we account for these sociologically, or do we by-pass the cultural evidence, which is all we have, and assume that such women are biological mutants?

The penis envy hypothesis of Freud (denied by Karen Horney, but she was a rank heretic) is still a powerful element in the psychoanalytic theory of female psychology. It is defended by many who claim to have seen it operating in their work with their female patients, though some psychotherapists who believe it exists, think it is sociologically produced. Females feel inferior because they lack a penis, they feel incomplete (when grown up, according to Spock, they have less sexual desire than men). Some women compensate negatively by assuming masculine traits, they want careers or to boss people about or set the world straight and similar 'unfeminine' things. 'Normal' women compensate positively by developing true femininity: they resign themselves to their lack of a penis and concentrate on what they have such as charm, and develop a strong sense of vanity together with passivity (aided by their less intense sexual desire), dependence, and a masochistic tendency to be dominated. The 'normal' woman accepts what man provides and from that she makes a home and rears the children. Psychoanalysis has liberated a lot of things but it has not freed women from the *Kinder, Küche, Kirche* creed of femininity in which woman fulfils herself through the achievements of man (6). Women who do not accept this faith are those who have not adjusted to the reality of the penis situation; if they want more than minimal education, it is only penis envy that drives them on to do well at school and university. Taken to its logical conclusion, it is a biological and psychological crime to educate women or encourage them to want education, careers, and so forth (unless there is a war on).

Spock tells us: 'The thing that I'm concerned about these days is that quite a few women nowadays, especially those who have been to university, find the life of taking care of their babies and children all day boring and frustrating. . . . It is much more creative to rear and shape the personality of a fine, live child than it is to work in an office or even carve a statue' (7). Whenever a psychotherapist becomes deeply involved he tends to express his values as if he were making sure of being printed in the digests. Women, when denying their instinctual make-up, do the oddest things apart from working in offices and carving statues, they 'drink, shout, backslap, use obscenities, and tell dirty stories like men. In these respects I think they have been motivated more by rivalry than by natural inclination' (8). Bettelheim is in agreement: 'We must start with the realization that, as much as women want to be good scientists or engineers, they want first and foremost to be womanly companions of men and to be mothers' (9).

These views fit the popular stereotypes about women that are still current in the West and although they represent a fair consensus of the views of psychotherapists, they have no evidence to support them save that provided by the culture within which such dependent and servile women live. It is one thing to agree that these views represent the cultural norms of our kind of society and quite something other to claim that these cultural constructs are based on immutable and inalienable facts of biological and psychological constitution.

All societies confer certain attributes on male and female as well as a division of labour based on sex. There is no need to quote the findings of anthropologists on the wide variations on what is believed seemly for a sex in a given society—that they have found that the attributes of the sexes differ from one society to another is well known, and the theme of sexual relativity is commonplace. But every society has a set of preferred attributes that are assumed natural to each sex, and in our type of society the feminine attributes contain 'among others', 'personal warmth, empathy, sensitivity, emotionalism, grace, charm, compliance, dependence and deference'. After she has become a wife, the woman becomes the centre of the home and displays the virtue of fidelity to her husband while maintaining the harmonious co-ordination of house and family; in doing this she gratifies man's demand for order and relaxation after work. Her talents are defined socially and she is endowed by her culture with intuition and a gift for dealing with interpersonal relations, but her emotionality (that she cannot control and thus channel into 'productive' areas) is her great handicap (10).

The female is warm, nurturant, acquiescent and lovable though not very bright—this is the basic stereotype of Western woman, a combination of loving mother and dumb blonde. She accepts, because it is her nature to do so, the domination of the male, though she occasionally shows signs of resenting it. Her negative attributes are that she lacks aggressiveness, personal involvement and egotism, persistence and ambition, though it is conceded that when the interests of her family or of a family member are involved she may show the possession of all the attributes that she is reputed to lack. Thus the patterns of behaviour are divided between the two sexes, each having the other's opposite traits.

Women are alleged to be difficult to get on with and to display 'cattiness' towards each other. They are also accused of having weak loyalties; this is because they become emotionally involved and put their feelings before everything else. It is interesting to observe some differences in the stereotypes between the USA and Britain in respect of mass media entertainment. Popular films and television dramas in the USA usually portray the 'good' wife or girl-friend remaining loyal to her criminal or subversive husband or lover only until such time as the police, FBI or some other security

I

or law enforcement agency demonstrate convincingly that he is a 'baddy', in which case her love for him promptly disappears. Similar British productions usually show the woman remaining loyal to her man in spite of proof that he is a bad lot.

According to Friedan, women who work and career women are shown in popular fiction as being frustrated and unhappy until they find the right man, marry, and settle down to making a home; she entitles this stereotype 'the happy housewife heroine' and she is as much a part of the short story material in British women's magazines as she is in those of the USA (11).

Social scientists, in particular sociologists studying the family, have been accused of furthering this stereotype of women by their selective appropriations from the literature of social anthropology and psychoanalysis (12). Epstein accuses such sociologists of trying to prove that women perform 'expressive' (emotional, supportive) functions within the family, while men exercise the active 'instrumental' ones (economic bread-winning activities). These writers participate in a great cultural conspiracy designed to keep women in their place and brainwash them into accepting this place. Epstein tells us that intellectually aggressive women are stigmatized as deviants, there is something odd about them, they may even be lesbian; and the game is maintained by categorizing tender and 'expressive' men as equally deviant, possibly homosexual. Much of the present trend towards what Winick calls the depolarization of sex roles is concentrated on the dissolution of the traditional stereotypes. Winick (13) lists a number of tendencies in America that have been reproduced in Britain and to a lesser extent in Europe since the end of the Second World War. They are: the appearance (dress, hair styles, adornments), first names, and play of boys and girls, adolescents and young people have become less 'gender-specific'; girls are showing the sexual precocity and aggressiveness once only associated with youths; not only are clothes and appearances becoming 'ambisexual' (unisex) but family roles, work and recreational activities are losing their gender-specificity. This is all rather ominous, thinks Winick and he refers to Talcott Parsons' (doyen of the 'systems' status quo apologetics brand of sociology) observation that the social structure is composed of a 'subtly interrelated and almost homeostatic series of interrelationships' (14) so any upsetting of this interrelationship will have bad consequences, but Winick is enough of a 'liberal' (in the American sense of the word) to concede that women's emancipation has been long overdue and that no one kind of family structure is inherently healthier than another; he also admits that 'overly explicit roles can be pathogenic, because they do not permit the expression of individual differences or a personal style'. But, he adds, although any male-female role structure is possibly viable, there must always be a 'clear division of labour and responsibilities' based on sex and he stresses the 'unique capacities' of each sex and that 'equality does not mean equivalence'. Unless there is this sexual division of labour and responsibilities and an acknowledgment of the unique capacities of the sexes, the future outlook is 'disquieting', though exactly why, he omits to tell us. Most of the sociologists of the kind that Rossi and Epstein attack content themselves with anxious observations about the danger of 'role conflict', 'role confusion' and 'neurotic disturbance' if people have not clearly defined sexual roles, but Winick seems afraid that the very foundations of our civilization will be sapped if girls continue to wear long boots and young men have long hair.

The counsellors and psychotherapists have not shown much sympathy with this movement though they have utilized it with considerable skill. Apart from a few social workers and probation officers who dress up like their younger clients to offset hostility and show that their hearts are in the right places, the counsellors, for the most part, have concentrated on using the 'pop and drug' scene to underline how much they are needed and how much they can do. In the case of the use of drugs such as cannabis and LSD, many of them have directed their fire at those who claim that 'drug addiction' is a 'problem' in the sense that political conservatives mean. Quite rightly, they have pointed to the much graver social consequences of dangerous driving, alcoholism, gambling and all the other socially sanctioned 'addictions' of our society but all they are really saying is, 'society is sick because it is composed of sick individuals, therefore turn the sick individuals (delinquents, drug addicts, etc.) over to us rather than the law, because we are the only ones who know a road out of this wasteland'. Others, however, have fully subscribed to the 'social problems' approach.

259

The attribution to women of these special qualities makes it extremely difficult for any women who seeks an independent identity outside 'woman's realm' of home, family and marriage. She has to face opposition from masculine vested interests plus the equally powerful resistance of other women who are fully socialized in the prevailing social conformity. If she shows no strong wish to set up a family, remarks are passed by women as well as men indicating that there is something wrong with her and the potent magic words of the psychoanalytic vocabulary are adopted to put her in her place by devaluing and questioning her motives. Women in male occupations or those who have career ambitions, sometimes even within the occupations conventionally reserved for women, are described as 'castrating' and suffering from an overdose of penis envy. A woman who rejects or questions the primacy of her domestic role is branded as a cultural deviant (if nothing worse), and psychotherapists urge their female patients to try to live contentedly within the conventional familial and sexual roles.

But women have gained sexual equality (or almost). They have the right conceded to them of demanding that sexual intercourse be enjoyable for them too; they have achieved, in some Western societies, a quasi-right to abortion (provided that they have the cash), and a right to contraception (though the 'Pill' is under constant attack as being a danger to health and one cannot help wondering if this ploy is more motivated by the wish to scare the women off them by medical motives; the contraceptive that men—and the anti-feminist women—would prefer is the chastity-belt). Sexual equality, however, has not meant social or status equality, and inequalities in these areas are supported by the *apartheid* doctrine of 'separate but equal' (as Winick says, 'equality does not mean equivalence'). This view is nothing more than the old special and unique sexual attributes argument and implies that women are honoured in their special womanly achievements, i.e. family, bringing-up children and providing the comfortable and emotionally secure background for their husband's achievements. Epstein argues that this is not so; women in the West are not even honoured for their 'feminine' accomplishments and if they want status they have to gain it by 'masculine' achievements such as making money or obtaining power over other people, that immediately opens them to the accusation of being 'unfeminine'. Even highly successful women athletes sometimes have their sex queried. If the feminine accomplishments were to be honoured, we should expect something like the Nazi *Mutterkreuz* or the Soviet 'Mother of the Year' to appear in the Birthday Honours list.

In the West, women are expected to be able to provide an answer to the question 'why they are working' if they are not just sitting at home. Their answer is usually that they are working for financial reasons, which is a confirmation of the stereotype: their husbands must have let them down by not earning enough and if this were not so, they would be able to stay at home and be truly feminine. The cultural attitudes prevalent today constitute part of a self-fulfilling prophecy; if women only work when they have to or while waiting for the right man to come along and marry them, then they will have little incentive to train or become highly educated and so there will be fewer women coming forward and offering themselves for posts in the male-dominated occupations.

The psychotherapeutic ideology does not contain anything inimical to the conventional views on the nature of women, it brings no liberation or emancipation with it. Those processes which have the effect of confining women within these conventions are: early and differential socialization; training in dependency, role requirements, and 'female' occupations, but they are weakened by (*a*) the ambiguity that our society creates in sex roles during later socialization at school where girls are encouraged to compete for the same academic qualifications as boys, and (*b*) the necessity for most young girls to earn a living during the period between leaving school and marriage.

The opinions of the psychotherapeutic ideologists on the nature of women are based on the Freudian notion that women are not aggressive or really capable of serious thinking (15) and the so-called 'scientific' psychology of personality based on clinical experience and selective elements taken from anthropological studies. The psychotherapeutic view is succinctly put by the psychiatrist Joseph Rheingold: '. . . when women grow up without dread of their biological functions and without subversion by feminist doctrine and . . . enter upon motherhood with a sense of fulfilment and altruistic sentiment, we shall attain the goal of a good life and a secure world in which to live it' (16). He puts all the blame for the world's ills on women and even St Paul could not have said it better.

As far as the counsellors are concerned, their interest in marital casework was based, and probably still is, on the assumption that it is not a good thing for marriages to break up, sometimes supported by the justification that it was bad for the children of the marriage. Although the techniques have altered, the basic orientation does not appear to have changed substantially. Present techniques, or rather the ideal form of them, are based upon the counsellor indicating to the marriage partners the various courses they can pursue and the means available while leaving the decision of choice to them; this is what takes place in theory if not always in practice. A change is, however, coming about, Noel Timms tells us, in which the two main dangers of the earlier and present techniques can be avoided: the dangers of too much or too little help. We are now witnessing a developing situation in which an increasing number of counsellors is seeking to understand the nature of the marital relationship in terms of an understanding based on the principles of psychodynamics (17).

Marriage, according to the psychodynamic approach, is 'deeply purposive' and this implies not only overt expectations such as those of sexual satisfaction, a home, financial security, status, children (18) but also all the 'unacknowledged purposes in all marriages, including those that seem to be unsatisfying or unsatisfactory' (19). Of all these purposes, tacit or otherwise, one must assume as fundamental a relationship of reciprocal love between the partners. Timms argues that marriage 'alone offers the adult in our society a relationship in which he can be accepted and involved *as a whole person*' (20). This notion of the whole person is central to the psychotherapeutic approach and seems to mean the individual not as a role-player or in his many and separate relationships with others but as all these plus the traits that he considers 'bad, destructive and worthless and which he struggles to disregard or to disown' (21). The whole person is thus the total set of roles and relationships together with the bad parts that the individual tries to reject. It is in marriage that these 'negative' traits become manifest and are accepted as a kind of currency to be used by both partners according to the interior needs of each. In the jargon of psychotherapy, the husband and wife when reacting positively to the situation, make 'contact' with and love the parts of each other that each thinks is unworthy and tries to disown. Marriage then is the situation in which the partners can enjoy 'the closest physical and emotional intimacy since their own infancy, and it marks at the same time the final stage in their evolution towards social maturity' (22).

The new counselling approach is thus a rejection of the older analysis of marital relations based on assigning blame to one partner or of classifying marriages according to the alleged personalities of the participants. The new analysis is based on a study of the interaction between the partners which takes the form of a collusion between the married couple to maintain some kind of marriage or the failure of such a collusion. In the everyday life of married people they complement each other in a variety of complicated ways, projecting their own bad aspects onto each other or accepting them in such a way as to bring about a viable (though it may be precarious) relationship in which they play roles that are complementary.

In his understanding of this complex process, the counsellor can disentangle the positive from the negative feelings and encourage the pair towards self-understanding and a comprehension of their own joint situation which might help them to 'think through' their problems and even resolve them. This technique is considered an improvement on past methods since it avoids the pitfalls of aggressive help, i.e. advice couched in imperatives, and too little assistance that comes from merely indicating courses of possible action.

To what extent the psychodynamic view of marriage reflects existing situations is anybody's guess. It is, after all, an ideal, a 'should be like this', a value judgment, and not a statement of fact. That marital partners collude with each other to achieve a *modus vivendi* is something that novelists have known for generations and does not affect the validity or otherwise of the psychodynamic approach considered as a reflection of existing conditions. The fact that marriage guidance counsellors and family caseworkers in their texts for student social workers warn the readers of the difficulties of satisfactorily resolving 'problem marriages and problem families' might lead one to echo Thurber's observation that 'if wives were a good thing, God would have had one'. If all the information and statistics on divorce and separation are to be believed, then it rather looks as if marriage as we know it today has failed in a very large number of cases to approach anywhere near the psychodynamic ideal, and those who argue that conventional marriage, like the conventional family, may be an out-moded social institution could have a point.

The counsellor's attitude towards the family is fundamentally similar to his view of marriage: family break up is to be avoided. He cannot be faulted for holding such a view for as a social worker he is called upon to prevent this happening. But this does not alter the fact that his orientation serves the industrialized society as the family is now the only major socializing influence as well as the most available, and for many the only available, source of individual identity. As Waller says: 'In our society the family furnishes the basic environment for personality' (23). In her paper, *The Social Worker and His Society*, Coyle argues that social welfare services fulfil the social goals that led society to establish them, and

'Our first and perhaps most clearly recognized function lies in the preservation and enhancement of family relationships. It is the family—its present instability, its loss of function, its confusion as to its authority and the roles of its members—which creates the most concern among observers of our social scene. It is here that social work has put much of its effort and has concentrated its most highly skilled practice. It is here that the use of psychoanalytic theory has made its most appropriate and deepest impact. . . . This skill and experience with the maintenance of families will remain and expand as one of our major contributions to social stability and individual fulfilment. What was discovered and started among the families of the poor is now available for use with necessary modifications in other parts of our society' (24).

This is the authentic voice of the psychotherapeutic ideologist, who is called upon by God (society) to fulfil certain functions that concern the revivification of what is apparently a moribund adjunct of the godhead, the family. By her special skills derived from the arcane knowledge originating in the cabinet of the psychoanalyst, she can penetrate the mysteries of the conjugal pair and lead them out of their blindness and into a true understanding of their interrelationship and thus hold society, the family, the marriage and all from falling apart and demonstrating the great gaping holes in our societal fabric, whose nature and significance defies analysis and reduces all this effort to mere whistling in the dark.

Most social workers are women. The focus of their attention is the family and marriage. Not only is social work a suitable occupation for women according to the canons of the psychoanalytic-psychodynamic school but the very nature of the areas with which she deals is 'woman's work'; what could be more suitable as a rationale for social work and the special qualities of womanhood? The psychotherapeutic ideology not only keeps woman in her place but provides a suitable and rewarding place for her to be in. She has become the high priestess of the psychotherapeutic ideology, her parish is made up of those segments of life in which her special womanly aptitudes, born of nature, are most appropriately deployed. Americans have feared a matriarchy but this is a paper tiger; women own more property in the United States than men do, but that property is mainly in the control of men, so there is no rational cause for fear there; if a matriarchy is to come about in the West it will not come from women owning property, it will come from women curing souls. The victory of the Faith of the Counsellors will be that of the women, but ironically it will be based on a set of ideals laid down by men. The social worker will ultimately become the soft hand of industrialized society and woman, with those unique qualities that serve her so well as wife, mother and homemaker will become the wife, mother and home-mender to us all in the person of the all-comprehending, empathic, non-directive social worker whose influence, persuasion and ultimate control is all the stronger for never being apparent.

That women are biologically constructed so that they can bear children does not require elaboration; that they must therefore assume conventional feminine roles and perform and have their children within the traditional family context of our culture is not self-evident. It could be argued that both the rules and the family structure are out-dated in spite of superficial continuities, that they are both a heritage from a time when social life had a fixed inevitability that it no longer has and that the sacred character of woman's nature and the sanctity of the conjugal family have little relevance today save in impeding social change. When Coyle asserts that the social work profession has developed in order to fulfil the social goals that led society to establish the welfare services, she is making an illicit assumption: society, that is an abstraction, establishes nothing for it is not capable of doing any such thing; people, groups of people establish things, and one of these groups is the social work profession itself which, like every group pretending to 'professional status', creates its demand for its services, and the values it reflects are its own, though they might also represent those of a large number of other individuals and groups, that is, they might represent a consensus, but the consensus can also be a product of the profession's marketing campaign. The values implicit in the traditional ideas of women, marriage and family in so far as they are held by social workers are their own values and not the values of some paramount chief called 'Society'.

If marriage, the family, and women's roles are going through a disintegrating process at present, it may well be an occasion for rejoicing. As the lemmings rush into the sea to solve their problems, so the break up of the traditional familial and marital structure may be our answer to the problem of over-population as all other methods have failed pathetically.

In addition, it could be argued that not only is the family structure that is being extolled archaic, but it is positively inhibiting. At a time when social paths to salvation are becoming fewer and the individual has to rely more and more on his own resources in the construction of an identity for himself and a meaning to life, the present marital and family structures make woman dependent and distort her personality by pushing her into a situation appertaining to the past rather than the present. At the same time, the husband assumes a pose of dominance that can be at variance with his position at work and outside the home. If this dominant role is not obtained by the man, he is then reduced, which is no better as a solution than is the dependence of the woman.

But the brute fact remains that there is no socializing agent of any consequence in our society save the family, so it must be preserved, even if it is a museum piece, as no one has suggested a practicable alternative as yet. This does not mean, however, that one must avoid searching for alternatives, just as the need to alleviate suffering and reduce unhappiness within an existing social institution need make us treat the institution as sacrosanct and unchangeable—unless we wish to think that way.

Notes and References

1 From a classified advertisement in *New Society*, 15 July 1971, p. 136.
2 Luckmann, Thomas, 'On Religion in Modern Society: Individual Consciousness, World View, Institution', *Journal for the Scientific Study of Religion*, Spring 1963, pp. 148–62, p. 61.
3 Bettelheim, Bruno, *Children of the Dream*, Thames and Hudson, London, 1969.
4 Erikson, *op. cit.*, p. 82.
5 Fromm, Erich, *The Art of Loving*, Allen and Unwin, London, 1957, pp. 39, 50.
6 One of the oldest and best accounts of the psychoanalytic view can be found in Deutsch, Helene, *The Psychology of Women*, Grune and Stratton, New York, 1944.
7 Spock, Benjamin, *A Young Person's Guide to Life and Love*, Bodley Head, London, 1971, p. 61.
8 *Ibid.*, p. 61.
9 Bettelheim, Bruno, 'Growing Up Female', *Harper's Magazine*, October 1962, p. 121.
10 Epstein, Cynthia Fuchs, *Woman's Place*, University of California Press, Berkeley and Los Angeles, 1970, pp. 18–30.
11 Friedan, Betty, *The Feminine Mystique*, Norton, New York, 1963, pp. 33–68 (Gollancz, London, 1963). As examples of the British genre: 'Twenty-Five Goodnight Kisses' in *Mirabelle*, 30 January 1971, pp. 10–11, and for the whole set of beliefs about sensible sex for married couples and familism in general see 'Adjusting to Marriage', a series of articles begun in *Petticoat*, 3 April 1971, pp. 6–7.
12 Rossi, Alice S., 'Equality Between the Sexes: An Immodest Proposal', *Daedalus*, Spring 1964, p. 611.
13 Winick, Charles, 'The Beige Epoch: Depolarization of Sex-Roles in America', *The Annals of The American Academy of Political and Social Science*, Vol. 376 March 1968, pp. 18–24.
14 *Ibid.*, p. 21.
15 Millett, Kate, *Sexual Politics*, Hart-Davis, London, 1971.
16 Quoted by Weisstein, Naomi, 'Woman as Nigger', *Psychology Today*, October 1969, p. 20.

17 Timms, Noel, *Social Casework, Principles and Practice*, Routledge and Kegan Paul, London, 1964, p. 142.
18 These overt expectations are dealt with in Beyfus, Drusilla, *The English Marriage*, Weidenfeld and Nicolson, London, 1968.
19 Timms, *op. cit.*, p. 143.
20 *Ibid.*, p. 144; italics in original.
21 *Ibid.*, p. 144.
22 *Ibid.*, p. 144.
23 Quoted by Timms, *op. cit.*, Waller, W., *The Family*, Dryden Press, New York, 1951, p. 33.
24 Younghusband, Eileen (compiled by), *Social Work and Social Values: Readings in Social Work*, Volume III, Allen and Unwin, London, 1967, pp. 39–54; pp. 39, 44.

Chapter 10

The Adjustment of the Adjusters

The application by its devotees of the psychotherapeutic ideology is not such a simple matter as one might think. The social worker and the psychotherapists are well aware that the facilities and resources put at their disposal by central and local governments and private agencies are insufficient for them to be able to carry out their programmes as they would wish. The welfare of the Welfare State is inadequate to meet the needs of their clients even in the satisfaction of material wants. Although some social workers are contented with the present state of their techniques most know that they are deficient and require more research and experimentation to improve them and the funds for such work are not forthcoming. But above all else, many of them know that the situations and conditions, both psychic and physical, that create a need for their services lie outside the field of social work and psychotherapy. They appreciate, not all, however, to the same degree, that they 'function' within a social structure that allows, even if it does not actually need, poverty and social injustice to exist in conjunction with a legal system that is far from perfect, and it is the legal system, together with the economic sphere, that impinges most frequently and forcefully on their fields of work. How then do they adjust to this frustrating and inhibiting situation? Because they do not merely hand out sums of money determined by official regulations but attempt to assist their clients to 'cope with' their troubles, they are unshielded from the temptation to think about the societal world in which they work; in fact, they cannot very well avoid doing so. Partly for this reason, they are particularly susceptible to the benefits to themselves of professionalization and bureaucratization. Professionalization enables them to retreat from facing the wider implications of their work and provides the opportunity of being apolitical or ethically neutral. After all, they are 'professionals', competent, trained experts who can legitimately concentrate on doing their jobs within the framework provided and as long as they focus on the narrowly technical aspects of their work they can manifest the same kind of detachment from the wider issues involved that certain scientists and technologists display when their achievements are used for military or other questionable ends. They can do a Pontius Pilate act and declare that the use to which their knowledge and know-how are put are neither their moral responsibility nor within their control and influence. The social worker can put forward a similar argument to the effect that he has to work to the best of his ability within a given social order that is beyond his control or power to alter.

This kind of situation could be construed as supporting Bell's end-of-ideology thesis in as much as this limited sort of professionalization leads to neutrality or indifference towards political philosophies. In the training courses, all of which are now oriented towards professionalization, there is a discernible tendency to eliminate as early as possible those candidates who are unlikely to conform to the prevailing agency beliefs and practices. Those potential non-conformists who manage to slip through the selection net are subjected to indoctrination at an early stage in actual training so as to weed them out. But some survive even this and carry their non-conformity into their world of work where, sooner, or later, they face problems of personal adjustment. Professionalization is often combined with a bureaucratic stance by which the practitioner accepts the dictates of the administration as the unquestioned framework within which he operates and the wisdom of which he takes for granted, though it emanates mostly from politicians and civil servants who probably do not as yet share his ideological views, or if they do, then it is in an attenuated form. Bureaucratization of the individual worker does not necessarily mean that he will become obsessed with the minutae of paper work but that the ultimate goal of those who opt for bureaucratization is to become an administrator and assume the outlook and attitudes of the civil servant.

Geoffrey Rankin has highlighted some of the problems imposed on the social worker by the type of society in which he works (1). As an occupation, social work is a creation of 'society' (i.e. of groups of people with sufficient power to impose their wishes on the rest) and it is supported and paid for by that society because it is believed that social work is in the interest of society. By its efforts, the anti-social and the asocial are encouraged to become socially-minded and stress on the individual and his family is reduced so that there is an all-round increase in productivity. The social worker mitigates the effects of bad housing and poverty and also alleviates the deleterious consequences of physical and mental illness. Thus, as Rankin argues, the social worker helps 'society' by making the socially sick less of a liability and more productive and thereby satisfying the economic criteria that are the bases of our culture. This interpretation could be called the general social justification for all types of social work.

But the structure of the society in which the social worker operates is based on a vertical system of social stratification, that is the members of the society are arranged in a hierarchy or layer-cake order in which the upper strata are more adequately rewarded than the lower. The rewards themselves are arranged according to ill-defined criteria, among which is 'productivity' (measurable for the lower strata but quite immeasurable for the upper). Competition is encouraged as a means of moving up the scale and low man on the totem pole is an unenviable position to be in. Monetary and status incentives are offered to induce individuals to make the effort required to move from one stratum to another. This is the shape of industry and trade and of the administration of which the social worker is a part. A social work agency with its directorate, supervisory personnel and rank-and-file workers is as much part of this hierarchial system as any factory; they are replicas in miniature of the encompassing society.

The psychotherapeutic ideology could well provide the ethic for such agencies but on the whole it tends to favour an approach that is very different. Some social workers, especially the élite of caseworkers and counsellors, like to subscribe to the belief that what they should be concerned with is not 'what is good for society' but what is good for those whom society disregards, i.e those who are handicapped, weak or underprivileged. This philosophy may be based on some notion of the rights of the individual or merely on a general tender-mindedness or even a Christian ethic of succour. Whatever its origins may be for the individual social worker, it is likely to convert him into an apparent champion of the individual whenever individual and majority interests clash.

Such clashes are bound to occur if only for the reason that our society classifies individuals into successes and failures, rough categories admittedly but clearly enough demarcated in any particular case. The persons with whom the social worker deals are almost always the failures in some form or another. But, and here is the rub, the social worker (no matter what his views may be) is a successful participant in this set-up: he has a salary, maybe insufficient but secure, and he has power over other people and therefore he finds himself in the anomalous position of rendering assistance to someone whose failure (assuming it is socially determined) is but the obverse of his own relative success. Failure, like success, must be considered relative; failures form a continuum from those who are inefficient workers to those who are economically totally unproductive and thence on to those who are delinquent and counter-productive. But as productivity is measured by monetary earnings, successful delinquents are clearly excluded; using Merton's terminology, successful delinquents are those who have achieved socially approved goals by socially disapproved methods but have escaped any penalties. The failures, partial or total, all end up, more or less, at the bottom of the social heap; most are poor (the rich social failures, and some successes too, go to private psychotherapists and pay large fees). On the whole, the social worker's clients are predominantly poor or in poverty, but in addition to this they fall into two categories that Rankin, using the terminology of the nineteenth century, calls the 'deserving' and 'undeserving' poor (2). Even failures have their successes and so the deserving poor are the aged, the physically ill or infirm, the physically handicapped, and a few unemployables, and those with markedly subnormal intelligence, in other words, those whom a Victoria puritan would have grudgingly conceded are where they are through no fault of their own. The undeserving poor are the unskilled, the inefficient producers, some people of subnormal intelligence, unmarried mothers (wicked and foolish), deserted wives (undeserving because the husband ought to maintain them), children (they have no right to be born poor or orphaned or maltreated), all the 'mentally ill', and all who have made a botch of their lives. The essential difference between the two categories is that the deserving would work if only they could, but they cannot overcome the handicaps that are not of their own making, and the undeserving who are either incapable of productive work or will not work. In the past these two categories would have suffered differing degrees of moral censure; nowadays, the censure is tacit but still there.

As the imperatives of our society are productivity and increasing productivity, a degree of compassion can be given to the deserving poor: they do not offend the canons of our society because they 'would if they could'. But a different situation exists for the undeserving; in strict accordance with our efficiency-productivity beliefs they should be treated as liabilities, but they are not, at least not totally because the Faith of the Counsellors has triumphed sufficiently to enable them to be *theoretically* in the category of those who should be helped. But this offends the basic principles of our society, and the question is asked, 'Whom shall we have to tolerate next?' The undeserving, the failures, lack 'moral fibres' of good quality so they can still be stigmatized as 'malingerers, scroungers, and criminals'. They are logically beyond the bounds of compassion but because of the spread of the Faith of the Counsellors they can no longer be locked in the stocks or given a good whipping and sent on to the next parish. In addition, they often have children (too often, in fact) and to penalize the parents means to penalize the children, thus the mantle of compassion must, in being spread over the children, in some measure also be used to cover the parents, and so the distinction between the deserving and the undeserving becomes blurred. The spread of compassion is due to something else, says Rankin, and that is the fear that if people are too severely punished for being social failures they will be driven to crime or even revolution or at the best flee into mental and physical illness. In the event of these fears materializing, the undeserving poor would become even more of a burden on the productive members of society than they are at present. It is in the interests of the more or less successful majority to provide a modicum of care for the children of the undeserving and to mitigate the hardships of failure for their parents and even for those who are childless. (It is not necessary to bother here with the nature of productivity or its measurement, we can conveniently assume a degree of rationality in our socio-economic set-up that does not exist.)

If he accepts this viewpoint, the social worker will have little cause for soul-searching, and he will believe himself justifiably an agent of 'society'. He can treat the psychotherapeutic ideology as only a set of beliefs about a technique and so cease to worry himself about its profounder implications.

But supposing the social worker does not believe that social failure emanates from personality problems that psychotherapy can solve? Suppose he believes that the work he is called upon to perform is the consequence of social conditions, of the 'system' and of 'alienation'? Rankin asks some pertinent questions of such a 'radical' social worker: whom is he attempting to help, is it the whole of 'society' or just the deserving and undeserving poor, even though helping the latter is against the policy of the majority? 'Is it', he enquires, with psychotherapeutic insight, 'a panic reaction to feelings of guilt because of the social worker's relative affluence?' (3) Such a question cannot be answered as there exists no way of proving or disproving such insightful explanations. If we assume that the radical social worker's attitudes are founded on goodwill, then there still remains the difficult question: how are the poor to be rendered less poor? This could be done by the traditional revolutionary solution: a redistribution of existing wealth by which the richer are made poorer and the poorer richer. Or it could be achieved by a means that is more favourably received by those whose revolutionary ardour is less: a more equitable distribution of an increased national product. The difficulty of this resolution of the problem is that an increase in the gross national product seems today to be taking on the characteristics of a cross between the Holy Grail and Pandora's Box. But, Rankin suggests, the championship of the poor is far less revolutionary than it seems; it could mean nothing more radical than that the social worker constitutes himself as a kind of information service so that he can ensure that each individual obtains all his rights and the full benefits of the existing welfare services according to the rules laid down by the administration.

It is extremely difficult for the social worker to see an acceptable way out of the impasse. It is one thing to believe that the undeserving poor are those born with an endowment of below average potential of 'strengths and skills into an environment that has aggravated these inborn weaknesses' (4), (a statement that has eugenic implications that come oddly from a social worker) and quite another matter to know what to do about it. A vertically stratified society has to have a base and the undeserving poor are automatically it. When social workers operate in organizations that replicate the social 'system' as a whole, i.e. in which the workers participate in a hierarchy of status and rewards determined by that 'system', then how can they be, in Rankin's words, 'beneficiaries of the establishment' and at the same time champions of the failures? But there is, he tells us, a compromise that offers a way out: by concentrating his efforts on the children and the families it is possible, in the short run, to differentiate between helping the deserving while giving minimal help to the undeserving (this might account in great part for the cult of the family and marriage). However, Rankin says, 'to reduce the stresses on the parents we have to identify with them against the competitive forces that press on them' (5); and so the internal conflict reappears. Rankin claims that new entrants to social work see themselves not as highly skilled therapists with built-in paternalism and inequality but as *community workers* whose client is not the sick individual but the sick society. If this is so, then wherein lies the special skills of the social or community worker? Even the most outrageously partisan advocates of social work have not claimed an expertise outside of dealing with the individual and have made no claims for techniques that could be applied to society itself. If the social worker abandons his tried techniques of individual therapy, he has little or no contribution to make *qua* social worker. When he reverts to traditional revolutionary views and stances, he has no more claim on our consideration than any other revolutionary. I suggest that there is little difference in the basic orientation of social workers who treat the sick individual and those who want to treat the sick society; in both cases, they claim to know best by virtue of the same set of techniques, i.e. those that constitute the core of individual psychotherapy. If social workers were really revolutionaries, it is most unlikely that the paying agencies would tolerate them for any length of time. But so far social workers have shown little sign of having a revolutionary programme other than the fashionable rebelliousness of many contemporary dissidents;

there is a world of difference between proclaiming that advanced industrial society is all wrong, and proposing to put something else in its place. For those social workers who are discontented with the present set-up in their agencies and with the rules under which they work, there seems nothing save Rankin's compromise: to become sources of information so that the poor may get whatever the administration of the day declares is their right (a valuable service as many do not know), and to assist the families and children so that the 'innocent' are not penalized.

Quite apart from the difficulties of conscience already mentioned and probably of far greater significance in keeping social workers within their agencies and not too far out of line with their colleagues is the social worker's sense of service. They tend to accept the ethical standards imposed by the concept of service almost or as strongly as their much prized professional expertise (with which it is, of course, closely connected). Their work brings them into more frequent contact with the grimnesses of social life than any other occupations save those of doctor and nurse, and this makes it very hard to evade or ignore the obligations of duty. These twin imperatives of service and professionalism both protect and shelter them as well as limit them. They cannot afford to waste too much time and effort on the sickness of society when they have clients in urgent need of their help. The ethic of service stems from a Judaic-Christian tradition that, in a society still possessing residues of this tradition, needs no justifying; 'I've got a job to do' can be a legitimate excuse for not worrying too much about solutions that are abstract when they are not pure fantasy. The imperative that is based on professionalism, although more tenuously based, probably has the greater influence, which is only what is to be expected since professional status is the foundation of any occupational claim. Additional to the imperatives of service and professionalism there is the pressure from the client that reinforces the imperatives. Clients are dependent (not in the sense that social workers *make* their clients dependent on them, though they sometimes do this) on the social worker because he is very often the only available source of assistance and the client expresses his need for the worker in a way that cannot be ignored without doing violence to the doctrine of service. Agencies and regulations usually impose limits on what the social worker can do for his clients (particularly where material help is in question) and if the worker identifies too strongly with his client, his sense of service can lead him into opposition to or conflict with his agency. If he has internalized the psychotherapeutic ideology, concentration on the individual case tends to stimulate the social worker into criticism of his agency and ultimately of the 'society' that provides such a bureaucratic structure. Service and professionalism are conducive to a critical approach while at the same time, they curb radical and revolutionary urges. Changing the social structure, unless the work in hand is to be disregarded, has to wait until the problems of the client of the moment have been resolved. Social workers are able to exert some influence on the 'development of social policy' and their indoctrination with democratic ideals leads them to put great faith in the beneficial results of discussion, conferences, and the gradual effect of their influence and these together tend to make them more 'conservative' and less radical. Apart from these factors, they, unlike most revolutionaries, have to live and work within whatever changes are brought about.

As professionalization develops and as the agencies become more bureaucratized and their directors more self-consciously part of the 'establishment' or power élite, so social work agencies and services will become less client-centred and more worker-centred as this is the apparently inevitable accompaniment to bureaucratization. Bureaucratization and the swallowing up of social work into the maw of 'administration' will probably result in a double set of ethical standards as the ideology clashes with the regulations. The directorates and supervisors of agencies will maintain the rules, while the individual worker's sense of duty and obligation will be divided between service to the client and the powerful pull of service to the agency. What occurs in such a situation is something akin to the 'collusion' that is alleged to be present in the relationship between the partners in a marriage. The worker and the supervisor collude in ignoring breaches of the rules (provided that they can be successfuly concealed) and in maintaining the fiction that the supervisor does not know.

To a certain extent the social worker is cushioned in his process of adjustment by his 'high-mindedness' or the 'holier-than-thou-syndrome'. The high-mindedness of the social worker is partly a product of his training in which he is indoctrinated with this ideology; partly the result of the conditions of his employment; and partly by the actual nature of the tasks he performs.

Social work training, as has already been indicated earlier, is a hotch-potch of bits of other disciplines, economics, psychology, social history, social administration (it is very questionable whether this is a 'discipline' at all) theories and practice of casework, and some practical training as well. It is very doubtful if more than a smattering of each of these is absorbed, but what is taken in large doses is the prevailing ideology that defines the counsellor and social caseworker as a paragon among the virtuous; it is not that he feels he is 'holier-than-thou'—he really is 'holier-than-thou' if he conforms to all the role expectations that his training prescribes.

One of the outstanding conditions of his employment in private or public agencies (but not in private practice but this is rare for social workes and usually comes only after considerable practical agency experience) is that his hours are long, his 'case load' heavy, his devotion to the task constantly required, and his pay relatively low. Quite clearly he does his work for something more than the monetary reward. This is not unique to social workers alone; to some degree or other, all the old established professions (law, medicine, church, armed forces) can claim that their rewards are nominal, though some have difficulty in proving this. Members of other non-profit making occupations (teachers, civil servants, the police) can also claim that they could earn more money if they went into business or industry. What all these occupations have in common with social work is that they are parts of a moral aristocracy whose occupational behaviour conforms to higher standards than those prevailing in business or industry. The incumbents derive prestige and satisfaction from holding an office rather than from what they do or what they are. All of this applies to social work but vis-à-vis certain occupations such as the law, teaching, and the civil service, social work is clearly in the same category as medicine and nursing; the law can be lucrative, the civil service has well-paid posts, teaching has long holidays and plenty of free time; social work is more akin to medicine and nursing in the demands it makes of its practitioners (6).

The nature of the work performed by social workers, especially the counsellors and caseworkers is also in a category not far removed from that of medicine and nursing. The social worker does not traffic in trivialities; he is concerned with the raw stuff of living; he deals with vital matters that affect his clients' lives and dependents, their health and sanity. But in a way, the social worker has a unique claim to 'high-mindedness': he can communicate with and understand the poor and the social failures; doctors, nurses, even lawyers might as individuals have this capacity but it is not a necessary part of their qualifications for doing their work, whereas it is for the social worker. In addition, the social worker can allegedly overcome his middle-class prejudices and his middle-class frame of reference in a way that is not essential to any of the other professions.

Thus the social worker, faced with the frustrations of his situation and attacked like any other believer by doubts is, in some measure, protected by the honourable character of his calling, its social utility, and the special qualities that it requires of its practitioners. He can adjust by merely fulfilling his role, playing his part, or to use an older and more perceptive term, by fulfilling his 'office'.

But playing his role is an ambiguous affair since his role is not defined with any more precision than are most other roles in our culture and he has a number of 'performances' available to him that provide him with more or less acceptable patterns of adjustment.

What has he to adjust to? Firstly, to disappointed expectations; all training courses lead the trainee to expect situations that are never realized in the form that he hoped for, and in the social worker's case the ideology of social work is particularly liable to create disappointments in actual practice. Secondly, to the equivocal position that Rankin has described. To summarize: the social worker is required to adapt to a job which has more than its fair share of the gross and brutal facets of human existence; clients that 'need' him and others that, need or not, regard him as an enemy; others so culturally remote in terms of education, moral standards and social thinking from him that communication and contact with them is very difficult (7); supervision by superiors, boards and committees, many of which are in his opinion, misguided, obtuse and obstructive; the depressing probability that most of the problems with which he is concerned are the consequences of a crazy society that he can do little to alter.

Within this setting, the individual social worker adopts one or more patterns of adjustment that enable him to survive with some degree of equanimity in the situation of having to work within a state, local government or private agency. Bensman, in his study of the work situation of social workers, lists nine such patterns of adjustment (8):

(1) The authoritarian mode. Some social workers identify themselves with the authoritarian aspects of their agencies and consider themselves to be the representatives of 'society' in its law and order function. They become part of the repressive machinery of the state. They penalize and censure clients on behalf of society, in other words they enforce, where possible, the distinction between the deserving and the undeserving. The possibility of adjusting in this way only exists in those agencies and welfare departments that have power to give or withhold material assistance or in which the social worker, e.g. a probation officer, can penalize the client. Bensman observes that such adjustment is not widely approved by colleagues.

(2) I'm on your side. This is the opposite type of adjustment and is radical. It takes the form of bending the rules and interpreting the procedures wherever possible in the client's favour. Again it can occur mainly in services that administer 'handouts' and assistance or can make life easier or more difficult as in the probation service. When this adjustment is clearly based on personal frustration and disappointment with the work situation rather than an attempt at an objective assessment of the client's needs and position, it is frowned on by colleagues. When it is overdone, the worker comes into conflict with his superiors and usually leaves (9).

(3) The-I-know-best-pattern. Adjustment through megalomania or as Bensman puts it, 'playing God'. The social worker expels all doubt of his own ability to diagnose and prescribe, and thus convinced of his own omniscience he can avoid thinking about the nature of the problems with which he deals and of the role he is playing. This pattern is particularly common among the counsellors and marriage guidance and family caseworkers. They have a great advantage on their side because their conclusions and

decisions cannot be checked. The overt display of this tendency is best avoided as colleagues disapprove of obvious megalomania, but if tacit the worker can go from triumph to triumph.

(4) The apathetic posture. A mode of adjustment that appears in every occupational situation and is in no way peculiar to social work; it consists in 'going through the motions' and doing as little as possible together with an undue concentration on paperwork. It has two adaptive consequences for the social worker: firstly, it helps him to adjust to situations in which the client cannot be substantially helped; secondly, it breaks no rules and so the apathetic worker may not be promoted but he is not branded as a non-conformist.

(5) Over there the grass is greener. This is the search for the fulfilled expectations and assumes the form of frequently changing one's job. The adjustment pattern emphasizes professionalism and helps to reconcile temporarily the ideology with the reality of the work. It is not usually successful as the worker rarely finds a post in which he can do his work as he would like to. The migration from post to post is 'not better pay or loftier causes, but the will-o-the-wisp, professional status' in the shape of being able to practice one's preofessional skills (10).

(6) Retreat to research. This consists in finding a post in an agency or organization that concentrates on a small 'intake' of clients that is carefully selected for the purpose of research and experiment. Ideologically this situation can satisfy the worker but the snag that might damage this satisfaction is the suspicion that in helping so few clients one might be depriving the many of valuable services.

(7) Narrowing the field. The social worker opts for highly specialized counselling, psychiatric social work or some other branch in which the psychotherapeutic ideology is more fully exemplified. The possibility of directly helping is greater, and in addition there is the possibility of taking on private practice. Sometimes the adjustment is completed by the social worker moving completely into private practice, often after taking a qualification as a psychotherapist, and thus escaping the bureaucratized organizational setting altogether.

(8) The flight into academe. One of the most satisfactory patterns of adjustment is to become a teacher of social work or of a

branch of it. This takes the worker out of the frustrating and inhibiting situation that may obtain in an agency and puts him in one in which he can feel that he is directly furthering the spread of his ideology. It gives him an influence over the formulation of policy and he is often consulted or asked to give advice on various matters that as an individual rank-and-file worker might never come his way. He can get the best of both worlds by taking a few cases to 'keep up his professional skills'.

(9) Adjustment through promotion. The social worker concentrates on promotion to a position where he can substitute paper for people and only deals with his subordinates. He becomes an 'administrator' and so ceases to be worried by the daily contact with clients and their problems. He solves his own difficulties by paper-work and administrative actions and rationalizes his position by saying that someone must do this supervisory and administrative work which is, anyway, ultimately to the benefit of clients. Another benefit, this time to him, is that he enjoys greater freedom and a lighter load of work; in social work as in academic life, the higher up the ladder one goes, the less work one *has to do* (11). Of course the careerist has to adjust to the jealousy and envy of colleagues left behind.

These are the nine major patterns of adjustment; they are not mutually exclusive and many workers adopt more than one at a time or change their patterns during their career. Some, of course, adjust by leaving social work for some other occupation, or if they are women they become housewives. Some adjust without following any of these patterns for some are selfless, dedicated and skilful with their clients and do their work adequately in spite of the difficulties experienced in the job and its setting.

Some of these patterns are likely to have unfortunate consequences for the clients and Bensman enquires whether or not there are any safeguards for them built into the practice of social work and he concludes that there are. The best protection that the client has comes from the ethical norms operative in social work and that are part of the psychotherapeutic ideology; they are, in fact, the only safeguards as the client is virtually helpless (sometimes, as in the case of the 'client' of a probation officer, he cannot even withdraw) and it is very difficult to check the activities of the social worker to find out what he is really doing. But Bensman also argues that it is very difficult to ascertain what ethical norms operate and how they do so as the social work situations are not directly observable by outsiders. Some practices are condemned outright by social workers and he thinks that those who are discovered to be doing certain things are liable to disapprobation. He quotes four practices: punitive moral condemnation or 'holier-than-thou' attitudes that the social worker enjoys; 'playing God'; failure to maintain minimal contact with the client; and using the client to work out one's own emotional problems (12).

Enjoying being censorious of clients is not approved by colleagues but it might be difficult to avoid. Even those social workers thoroughly indoctrinated with the dogmas of the client-centred approach cannot always be assumed to have been immunized against this temptation. If, as some observers think, social work is becoming more popular among men and such men are usually from lower middle-class or upper working-class backgrounds, some of these may be hard on those they feel have not 'made the grade'; their own upward social mobility could easily lead them to exaggerate their own achievement in comparison with those of recognized social failures (13).

'Playing God' is most likely to be the vice of the counsellor and although in theory it is condemned, in actual practice condemnation depends on how clever the practitioner is at concealing what he is up to; as long as it does not become embarrassingly apparent to colleagues and supervisors (the latter have special opportunities to play God), the he-who-knows-best is likely to escape disapproval (14).

Failure to maintain the minimum contact with the client that is necessary (a ploy of the apathetic) is plain dereliction of duty, while exploiting a client for one's own emotional needs is not only the greatest sin in the catalogue but also indicates that the training of the worker has been faulty, or even that the worker should never have been admitted to the ranks in the first place.

It must not be forgotten that aside from the upward mobility that social work represents for some practitioners, it is a job that brings with it respectability and an increasing social status and that for his client the social worker is a very important person with quite a lot of power, real or fancied.

Bensman suggests that there is an area of the social worker's world where the ethical norms embodied in the ideology do not operate very effectively: the area of supervision of subordinates. The supervisor of social workers is prone to use the techniques of social work on his subordinates; he can use devaluation to attack the motives, personality and self-image of his subordinate and if so inclined, he can go far to destroying or undermining their identities; no doubt other fields of work have administrators and directors, bosses and employers who do just the same, but the weapons in their arsenals are not as sharp as those in the hands of a trained counsellor dealing with other trained counsellors, only the megalomaniac (God-player) is likely to be impervious to this kind of treatment.

Are social workers too hard on their superiors? Bensman concedes that this is very likely. The ideology and vocabulary of social work is internalized by social workers to a high degree (if it were not, it would be hard to conceive of their being able to carry out their duties) and they believe in their democratic principles and in the doctrine of the sancitity of the individual personality, hence subordinates expect higher standards of their superiors than they are likely to possess, given the conditions surrounding the attainment of superior positions in any bureaucratic organization. This is a situation that leads to a hypercritical attitude on the part of subordinates that promotes a beneficial reaction in as much as it might be conducive to compelling the upper ranks to act and behave within the limits ordained by the ideology common to subordinates and superiors.

The adaptation and adjustment that the counsellor, caseworker, social worker, and psychotherapist working inside an organization have to make are probably greater than in any other occupation, not so much because of the gap between ideal and reality but because the social milieu in which they work has been but slightly affected by their faith. The surrounding social structures utilize their ideological actions but only as palliatives. The brute fact is that the society for which the social worker operates does not subscribe to his beliefs in the worth and significance of the individual and in his rights against the majority. The less the social worker believes in his own creed, the easier it is for him to come to terms with his agency or 'setting' and with the society that encloses it.

Notes and References

1 Rankin, Geoffrey, 'Professional Social Work and the Campaign Against Poverty', *Social Work Today*, Vol. 1, No. 10, January 1971, pp. 19–21.
2 *Ibid.*, p. 19. I have retained the author's terminology but slightly changed his allocation of specific groups between the two categories.
3 *Ibid.*, p. 20.
4 *Ibid.*, p. 20.
5 *Ibid.*, p. 21.
6 Pins, Arnulf M., *Who Chooses Social Work, When and Why?* Council on Social Work Education, New York, Ann Arbor, Michigan, 1963. This extremely interesting study of social work students does not, however, provide much information on factors influencing the career choice of social work students (as the study is concerned only with American students it is not easy to relate its findings to the situation in the UK; for example all the students surveyed by Pins were graduates and they had all had greater opportunities for failure in a previous occupation than British students would have had), or their reasons for choosing it. However, the survey did show that 14 per cent gave as one of their two reasons for choice: status and remuneration, while some 33 per cent gave the expected stock answer 'the important contribution of social work to individuals and society', and another 33 per cent offered as one of the two main reasons for their choice the equally stock response: 'enjoy working with people'. But a considerable number of social-work students intending to take up community work felt that 'social work makes an important contribution to society, *gives status and prestige, and provides job security*'. (My italics.) See also Henry, W. E., Sims, J. H., and Spray, S. L., *The Fifth Profession*, Jossey-Bass, San Francisco, 1971; Lubova, R., *The Professional Altruist, the emergence of social work as a career 1880–1930*, Harvard University Press, Cambridge, Massachusetts, 1965; Etzioni, A., *Semi-Professions and Their Organization*, Free Press-Collier-Macmillan, New York, 1969.
7 Pollak, Otto, 'Treatment of Character Disorders: A Dilemma in Casework Culture', *The Social Service Review*, Vol. XXXV, No. 2, June 1961.
8 Bensman, Joseph, *Dollars and Sense: Ideology, Ethics, and the Meaning of Work in Profit and Nonprofit Organizations*. Macmillan, New York, 1967 (Collier-Macmillan, London, 1967); the descriptive titles to each of the patterns of adjustment are mine, the *ideas* are Bensman's, to whom I make full acknowledgment for most of the material in the later part of this chapter. Also informative is Stanton, Esther, *Clients Come Last*, Sage Publications, New York, 1970.
9 *Ibid.*, p. 101. Bensman gives an entertaining account of the 'double rhetoric of social work' from which one is never dismissed but 'given the opportunity to develop one's interests and career in areas more

conducive to one's interests, personality, or flair'. He continues: 'Individuals "share" their interests instead of talking. Subordinates do not disagree; they resist or have problems, especially authority problems. Clients are never manipulated, they are involved. And authority does not exist. Obedience is defined as cooperation. Practice in linguistic virtuosity not only expresses irony, it is also training.' Marion Sanders (see note 10 below) also provides a useful working glossary for those unfamiliar with the language of the counsellors: 'a social worker never tells you anything, she "shares information" with you. Helping you find a job is "environmental manipulation". Instead of publicity, selling an idea requires "interpretation". The social worker is not employed in a school, hospital or welfare organization but "functions" in a medical, education, or agency "setting". She does not care whether you like her but hopes you will "relate" to her.' *Op. cit.*, p. 58.

10 Sanders, Marion K., 'Social Work: A Profession Chasing Its Tail', *Harper's Magazine*, CCXIV, March 1957, pp. 56–62. Writing of a woman with a master's degree from the New York School of Social Work, she tells us:

'In 1938 she (Hester, with the Master's degree) decided to quit this job and join a private agency. It seemed natural enough to want to escape the endless, grinding burden of human misery (in a city relief bureau). "That's not the reason," she explained. "I am losing my professional skills giving economic assistance to all those people. I must get back in a setting where I can function under proper supervision." Since she had been bossing a large staff herself for some time this sounded strange. But there were other troubles too, linked to the Great Ideological Schism then rending the social-work world. The chief of the city bureau had studied at the University of Pennsylvania and was Rankian (following Dr Otto Rank) and Functional. Hester, being Freudian and Diagnostic, could not risk the continuing peril of contamination by a deviationist. . . . This restless hunt led her, at one point, to what was called an Interdisciplinary Team. She was then a *psychiatric* social worker, which was long considered the classiest category in the field. Later she ventured into "private practice" calling herself a "casework counsellor". This project paid off well. Friendly psychiatrists sent her some of their leftover cases and a lot of people came on their own steam either because they were too snobbish to patronize social agencies or too distraught to sit out their terms on waiting lists. Hester finally left private practice: "I do not wish to acquire status at the expense of my professional identity," she said. "I shall return to social work and find it there." On returning to an agency, she became a "Supervisor of Supervisors and diagnoses clients whom she never sees".' (Pp. 57–8.)

11 Many administrators in all occupations make work for themselves.

It is part of their 'image' to be seen to be busy day and night, week-ends and holidays. But they might also make work for themselves because they feel a little guilty or it is just a habit that they cannot break: having in the early part of their careers impressed superiors by being such eager beavers, they are no longer able to relax. See Oates, Wayne E., *Confessions of a Workaholic*, World, New York, 1971.

12 He also refers to exploiting clients sexually, but this is probably so rare that it can be ignored.

13 See Peters, Helge, *op. cit.*, and Pins, Arnulf M., *op. cit.* Pins' findings agree with those of Peters, though the former's refer to the USA and the latter's to Western Germany. Pins found that more men were coming into social work: in the period 1931–3 only 12 per cent of the total casework students were men but the percentage had risen to 34 per cent in the years 1953–5 and to 40 per cent in the years 1960–1. He also found that they were upwardly mobile: they came from lower-middle class homes (p. 126) and as a group their socio-economic background was higher than the national average, but when the education and occupation of the students' parents were compared, social work students were seen to come from a somewhat lower socio-economic group than did all graduate students as a group. In addition, they were not so bright (as measured by passing grades): 'The undergraduate grades of social work students were substantially lower than the grade averages of other graduate students in higher educa-cation' (p. 130).

14 I recall hearing, at a student selection conference, a discussion be-tween a sociologist and a psychiatric social worker on the desirability of admitting a certain candidate to a social work course. The discussion became more acidulous as it proceeded and the sociologist finally brought it to an end with the words: 'The real difference between us, Miss X, is that I can tolerate deviance and you can't.'

Conclusion

The psychotherapeutic ideology has already achieved a notable degree of success and among the reasons for this are: it ameliorates the harshnesses of technicized society; it reduces the tensions and resentments occasioned by that society; it appeals to the residues of the Judeo-Christian ethic in our culture. It is, moreover, in keeping with the prevalent intellectual mood that is highly favourable to technique, and the psychotherapeutic ideology is above all else a faith in a technique. Since it is clearly of value to industrial organizations and their chiefs, and because it does not offend the current worship of technique it is welcomed as a stabilizing influence, almost as a counter-revolutionary ally by business and industry as well as by the state and local government. It reconciles the individual to society and simultaneously it recreates the conviction of self, the belief in the reality of one's own existence, that the processes of industrialization destroy. It provides an inner light by which the individual's identity (or semblance of identity) is illuminated against the obscurity and opacity of the social world surrounding him.

These are the good consequences but psychotherapy has some grim concomitants to the benefits it brings. It can easily become the instrument of political and social repression; not perhaps in the sense of the tyranny that Rieff warns us of, and not in the sense of the pressures that feelings of guilt create when the new orthodoxies of familism, child-rearing, adjustment, maturity and so on are disregarded, but in the use to which the governing forces can put it. The trial of the editorial staff of *Oz* in London in 1971 was a case in point. After the verdict of guilty, but before the sentence was passed, the three convicted men were submitted to 'psychiatric examination'. It is pertinent to inquire why this was done. They had not committed any acts of violence or manifested behaviour that could indicate insanity. Perhaps the stigma of a psychiatric examination with its implications of insanity could give legitimacy to a legal procedure that had aroused considerable public discussion and some questioning of the motives of the authorities. It seems to have been an early Anglo-Saxon step in the direction of similar psychiatric-judicial procedures already familiar in the USSR. The argument for psychiatric participation in affairs such as this is simply that 'who does not agree with us and our type of society must be mad' and psychiatrists and psychotherapists are so used to playing God that even when they would not subscribe to such notions if plainly stated, they are so flattered by being called upon that they ignore or blind themselves to the implications. Whatever the motives behind this judicial procedure were, the procedure was an ominous sign of the probable consequences of taking the psychotherapists at their face value.

J. A. M. Meerloo (1) has accused psychotherapy of being a powerful instrument for the domination of one man by another. The psychotherapist can reconstruct the personality of his subject so that it becomes a reflection of his own, or he can disintegrate the personalities of certain people (this does not apply only to the therapists and practitioners of the psychoanalytic school, it is just as applicable to aversion and learning theory therapists). In some instances, the processes can result in 'brainwashing' which, even disregarding the exaggerated claims made on its behalf, can still result in quite drastic personality changes.

Rogers (2) defends psychotherapy by pointing out that it can be more than this and he is, of course, right but the dangers are still there. He produces a rather weak argument to show that such abuses are not likely. It is primarily, he says, a liberating process and the safeguard lies in the concept of 'client-centredness'. When the therapist adheres to the requirements of this technique, the results are beneficial: 'Greater maturity in behaviour, less dependence upon others, an increase in expressiveness as a person, an increase in variability, flexibility and effectiveness of adaptation, an increase in self-responsibility and self-direction' (3). All no doubt, possible but hardly the kind of consequences that are scientifically verifiable as Rogers claims they are.

In spite of Rogers' assurances, it cannot be assumed that all psychotherapists, counsellors and caseworkers will adhere to the rules of the game and will not misuse their influence and power either for their own ends or for the ends of some organization or the state. They are just as likely to suffer from the effects of the

K

blind faith in the technician as is any other group of technical experts, and that is where the real danger resides: in the expert believing in his own expertise. This aspect of the spread of the psychotherapeutic ideology becomes increasingly important as it gains ground. It is true, as Kogan says, that at the moment the top posts in the civil service are not held by men with training in the social work field and that top posts are not even held by men from the social service departments, and it is also true that administrative decisions are made from the financial point of view rather than from the viewpoint of social policy (4), but there is no reason to assume that the influence of the ideologists will not grow; the recent creation of the highly paid posts of directors of social services in local government is an indication of this growing influence.

But it is probable that these matters are of little consequence when compared with those factors that are the prime driving impulses to the inevitable victory of the psychotherapeutic ideology. The first, and of lesser importance, is that the creed and the technique appeal to a long-standing sentiment in the classical-humanistic tradition that is as important in our culture as the Judeo-Christian, namely, the belief that man has inner powers that enable him to rely on himself and his own efforts. Basic to the techniques of counselling and psychotherapy is the belief that human nature contains within itself its own therapeutic mechanisms which can be brought into action by the special relationship that is established between counsellor and client, psychotherapist and patient. Once this relationship has been established, the client makes his own decisions and solves his own problems with the least possible amount of direction and intervention by the counsellor-therapist. Thus the technique re-establishes the humanistic value of the individual.

Secondly, and this is by far the most important, the psycho-therapeutic ideology and the techniques associated with it, in spite of their dangers and drawbacks, offer the only way out of the mess that is our society. When Joseph Goebbels, shortly after the Nazis came to power, said 'You are at liberty to seek your salvation as you understand it, provided you do nothing to change the social order' he was speaking of something (changing the social order) that in those days was, perhaps, still a possibility. Who today can seriously believe that the social order can be changed save as a result of a nuclear war or some equivalent natural catastrophe? The essentials of the contemporary social order do not reside in classes and strata, in the opposition between bourgeoisie and proletariat or in the dominance of a political élite, but in the processes of machine and technical production, in the bureaucratization of organizations and in the supremacy of techniques. The material rewards that this situation produces are so great and so attractive that only natural or military catastrophe could put the clock back or forward, unless we are to believe in some fantasy of men becoming more rational, and the history of the past thousand years offers scanty supporting evidence for such a belief. All prediction in the social sciences is mere prophecy, but even prophecies have a habit of fulfilling themselves and it seems that the technicization of society will continue and that the present characteristics of our society will become more accentuated as time passes. A few rebellious demonstrations prove nothing more than that the members of our society need better outlets for repressed feelings than football matches and pop festivals provide. The triumph of the technician is inevitable and we shall have to live in the world he has created until such time as he blows us all up, or destroys our environment; in the meantime the psychotherapist can make us feel better.

Ever since the unified, enchanted world of Christendom was destroyed and man's certitude with it, man has been alone with no one to mediate between himself and God. The characteristic feature of man's situation in technicized society is not that he is alienated but that he is *isolated*. Technicized society is inhabited by isolated man. Given the impossibility of a return to older forms of religious belief, the therapeutic ideology is the only creed available that can give man the illusion that he is not totally alone, that even if God's grace is not vouchsafed to him, then man's is.

The meaninglessness of work, the fatuity of leisure, endemic violence and crime, acquisitive and competitive relationships engendered by the industrialized society can be rendered less noxious by psychotherapy. The 'progress' of industrialization cannot be halted, impeded for more than a brief space, or replaced. We have to be thankful that events and circumstances have thrown up the psychotherapeutic ideology and its techniques, for without

K

them we would be in even a worse fix than we are. The psycho-therapeutic ideology provides the only path to personal salvation. That it is apolitical, anti-radical, and supports the status quo is not important when compared with its positive contributions to human well-being. That its practitioners play God and are convinced of their own virtue and rightness is likewise of little importance: we have always had priests and mentors confident in their own holiness. The inestimable service that the psycho-therapeutic ideology supplies is that it gives the individual the feeling that somebody cares—even if it is not true.

Notes and References

1 Meerloo, J. A. M., 'Medication into submission: the danger of therapeutic coercion', *Journal of Nervous and Mental Disorders*, 1955, 122, pp. 353–60.
2 Rogers, *op. cit.*, pp. 397–8.
3 *Ibid.*, p. 398.
4 Kogan, Maurice, 'Social Services: Their Whitehall Status', *New Society*, 21 August 1969, p. 282.

Index

Abrams, Philip 60n
acceptance 67
activist approach 107
adaptation 123–4, 126, 134, 136, 205;
  definition 119
adequacy and inadequacy, sexual 234
adjustment 69, 82, 109, 119–14, 224;
  aim 130; attributes 120–22; counsellors 269–87; definition 119, 138;
  process 120, 122
advertising 216–17
Alberoni 217
Aldington, Richard: *Death of a hero*
  252
Alexander, Franz 135–6
alienation 183–4, 209–11, 225n
American Dream 137
anomie 183–4
aptitude testing 201
Ardrey, Robert 42
Arendt, Hannah 213
Aron, Raymond 181–2
authority 151–2

behaviour 104–5, 230
Bell, Daniel 172n, 177, 179, 270
Bendix, Reinhard 153
Benedict, Ruth 124–5
Bensman 280, 282–3, 285–6n
Berger, Peter L. 18, 21, 24, 26, 27n,
  41, 62n, 96n, 201, 210
Berle, Adolf A. 151
Bertalanffy, Ludwig von 42, 61n
Bessell, Robert 56–7, 62n
Bettelheim, Bruni 252, 256
Biestek, Father Felix P. 91–2
Binswinger, Ludwig 38, 60n
Birbaum, Norman 149
Bisno, Herbert 90
Blauner, Robert 154–5
bourgeois virtues 217
Brim 140–1

British Association of Social Workers
  31
Brown, Marjorie A. 95n
bureaucracy and bureaucratized
  society 22, 79, 85, 267–70, 277, 291
Burns, Tom 217–18
business 84
Butterfield, Herbert 60n

capitalism and capitalists 34, 151, 183
central-life interest 154–6, 215
Chandler, Raymond 177–8
character neurosis 132
childhood 24, 105, 251
Childhood and Society (Erikson) 104
Christianity 189–90
class struggle in society 211–14
client 48–52; response 66–7
client-centres practice 107, 109
coal industry 158
Coleman, Jules V. 72, 93–4n
communist in industry 161–2
community 195–7, 214, 226n
compassion 273
competition 197
Comte 177, 181–2
conformity 179
control-release system 33
counselling: adjustment 269–70; business and industry 145–75; definition and aims 63–96, 119, 271–2;
  education 43–7; mystique 63–96,
  role in society 84, 269, 271; sex and
  family 229–30; techniques 49–52,
  71–2; training 63–5, 270, 278–9
Counselling in a Changing Culture 44–7,
  97
counsellors 38, 246–7, 274–5; adjustment 279–85; aims 142; attributes
  47–9; caseworkers 43–4; definition
  29; family 264; function 47–9, 54,
  56, 63–96, 279–80; motivation 90–1,

293

counsellors—*contd.*
  promotion 282; relationship with
    client 48–52, 66, 81–3, 90–1;
    satisfaction 83; skills and qualities
    63–8; training 31; transmission of
    values 29, 62; women 260–1, 265–6
Coyle: *The Social Worker and His
  Society* 264, 266
craft workers 159
crime 131, 218

Dahrendorf, Ralf 60n, 96n, 148,
  152–2, 157, 165
Davies, Bernard D. 97, 109–11, 114
de-alienation 211
Death of a a Salesman 36
devaluation 85–6, 98–9, 244
Devereux, George 133
Dewey 119–20, 143n
Dubin, Robert 154
Dumazedier, J. 216, 227n
Durkheim 26, 40, 148, 177, 183–4

economic techniques 188
education 199–200; counselling 44–5;
  counsellors function 64; students
  213
Eissler, Kurt 133, 144n
Electra complex 230
elitists 43
Ellis, Albert 74–5, 94n
Ellul, Jacques 185–6, 188–9, 191–4,
  196, 200–3
emotions 219
empathy 66
employees and workers 154–60
enculturation 120–1
entertainment 201–2, 219–20
environment: change 112; machine
  made 186
Epstein 258, 260
Erikson, E. K. 48, 103–4, 106–7, 114,
  132, 230, 233–4
eroticism 233, 237
European technological society 191–2,
  204–5
existential vacuum 19, 27n

failure 272–5

faith of the counsellors 18, 273
familial sexuality 20, 27–8n
familism 24, 37–8, 229, 251–68
family 21, 37, 134, 228, 230, 251–2,
  266; function 252
Farber, Leslie H. 99, 115n
Fasching 219–20
fatherhood 254–5
Foote, Nelson 251
Fourier, François Charles Marie 141
France 212
Frankl, Viktor 19, 26–7n, 85, 233, 237
French Revolution 176–7
Freud, Sigmund 18, 25, 28n, 32–5,
  59–60n, 73, 76, 94n, 100–2, 114,
  128, 229–31, 233, 237–9, 242, 246–7,
  253, 255
Friedan, Betty 258
Friedmann, Georges 145, 157, 171n
Friedrichs, Robert W. 60n
Fromm, Erich 134–5, 168, 231, 254
functionalist church 42

gambling 219
Gans, Herbert J. 28n
Gehlen, Arnold 18, 27n, 205–6
  208–10
Gellner, Ernest 22, 28n
generation gap 45
genitality 234, 245
Germany, West 31, 138, 164; industry
  156, 158; poverty 59n
Gibson, Alan 97, 109–11, 114
Giedion, Siegfried 195, 226n
Ginsberg, Morris 38
Goebbles, Joseph 290
Goldthorpe, J. H. 159
Goode, W. J. 31, 59n
guilt 105
Guntrip 232
Guttsman, W. L. 148

Habermas, Jürgen 205, 212
Halmos, Paul 18, 27n, 29–32, 35–7,
  55, 146, 164, 247
Hamilton, Gordon 70–2, 93n, 119,
  122, 124–5
Heasman, Kathleen 55, 62n
Henry, Jules 22, 28n